READING STRATEGIES
Focus on
Comprehension

READING STRATEGIES
Focus on Comprehension

YETTA M. GOODMAN
UNIVERSITY OF ARIZONA

CAROLYN BURKE
INDIANA UNIVERSITY

with **BARRY SHERMAN**

Holt, Rinehart and Winston
New York   Chicago   San Francisco   Dallas
Montreal   Toronto   London   Sydney

Library of Congress Cataloging in Publication Data

Goodman, Yetta M   1931–
        Reading strategies.

        Bibliography: p. 236
        Includes index.
        1.   Reading comprehension.   2.   Reading.
I.   Burke, Carolyn L., joint author.   II.   Sherman,
Barry, 1938–   joint author.   III.   Title.
LB1050.45.G66   428.4'07   80-10257
ISBN 0-03-044011-4

Preface

Reading Strategies: Focus on Comprehension is a practical book, applying psycholinguistic concepts to reading with specific lesson plans. The book is appropriate for use in courses in reading diagnosis, reading comprehension, and methods in reading at both the graduate and undergraduate level. It is also written for classroom teachers who want to keep reading in a whole language context, rather than focusing on isolated skills, and is particularly well suited to the development of individualized reading programs.

Researchers in reading began to devise models or diagrams of the reading process based on new insights from linguistics more than a decade ago. These models are intended to help answer the questions: How do people read? How do people learn to read? What factors affect reading and learning to read? As new insights about reading reach teachers who are working intimately with children learning to read, it is natural for these teachers to ask, How can I take all this new knowledge and put it to use in my classroom? It is to this question that we have addressed this book.

Our research and that of others has led us to adopt the point of view that the reader's focus must always be on constructing meaning from the author's message. We believe that the reader's search for and construction of meaning occurs naturally as the reader develops. We also believe that teachers can organize a literate environment for children from the very beginning of reading instruction so that the natural reading process is nurtured.

Reading Strategies: Focus on Comprehension has two parts. Part One sets the theoretical perspective, which places reading—where we believe it must be—within a language framework. We explore the process of reading as it relates to the other language processes of listening, speaking, and writing, and use knowledge about language and learning to develop a rationale for reading instruction. In this section we attempt to explain why we believe a comprehension-focused program is the most effective way to teach reading.

Part Two presents specific strategy lessons growing out of this theoretical framework that can help readers become secure in their quest for meaning.

The text for each reading-strategy lesson explains why the lessons are important; suggests the kind of readers the lesson will benefit; provides additional understandings about the relationship of these lessons to our views of reading and curriculum; and suggests a classroom procedure through which the lessons can be presented.

The text is appropriate for teachers with varying degrees of experience and expertise in the teaching of readers. Below we have suggested a variety of ways to work with our material which may facilitate use of *Reading Strategies* by more and less experienced users.

If you are new to a comprehension-centered approach to reading and you are a preservice teacher

1. Read the first three chapters
2. Read the general rationales that precede the various strategy lessons
3. Find one or more students who might benefit from the lessons
4. Read the specific rationale and strategy lesson when you are ready to present the lesson to the student(s)

If you are new to this approach and you are an inservice teacher

1. Read the first three chapters
2. Select students from your class whom you wish to help
3. Find the strategy lessons written for students who have a profile similar to that of the students you have selected
4. Read the general and specific rationales, and follow the lesson plan, making appropriate adjustments for your particular situation

If you are not new to this approach

1. Review chapters 1 and 2 quickly
2. Read chapter 3, as there may be some things that are new to you or that are organized in a new way
3. Select the students you plan to work with
4. Find the strategy lessons written for students who have a profile similar to that of the students you have selected
5. Read the rationale and follow the lesson plan, making appropriate adjustments for your particular situation

The more the reader knows about an author's background and experience, the easier it is to construct the message being presented. For this reason, we would like to share with you some of our background, experience, research perspectives, and instructional focuses.

We have had considerable experience teaching children and young adults in elementary and secondary schools, as well as teaching in teacher-training institutions, colleges, and universities. Yetta Goodman taught at the elementary- and secondary-school levels for ten years, primarily in grades five to eight; much of her teaching was in Los Angeles, California, and Detroit, Michigan. She has been involved in higher-education programs for more than fifteen years. Carolyn Burke spent the first six years of her professional career teaching in the primary grades in Highland Park, Michigan, and since then has taught in university teacher-education programs. Barry Sherman has taught secondary school and college students for many years, often working with bilingual students.

Our teaching experiences have been augmented by personal involvement in reading research. In association with Kenneth Goodman, Yetta and Carolyn have been involved in miscue research projects, taping the reading of hundreds of readers of various ages and proficiencies and analyzing their miscues in order to gain insight into the reading process. Most recently Yetta has been involved in research focusing on emergent reading among preschoolers, and Carolyn has been examining readers' personal views of reading and the effect of these views on reading behavior.

All of us have been concerned with relating research to practice. We have been interested in determining the kinds of experiences and knowledge needed by teachers of reading, and the kinds of experiences and materials needed to support children as they learn to read. We have designed and conducted successful inservice training programs for teachers who work with students with reading problems. Through such programs we have gained the insights necessary to develop lessons focused on comprehension to support the reader's own developing strategies. All of our teaching and research experience has led us to view the reader's search for meaning as the primary focus of reading. When reading instruction also is focused in this way, the natural search is supported and reader's energies are not diverted to unproductive activity.

We believe that within the school the teacher plays the most significant role in helping children learn to read. No reading material or program can teach children to read. Materials and programs are only tools. In the hands of a master artist good tools can be used to produce a great work of art. In the hands of an insecure or weak artist not even superior tools will be very helpful. The artist must bring to his or her work a knowledge of perspective, color, line, space, and theme, as well as a technique implemented with mallet, chisel, or brush. A teacher, to be a master, must bring to reading instruction a knowledge of language, of the reading process, of the cultural and experiential language differences of readers, and of subject-matter content, as well as expertise in using teaching methods and materials. We hope that *Reading Strategies: Focus on Comprehension* can provide some of this background knowledge and, at the same time, provide suggestions for the selection and construction of reading materials.

We believe that teachers are decision makers. This book is not meant to tell teachers what to do. Instead, it provides a framework for what we believe about reading. We provide examples and samples of possible lessons, which are intended to serve as guidelines for new teachers or those teachers new to a comprehension-centered reading curriculum. As teachers come to understand the issues and concerns related to this view of reading, it is essential that they personalize these lessons and develop others based on their individual philosophies and the specific knowledge they have about the students whom they are teaching.

Remember, this book is a guide for teachers. Be selective in your reading. Use this book as a tool. Use your own professional judgment to adapt the lessons as you gain greater confidence and understanding. When you have written some of your own strategy lessons, we would be pleased to have you share them with us.

The concepts behind *Reading Strategies: Focus on Comprehension* started to develop in 1973. Since that time the book has been modified and developed through the help of many friends and colleagues who have reviewed our manuscript in various stages of development. We appreciate the benefits of their experience and well thought out opinions. Although there are too many to thank individually, we do wish to acknowledge the help we have received from so many. Above all we owe a great debt to the readers and their teachers with whom we have worked over the years to test out and critique the strategy lessons.

Yetta Goodman
University of Arizona
Program for Language and Literacy
Elementary Education Department
Tucson, AZ 85721

Carolyn Burke
Indiana University
Reading Department
Bloomington, IN 47401

Barry Sherman
6185 Orchard Station Rd.
Sebastopol, CA 95472

Contents

READING STRATEGIES
Focus on
Comprehension

Part I

A Theoretical Framework

Chapter 1

Reading and Reading Strategies

THE READING PROCESS

Reading is a problem-solving process. As readers, we try to discover what the author means while, at the same time, we build meaning for ourselves. We use our own language, our own thoughts, and our own view of the world to interpret what the author has written. These interpretations are limited by what we know.

When authors create, they project their language, their thoughts, and their meanings into producing text. Their creations are limited by what they know. Because of the obvious differences between the language, thoughts, and meanings of an author, and those of the reader, reading can never be an exact process. Because the reader's own language and thought become involved through interaction with the language and thought of the author, readers can never be certain that they have discovered the meaning the author intended. However, since readers are compelled to understand what they are reading, they interpret actively while reading in order to gain meaning, which is their ultimate goal. *The reader is as active in searching for meaning as is the writer in creating written language.*

The model of reading presented here is an attempt to represent in graphics a verbal form of the reading process. To help solve the major problem confronting everyone who reads—*What do I think the author means?*—the reader uses a number of complex plans or *strategies*. The significant strategies in the reading process involve *predicting*, *confirming*, and *integrating*. These strategies are used by all readers with varying degrees of proficiency, from the very beginning of reading. In most cases, readers have no conscious awareness that they are so proficient in their attempts to comprehend what they read.

Predicting Strategies

As readers we use our language proficiency and knowledge about the world to make tentative decisions.

1. *Is the material I am going to read a piece of fiction, a recipe for making fudge, a description of an event, or . . .?*
2. *Since this is fiction, is it a love story, historical fiction, science fiction, or . . .?*
3. *Will the next word I read be a noun, a verb, an adjective, or . . .?*

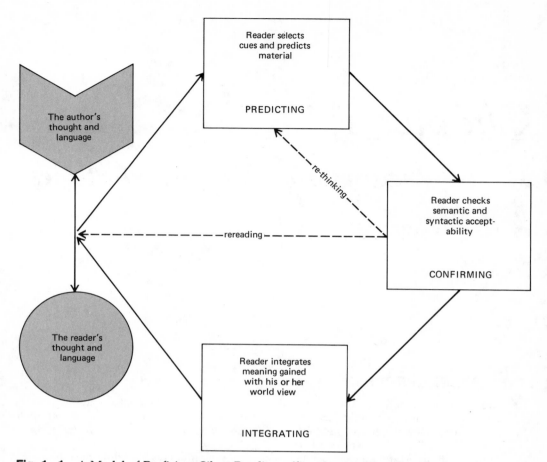

Fig. 1–1 A Model of Proficient Silent Reading—(focus on reader and author)

4. *Is the letter following that* q *going to be a* z, n, o, *or . . .?*
5. *Is the next event in the story going to be happy, sad, perplexing, or . . .?*
6. *I wonder if "extenuating circumstances" means "long and drawn out" as in "extended"?*

This type of hypothesizing or predicting generally occurs without our conscious awareness and certainly not in such specific language, but nevertheless it does occur.

Consider the following:

> [lag] v. lagged, lagging. 1. To fail to keep up a pace; fall behind. 2. To fail or slacken; flag.— n. 1. A falling behind; retardation. 2. An interval resulting from this.
> la-gniappe [lan-yáp, lan yắp] n. An extra or unexpected gift. [Amer Span la nắpa.]
> laid [lad]. p. t. & p. p. of la‚.
> laissez faire [leś a fâr]. Also lais·ser faire. Noninterference, esp. the doctrine that government should not interfere with commerce. [F. "allow them to do."]— laiś sez-faire adj. — laiś sez-fairé ism' n.[1]

The moment you glanced at the sample of written material above, you started *predicting*. You tapped the knowledge you have constructed because of your years of experience with written language. You not only predicted what kind of reading material was being presented but began to predict what purposes you might have in using these dictionary entries. Even though you were asked to read the passage, did you choose not to read certain parts? You probably

[1]*The American Heritage Dictionary of the English Language*, ed. Peter Davies (New York: Dell Publishing Co., Inc., 1970), pp. 396–97.

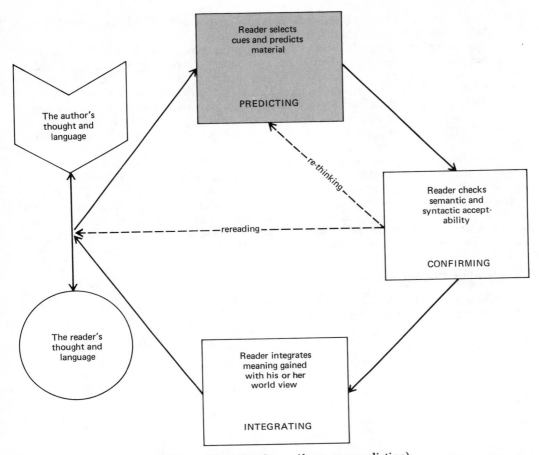

Fig. 1-2 A Model of Proficient Silent Reading—(focus on predicting)

ignored the pronunciation marks because you knew you would not need to pronounce the words, or you knew how to pronounce them and so did not need the marks. You may have skipped the whole example and read this paragraph first because you could not predict our reason for asking you to read the example. You wanted a purpose for reading before you wasted your time on too careful an examination. The decision to read or not to read is based on your predictions of what aspects of the material are going to be significant for your purpose. Did you react differently to the unknown words than you did to the familiar ones? Were they all equally familiar? Your various reactions to specific words were based on your predictions of how much you would know about the words. You were probably not concerned about the incomplete sentences ("Also 'lais·ser faire") and lack of parallel grammatical construction ("A falling be-hind; retardation") because you predicted just this kind of grammar in a dictionary. If this had been the beginning of a novel, such language units would have been jarring because you would have predicted complete sentences. Were you immediately aware of the words that were not common English spellings? Once again your years of being an experienced language user provided you with the necessary *predicting strategies* to recognize quickly non-English or unusual spelling patterns.

When we read, we do not make predictions on the basis of looking at every punctuation mark, letter, word, or sentence. Instead we select certain aspects of the available language. Because of background and experience, accumulated over the years, we know what is usually significant and select only the most significant cues to make predictions.

We react to all aspects of language as we predict. We interact with our knowledge about the relationship between the letters and sounds of the language as we predict graphophonic units of language. Our knowledge of the rules of grammar is brought to bear as we predict the syntactic system of language. Our understanding of the world around us helps us predict what the author means as we use the semantic system of language.

Even young beginning readers are able to make appropriate predictions based on their experience with print found in a variety of environmental settings. They use cues surrounding the print, such as pictures, symbols, color, and graphic design, as well as information about the relevant contextual setting, in order to predict what the print might say. For example, a preschooler might predict on the basis of the stylized, multicolored letters, shape and design of the carton, and the functional setting that the print reads "Crest" or "toothpaste." Although beginning readers use a wide range of relevant cues for prediction, they know that the print "says something"; that it communicates.

Readers select the most significant graphophonic, syntactic, and semantic cues and predict what they believe subsequent graphophonic, syntactic, and semantic structures are going to be. No reader uses all of the available cues. Reading would be too slow and inefficient if this were done. Nor are the cues selected in any consistent order or sequence. The weighting and significance the reader gives to individual cues vary with the experiences and language information he or she brings to the text and depends on the reader's specific purpose. The interaction of these cueing factors within the reading process occurs so rapidly as to appear simultaneous.

Confirming Strategies

As predictions are made, readers test these hypotheses to see if they are meaningful. To do this, we *confirm* or *disconfirm* our predictions.

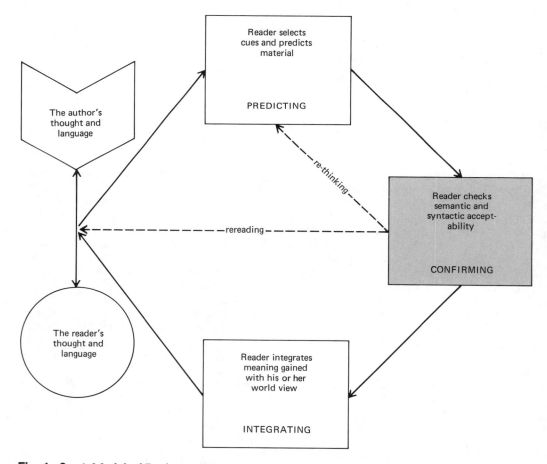

Fig. 1−3 A Model of Proficient Silent Reading—(focus on confirming)

As readers we ask ourselves two questions to test our predictions or hypotheses: *Does this sound like language to me?* and *Does this make sense to me?* If the answer to both questions is yes, and if we decide the material is worthwhile, we continue to read. However, if the answer is no, certain optional strategies are available:

1. Stop and rethink the problem.
2. Regress, reread, and pick up additional cues until the material makes sense.
3. Keep reading in order to build up additional context; in so doing, you may generate enough understanding to decide what went wrong.
4. Stop reading because the material is too difficult.

Consider the following passage:

Shirley was a beautiful yellow canary. He was loved by his family but they were all disappointed because he didn't sing very much or very often.

Shirley would welcome the members of the family with tiny tweets whenever they came home. He chattered whenever he heard people talking but he never sang.

One day the man who gave Shirley to the family came to visit. They told him that they loved Shirley but wished he would sing. He went to the cage and held Shirley in his hand.

He called out, "Shirley is a female canary, not a male. I must have made a mistake when I gave her to you. Female canaries don't usually sing."

The family continued to call the canary Shirley but began to refer to him as "her."

Would you now reexamine the selection and with a pencil place a check mark at any point in the reading where you regressed for any purpose or where you were puzzled by what you were reading.

It is difficult to help you discover what you confirmed or disconfirmed while reading a written context like the example above. Each reader brings a unique background and experience to the written material, and there are many places where you might have been aware that you wanted to confirm or disconfirm your predictions. Let us examine a few of those possibilities.

If you predicted that Shirley was female, it probably startled you, at least momentarily, if you noticed the male pronoun referring to the canary. You might even have read *she* for *he* at the beginning of the second sentence and had to reread to disconfirm your prediction of female canary. Some of you might have stopped to rethink the relationship between the male pronoun and a name that is not commonly used for men in our time.

Did you predict that the family in the story was a bird family or a human family? If you predicted human family, subsequent information confirmed your guess and you had no rethinking to do. However, if you predicted bird family, you had to reorganize your notions about the story when you got to the third paragraph and disconfirmed your prediction.

In the third paragraph there are ambiguous references to "he." Did you get confused and think the paragraph was badly written because of the ambiguity? Did you have to rethink or reread in order to confirm or disconfirm who was doing what in the story?

Some of you may have knowledge about canaries that helped you predict the reason the bird was not singing. You probably felt good about your prediction when you confirmed it at the end of the story.

Did you want to intone the last sentence so that it became two sentences? Did you try to create a first sentence that ended with *canary* and start a second sentence with *Shirley?* If you did, you had to rethink the structure and change it back into a single sentence.

Look at your check marks. Using reasoning similar to the above, can you explain why you reacted to the particular language units as you did? Think about how your knowledge of language and the world interacted with the print, the grammatical structure, and your thoughts about what the author was trying to say.

Beginning readers also test their predictions while they read. The more cues they have available to them as they interact with print, the more appropriate their predictions and confirmations will be. For example, illustrations accompanying stories are important sources of information that beginning readers utilize in order to test their hypotheses about story content. It is these interactions that are involved as readers *predict* and *confirm* as they read.

Integrating Strategies

As we read, we are continuously making choices about which chunks of information are to be remembered. These choices are always related to the purpose we set for ourselves. We then build a meaning for what we are reading, which we incorporate into our storehouse of knowledge or our schema.

We use various criteria to integrate what we are reading into our own system of knowledge. These criteria are dependent on our purpose for reading and our belief system, among other factors.

1. My purpose for reading:
   a. *This is not important for my purposes, so I'll forget it.*
   b. *I'm not sure whether it's important for my purposes, so I'll remember it for a while until I have enough information to make a better decision.*
   c. *This is very important for my purposes, so I will keep it in mind and add it to things I already know.*
   d. *The information is not exactly what I expected, and I have to rethink my purposes for reading and perhaps set some new purposes.*
2. The relationship of what I am reading to my view of the world:
   a. *This information is similar to what I know and fits into my belief system, so I can easily assimilate it to my view of the world.*
   b. *This information is new to me, but can fit into my belief system. I will have to think about it for a while, but it will help me expand my view of the world.*

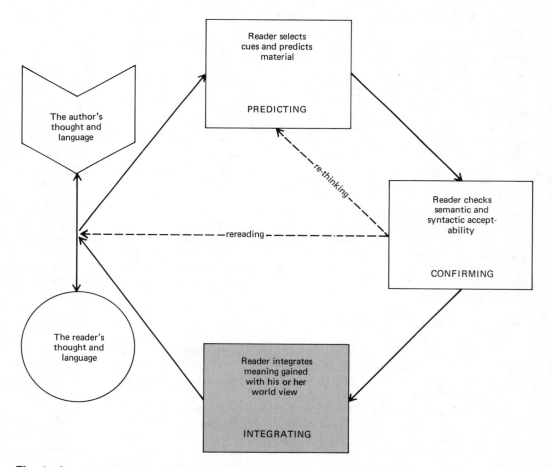

Fig. 1—4   A Model of Proficient Silent Reading—(focus on integrating)

    c. *This information does not fit into my belief system. If the author makes a strong enough case, I may have to alter my belief system completely.*
    d. *This information does not fit into my belief system. If the author does not make a strong enough case, I must either reject the information or distort it to fit my own view of the world.*

The following examples may help us explore some of the preceding statements about *integrating strategies.* Suppose you were to read:

1. "As I approached the corner, the traffic light turned green, so I crossed the street."
2. "As I approached the corner, the traffic light turned purple, so I stopped."
3. "As I approached the corner, the traffic light turned red, so I crossed the street."

The first example can be easily remembered from reading because we understand most easily information that fits our view of the environment or the schema we have already developed. Even if we were to skip this part in the reading or forget it because it is insignificant, we would nonetheless believe we had read it and be able to discuss the information with others because it is information we bring with us to the reading.

    The second example, however, poses a different problem. We know that traffic lights are usually red, yellow, or green. A purple traffic light is new information, but we may still be able to relate this to our belief system because we have other knowledge that permits us to accept this information: (a) Purple has red in it; perhaps the author is stretching the truth for some reason that will be disclosed to us as we continue reading. (b) Maybe the author is going to talk about color blindness, and since we do not know much about color blindness, it may be that color-blind people see red as purple. (c) Perhaps this is a new or a strange world and we are reading a science-fiction story. We also have the option of rejecting or distorting the information.

    If we think of jaywalking as a possible cause for the third example, we may follow a procedure similar to the one described for the second example. However, if all our lives we have stopped for red lights and crossed on green lights, this information may jar our belief system. We may be so comfortable with our belief system that we read *green* for *red* or read *didn't cross* for *crossed.* Another possible option we have is to think that the printer has made an error.

    Reading can also change belief systems, of course. If the author of the third example makes a strong enough case for this new system, we may come to accept the notion that there are times when we can safely cross the street on a red light. We may integrate this into our knowledge system or schema, or we may build new schemata in response to the new information, reasoning that perhaps a scramble system is being described in which all cars must stop on the red light and the pedestrians can cross the street in any direction.

A MODEL OF READING

Predicting, confirming, integrating—these we have identified as the key operations within the reading process. Now let us observe these operations as they interact within a reading instance.

    Read the following paragraph through once and only once. Then, without rereading, write down everything that you remember you have read.

        The king called the assembled to order. He stood regally waiting for silence. As the noise ceased, he spoke.
        "Tomorrow, I invite you all to the place. There we will make the decisions necessary to overcome the enemy."

Write down everything that you remember of what you just read.

    Look back over your representation of the paragraph and compare it with the versions of other readers if possible. Compare these versions with the original passage. Can you identify, through your observations, the various operations of the reading process?

    Which cues did you select as significant, and which did you discard? *Regally* is often omitted. Because readers assume that kings are regal, the word becomes redundant. Few people write both *waiting for silence* and *the noise ceased.* These, too, are redundant statements and a reader needs only one, or some combination, of them to integrate that information into the meaning being constructed.

Can you provide evidence from your written statement that you were predicting and confirming? Upon arriving at *assembled* in the text, did you realize that you had actually anticipated *people, courtiers,* or *meeting*? Does your version contain *palace* instead of *place*?

At this and similar points in text, you might have felt the need to reread even though the directions told you not to do so. Some readers disregard these directions and reread. Others follow the directions and are frustrated by them. Both cases are instances of the use of confirming strategies. These are places where readers encounter unexpected cues or where they want clarification.

Did you notice that the words and sentences of your version were more different from the versions of other readers and from the original text than were your meanings? There will always be some minor variations in meaning attributable to reader experience and background. The search for and development of meaning is the basic function of reading, and it is achieved through the use of predicting and confirming strategies.

Reading a short paragraph and then writing down what you remember of what you read is not like continuous silent reading, but it can provide some insights into the reading strategies that all of us use. Reading begins when we interact with an author through the medium of printed material. We select the appropriate language cues needed to *predict*. Then based upon our language knowledge and background experience, that is, our schema system, we *confirm* our predictions by checking the syntactic and semantic acceptability of what we think we are reading against our knowledge of language and of the world. We *integrate* what we believe to be significant into our established meaning system. This process of predicting, confirming, and integrating proceeds continuously and interactively. As we read, we continuously add to, alter, or reorganize our meanings. We are expanding the universe of our knowledge.

LANGUAGE AND ITS SYSTEMS

Children come to school already in possession of a great deal of language knowledge. They are proficient users of the language of their home. They have already begun to make use of written language and are aware that print can communicate such enticing messages as McDonald's or Coca-Cola. Many of them have had the experience of being read to from books by parents, nursery-school teachers, or librarians and of paging through the books themselves, using pictures to recall the story. They have this accumulated language knowledge to apply as they begin to interact with the language of an author (that is, the printed material). A clear relationship between the language and meaning of the text, and the children's own language and knowledge, makes material predictable. The more this reading material reflects the whole and intensely meaningful language they use already, the more proficiently will they apply their accumulated language knowledge and world view to the construction of meaning. In the process of constructing meaning, they, like all readers, will make use of the three language systems: graphophonic, syntactic, and semantic.

Graphophonic System

The *graphophonic* system refers to the relationships between the sounds of language, and the written form of language. Contrary to a good deal of popular opinion, the English spelling system is quite regular and not at all haphazard. However, there is no simple one-to-one correspondence between the written language and the sound system. There are language features that exist in written language and do not exist in the oral language. *Once upon a time*, frequently found in storybooks, is seldom used in oral language except in storytelling. Clauses such as *said Mother* or *John laughed* preceded or followed by a quotation are common in written language, even in beginning reading material, yet are not frequent in oral language at all. In addition, there are other influences that do not permit a one-to-one relationship between written and oral language.

Because of its long and complex history, as well as influences from several other languages, the English spelling system has more than one spelling pattern that relates to the same sounds. Examples include *ai* as in *bait* and *a-e* as in *hate*. Although English is to a large extent spelled in a standard way, there are different ways to pronounce the same written words. To some speakers of English *Mary, merry,* and *marry* are homophones—pronounced exactly the same. For other speakers only two of those three words are homophones, and for still others all three words are pronounced differently.

People say what sounds like "cuz," "watchamacallit," "jeet," and "gonna," and must learn to recognize their counterparts in written language as *because, what you may call it, did you eat,* and *going to.* Each reader must learn the set of relationships that exist between his or her oral language and its written counterparts. The relationships are not the same for all speakers because of differences in dialects, as well as idiosyncratic differences.

In recent years research on young children's spelling patterns has provided us with evidence that despite the complexities of the English spelling system, children's understanding of the relationship between the sound system of oral language and the graphic system of written language develops in a logical and rule-governed way. Beginning readers use their proficiency in the sound system of their language, and their developing understanding of the symbolic nature of print, to build relationships between oral and written language. Because the purpose of reading is communication—comprehending the meaning of the author—readers use the syntactic and semantic systems available to them in order to build the relationship between the sounds of language, and written language.

Syntactic System

The phrase *syntactic system* refers to the interrelationships of words, sentences, and paragraphs. It includes the interrelationships of word order, tense, number, and gender. *Grammar* is the more common term for *syntax.* All children can use the rules of their own grammar system rather proficiently by the time they come to school.[2] When five-year-olds are asked to complete the sentence "A boy is sliding down the _____," they will always supply some acceptable noun or noun phrase at the end of the sentence. They will not be able to call the word they supply a *noun* or know the definition of *noun*; nevertheless they know where nouns go in English sentences. When we use the terms *syntax* or *grammar,* we refer not to the rules imposed on the language by grammar books but to the rules people know intuitively by virtue of being language users.

For many of us, there is no question that we say: "I am going to college," "I am going to the university." How do we know that *the* is used before *university,* but not before *college*?[3] There are few grammar books that provide rules about when we should use the determiner *the* and when we should not, since no clear-cut rule system has been discovered concerning this phenomenon.

Consider each of the following sentences. Would you use the determiner *the,* or would you not use it? Could you say the sentence both with and without *the*? If so, in what instances would the meaning be changed?

I went to (the) hospital.
I went to (the) school.
I went to (the) town.
I went to (the) library.
I left (the) home.
I left (the) house.

The awareness you, as a speaker of your language, have that a sentence sounds right, or that it does not, is your *intuitive knowledge of language.*

When written material has sentence structure similar to the syntax that students have *heard* or *used,* they are able to predict the language and know whether a particular sentence sounds appropriate.

In a list of words with only graphophonic cues available, students may have difficulty

---

[2]We refer here to the grammar system of their own dialect.

[3]In some dialects of English people do say, "I am going to university." And speakers who usually say, "I am going to college," could, in some settings, say, "I am going to the college," changing the meaning of the original sentence.

remembering how *merry, Mary,* and *marry* are different and often may be unable to provide a grammatical function or a meaning for each word. However, as soon as syntax is available, readers can use that syntax to support their predicting and confirming strategies. Even if many of the other words in a sentence are nonsense, they can determine how the word functions in the sentence.

> Mary femped to the plurn clumbly.
> The lum and the sanin flis to marry.
> Jif blees a merry rount.

The syntax of written material provides significant cues for readers. They are able to ask, *Does this sound like language to me?* They can use syntax to predict and then to confirm the acceptability of their predictions. But in order to comprehend, they must also have the *semantic system* available.

Semantic System

The semantic system is at the heart of the language. It includes the relationships within a language that establish meaning for the user. Everything that the user has been learning and thinking about the world is also involved in establishing meaning.

People who live in apartments, trailers, or box cars that are secure, warm, familiar places have established the various meanings of *house* and *home* through their own living experiences and their use of language in various real-life settings. Regardless of where they have lived, they have said to others, "Come over to my house after school today." "Take this home to your mother." They may therefore have difficulty with lessons that try to explain the traditional meanings of *house* and *home* or may not understand why a poet would rhapsodize, "It takes a heap of living to make a house a home." Marlene, who has traveled from New York to Los Angeles in five hours to visit her grandmother, and speaks to her grandmother on the phone a number of times a year, may have difficulty understanding the total break of family ties and the trauma involved during the migrations of the Westward Movement. The closer the content of reading material is to the life and experiences of the students, and the closer the concepts of reading material are to what students already know, the easier it is for them to understand the meaning relationship in the reading material.

At the same time, reading must expand students' knowledge and view of the universe. If the material to be read has many known concepts along with some unknowns, readers can use what they know in order to understand better the unknown content or concepts. Therefore, in order to provide opportunities for expansion of experiences and broadening of concepts, teachers should encourage students to read material that involves some unique experiences and that is to some degree beyond their own knowledge. However, if too many of the experiences or concepts are foreign, the reading will be nonsense to them.

Only when the semantic cueing system is available, in addition to the syntactic and graphophonic systems, is there the necessary support for developing reading strategies. Readers can then predict and confirm language experiences based on graphophonic and syntactic information and can make intelligent predictions and confirmations because they have the necessary semantic information available. In addition, they can integrate what they are reading with what they know in order to comprehend.

When we add semantic meaning to the examples of spelling patterns presented earlier in the chapter *(Mary, merry, marry)*, we can examine the significance of the semantic system:

> Mary ran to the store quickly.
> The man and the woman want to marry.
> Jeff sees a merry clown.

The more context available to the reader, the more support there is for understanding and comprehension.

Mother needed milk for dinner. She asked Mary to go to the store for her, but Mary was playing with her friend and did not want to go.

"If you go to the store, you don't have to do dishes tonight," Mother told her.

Mary ran to the store quickly.

We know Mary much better now than we did in the preceding sections on graphophonics and syntax, or even in the sentences we composed to introduce semantic meaning. The semantic system helps the reader support the development of the most important of all reading strategies: *"READING IS SUPPOSED TO MAKE SENSE TO ME! NOT TO MY TEACHER, MY FATHER, OR MY CLASSMATE, BUT TO ME!"* It is important to keep in mind that language systems and reading strategies operate in an interrelated fashion. When readers are dealing with any one of the individual strategies, or focusing on any one of the language systems, all the other strategies and systems are still operating. Although proficient readers balance their use of reading strategies and cueing systems successfully, beginning readers may need some extra support in order to achieve this ability. They may need to be directed away from overreliance on one cue system, and underutilization of one of the reading strategies. With experience and guidance, beginning readers learn to integrate all the strategies and cue systems effectively and efficiently.

The reading strategies and language systems introduced in this chapter are discussed in greater detail in appropriate sections of the specific reading-strategy lessons. The bibliography lists sources that supplement the information provided here.

Chapter 2

A Reading Curriculum: Focus on Comprehension

How do readers use the language process? How do they develop reading ability?

The first question, which we discussed in chapter 1, is concerned with developing a model of reading as a language process. We have examined the relationship between author and reader—that is, the processing of the three language systems and the strategies that readers apply to achieve their purposes, which are to gain meaning.

This chapter examines the second question, which is concerned with merging our model of reading with a philosophy of education—teaching and learning. We will examine the relationship between reading, reading evaluation, and reading instruction, and in so doing will provide information for use in creating instructional materials and determining the teacher's role in supporting the development of reading ability. As we consider all of these elements, we will also be creating an outline for a reading curriculum.

PUPIL AND TEACHER

Much like the old saying "You can lead a horse to water but you can't make him drink," a person can, we believe, learn to read but cannot really be "taught" to read. Both the horse and the person must be active in their specified endeavors. When the horse will not drink, its behavior is fairly obvious, and we are immediately aware of the situation. Sometimes students' responses to a learning situation are just as direct. They will not do homework or they refuse to answer questions or they fail to participate in discussions. But at other times behavior is more circumspect. Students memorize a list of words and pass the spelling test based on that list but never use the words in speaking or writing; they successfully complete the computation of fractions but are unable to adjust a recipe to a varying number of guests; or they read assigned stories with a minimal number of oral miscues and some retention of facts but develop no facility for applying the information to similar situations or show no interest in seeking solutions to problems through reading. The role the learner plays in his or her own learning will have an impact on the quality of that learning.

The Right To Be Involved

Circumstances such as those described in the previous paragraph can be forestalled only if teaching and learning are considered a cooperative venture between teacher and student. The

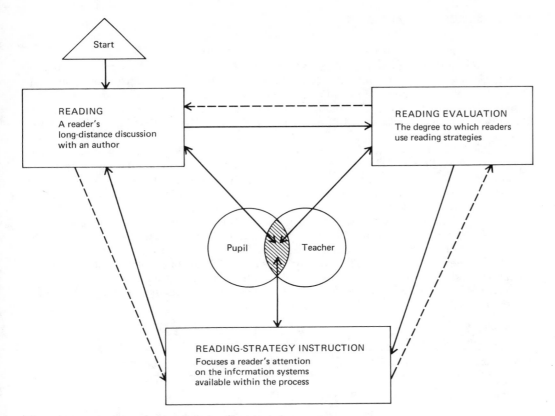

Fig. 2–1 Comprehension-Centered Reading Curriculum

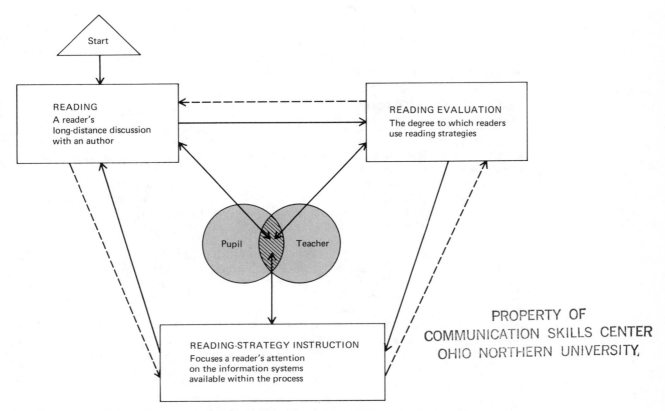

Fig. 2–2 Comprehension-Centered Reading Curriculum (focus on pupil–teacher)

teacher's role becomes one of guiding and facilitating learning more than one of imparting knowledge. Decisions concerning the concepts, content, and focus of instruction come from three interrelated and equally important factors: (1) the students' interests and concerns, (2) cues to strategy needs that the teacher picks up from evaluation of student work, and (3) the teacher's knowledge of language and thought processes, and the strategies that facilitate their development.

As active participants in the teaching-learning process, readers need to be aware of their strengths and weaknesses. They need to develop the ability to evaluate their personal reading needs. The teacher becomes responsible not only for helping students develop as readers but also for organizing the instructional environment so that pupils will develop a conscious awareness of and responsibility for their personal involvement in the process.

The learners' conscious awareness must not be confused with superficial verbalization. It is not memorizing the geometry theorem, The measure of an inscribed angle is one half the measure of its intersected arc; or stating, Nouns are the names of persons, places, or things; or being able to respond correctly to the question, What is the theme of this story? It is being able to recognize, and so make purposeful use of, relationships underlying the process in use. It is a seven-year-old reader correcting *roorshed*, which sounds like it rhymes with bushed, for *rushed* in the sentence

© *roorshed*
↳I rushed up the front stairs,[1]

reasoning: "As soon as I saw *stairs* I knew it had to be rushed"; or another young reader reading *lōsē* (producing the long *o* and long *e* sounds as marked) for *lose* in the context

His mother said, "You'll lōsē your ticket!"

but reading it appropriately minutes later in a new context, after references to losing and finding things:

He was careful not to lose his money,

and exclaiming, "Hey, that's the word I didn't know before." Both of these readers are developing an awareness of the role that context plays in the recognition of lexicon. Because they discover this relationship, they are able to maintain control of its use. They are conscious of the application that they can impose on the process.

The Right To Be Wrong

Students must have the right to make mistakes. This is a significant prerogative for two reasons: (1) Reading is not an exact process and always, for all readers, involves miscalculations; and (2) as learners, we develop an understanding for the parameters of a process by exploring them. If reading were a mere parroting of memorized items, accuracy would then be the appropriate measure of a reader's success. But as the reading model presented in Chapter 1 indicates, we are dealing with a much more complex process. Readers screen the language and thoughts of another person through their own language and thought processes. They must expect to vary from the author's intentions. Readers' willingness and ability to risk such variations thus become of central importance.

A concern for accuracy can actually mask a true breakdown in the reading process. Of necessity it causes readers' attention to be more highly concentrated on individual words than on the text as a whole. The focus is on "handling" each item—producing an appropriate sound, developing a word-level definition. The different ways in which one eleven-year-old reader handled *contented* and *tassels* within the context of one story demonstrates this point.

In reading the sentence "The sunshade was turquoise with golden tassels hanging from it," Gary paused after *golden*, mumbled under his breath, and finally produced a word that sounded like *tessels* (which rhymes with wrestles). Reading "The king was contented," he first produced *con' tented*, paused in dissatisfaction, and then produced the expected response,

---

[1] © ↳_____ indicates reader reread underlined section and corrected the miscue.

conten' ted. If the ability to pronounce accurately and the ability to gain meaning are synonymous in reading, then we ought to be able to assume that Gary understood the feelings of the king but did not know what was hanging from the canopy of the king's sunshade.

In the story the king wanted to be the most powerful thing in the universe. Each time he saw something powerful, he thought it stronger than himself and wanted to become that thing. A wizard always gave him his wish. With each wish the king was sure that the change would bring contentment. But each time he would see something more powerful, grow discontented, and wish to become that new thing.

When asked to put the story into his own words, Gary was able to recount the sequence of demands that the king made, but no amount of questioning could get him to assign a state of mind to the king. Though he had accurately produced the word *contented* at one point in the text, he had assigned it no meaning.

Following the retelling of the story, Gary was asked if there were any words he was aware of that had given him trouble. He responded, "Oh yah, those goldlike fringes on the sunshade." In this case a near miss at pronouncing a new item was combined with an effective definition.

Students and teacher are committed to a teaching-learning partnership. But the right to make mistakes on the part of students should not be translated into a laissez-faire policy on the part of the teacher. It does indicate an acceptance of learning by doing, an acceptance of students as experimenters who must put thoughts to the test. Such an active learning environment is possible only when the teacher plans open-ended learning experiences, encourages discussion, and commits classroom time to exploration. Gary was able to work through his own reading difficulties with *contented* and *tassels*. This experience provided him and his teacher with specific information about his reading strengths and needs. For instance, Gary was able to use graphophonic (letter/sound) relationships to produce expected or near-expected oral language for two unknown items. In the case of *tassels*, where sufficient context was provided, Gary developed a functional meaning for the item. When this one instance of reading is combined with other experiences, Gary's strengths and weaknesses as a reader emerge.

Observation of uninterrupted reading situations provided Gary's teacher with information about the material he was reading. The fact that Gary was able to develop a meaning for *tassels* but not for *contented* was not a function of how Gary operated as a reader but of the structure of the material he was reading. An examination of the story text indicates that *tassels* were described by the author, but the king's desire to be *contented* never was. Gary's background and experience aided in his integration of the meaning of the story. His experiences with fringes on umbrellas, curtains, and scarfs aided his understanding of the concept of *tassels*.

Both Gary and his teacher must be active and alert—but patient—within the teaching-learning partnership. Gary must be willing to apply reading strategies and to continue reading. He must have the patience to hold some of his problems in abeyance and allow his understanding to develop as the text supplies additional clues. He must be willing to build what he can from any reading experience and add his new, budding knowledge to a developing schema.

Gary's teacher must be alert to ways of evaluating Gary's successes and limitations. She must be active in determining what instructional experiences will offer the most immediate benefit to him. She must have the patience to allow him his discoveries without immediately imposing her own knowledge and experience. She must understand that a definition is seldom fully developed the first time a new idea is encountered; rather it develops over a period of time through a variety of encounters with the same idea in different settings.

Permitting students to explore, to take risks, and to make mistakes involves a respect for their intellectual capacity and their investment in the learning process. It commits students to taking responsibility for their own decision making, for evaluating the effectiveness of the alternative paths they have explored, and for formulating at least tentative conclusions. Both student and teacher become focused on finding workable solutions and progressively more satisfying ones, not upon determining any final right answers.

ELEMENTS OF A READING CURRICULUM

A reading curriculum encompasses all school-related reading experiences—both those that are planned for and those that are incidental. The way in which the curriculum planner perceives the interaction among learning theory, educational philosophy, social and psychological needs, methodology, and the operation of the reading process will determine the planned elements of the curriculum. Based on our view of this interaction, we have developed a comprehension-centered reading curriculum encompassing three major elements: reading, reading evaluation, and reading-strategy instruction.

Reading

Any language interaction—discussing rules for playing blindman's bluff, writing an essay on the relationship between thought and language, relating the symptoms of a malfunctioning engine to a mechanic, ordering a meal from a French menu—is the culmination of one's facility with language, one's grasp of the context of a situation, and one's ability to mobilize thought and language forces. Language users, involved in the interaction, have a communication need—learning the rules of the game, developing the relationship, repairing the motor, eating the food; and they satisfy this need through use of available language and information resources.

It is on the basis of their success in such experiences that language users evaluate their proficiencies and needs. Playing blindman's bluff gives a new meaning for being "it," writing the essay causes the student to seek more finite and descriptive terms to define the possible relationships among oral language users, conversing with the mechanic convinces the driver to learn the names for more engine parts.

Reading can be defined as a private, ongoing, long-distance discussion between the reader and the author. There is no need for a third person (such as the teacher) to direct that discussion or focus its interpretation. The author has the major responsibility for introducing and interpreting ideas, and the reader the major responsibility for considering and integrating them. By no means is it a one-way stream. The reader and the author communicate with each other. Ideas are fed into the discussion by both participants.

For example, an author marshals facts for why T. J. Blowhorn was a significant president.

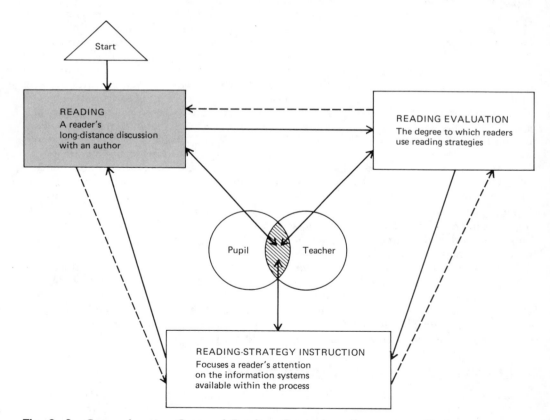

Fig. 2–3 Comprehension-Centered Reading Curriculum (focus on reading)

Noted are the series of treaties signed with foreign powers, the decrease in the national debt, the cultural-exchange program. The reader remembers that this same president also allowed a high level of unemployment, reduced federal funds to education, and used the presidential veto on an equal-rights bill, all matters of great concern to that reader. He concludes that Blowhorn was at best a mediocre leader and that his internal policies might have been damaging enough to make him a poor president in the reader's estimation. The author has introduced facts about T. J.'s presidency that the reader either has never seriously considered or had not known. She has placed these facts within a logical framework and interpreted them. The reader, however, is not limited to the author's information or logic. He applies his own knowledge, tests the author's logic against his own, and in this case decides to reject the author's views.

Given the understanding that reading is a long-distance discussion, the curriculum must reflect the following three attributes of reading: (1) It usually occurs *in silence*; (2) it is *done independently*; (3) and it normally involves the *reader's selection of materials*. It is also significant that reading and reading instruction *must* be viewed separately in the development of a comprehension-centered curriculum.

Readers read silently for several reasons, chief among them the fact that it is economical. They can visually and mentally process the information much more rapidly than speech will allow. This additional speed saves time and permits a greater retention and use of linguistic cues in processing and predicting the material. Many of the language cues picked up by readers—the shape of a word, the possible sound correspondence for a spelling pattern, the grammatical structure—provide short-term information whose only value lies in its function as a cue to create a meaningful whole.

If readers focus too much on any one cue or too many unrelated cues, they cannot hold them in short-term memory long enough to use them in constructing a conceptual unit. Reading then becomes merely a word-calling game in which the player obtains a high score by accurately reproducing a string of expected but relatively meaningless sounds and sound sequences.

Silent reading also encourages self-pacing. There are no intermediaries—no referees, no listeners—whom readers must consider. They need simply please themselves. They can speed up, slow down, reread, pause to think, all in an effort to make sense of the author's message. They do not have the added burden of attempting to present the message meaningfully to a third party.

Oral reading may be used in a number of situations. For diagnostic purposes a reader may read aloud to the teacher, a teacher may read aloud to children to share something with them, or children may read along with others or to others. Oral reading may occur to share something from the newspaper with others or to prove a point being discussed or debated. But for most purposes and for most of a person's reading time, reading is a silent receptive activity.

Reading is a private, individual, and independent process, not a team sport. Only two people, the reader and the author, can participate; and the outcome of the experience will vary as the identity of either participant changes.

Let us examine the foregoing statement through an example.

Several students from one classroom were all reading the same story. The plot revolved around a herd of sheep in danger of attack by coyotes. In the course of the story the coyotes were identified as being bigger than the sheep dog, having long sharp teeth, being able to climb over high rocky places, making loud howling noises, and having coats of long fur. When the students were asked what a coyote was, their responses included, "It's like a wolf," and "It's like a wild goat."

All were aware that their conclusions were tentative, for they prefaced their definitions with such phrases as "I think." They all had use of the same information supplied by the author. But their personal experiences—TV westerns, trips to the zoo, animal stories—varied. As the relationship between readers and author varies, so will the information derived from the reading vary. The outcomes of any reading experience are not totally predictable, nor can anyone make them so.

Readers must be on their own; they must be independent. Each student in the class described above developed as much of a concept of coyotes as their personal experiences and the information contained within the story permitted. These concepts were sufficient for the immediate reading purposes.

As soon as a third person intercedes, reading stops—even though learning continues. Readers may modify or expand their own reading interpretations depending on how they view the status of the teacher, other readers, or members of a discussion group who offer alternate interpretations. This may happen even if the other views are no more fully developed than those developed in the stories. When the teacher in our example asked the students to look up more information about coyotes in the dictionary, they found one popular pocket dictionary describing coyotes as "wolflike animals common in W. North America."[2]

More fully developed concepts can thus be formed about coyotes, and there may be greater consistency in those concepts than in those developed by individual readers. However, that learning would be the result of a language experience other than reading. The students in this case do not gain new information or develop new concepts through a reading experience. The way to obtain the best knowledge about coyotes would be to involve the students in a more concrete experience than reading—a trip to the zoo, or a movie. Younger readers, in particular, will need these types of concrete experiences to promote concept development. Involving young children in varied, interesting firsthand experiences will prepare them to cope more successfully with ideas and concepts they encounter in print. There are limitations on the learning that can develop solely from reading.

The focus on the reader brings us to the third attribute of reading. *Readers have both the need and the right to personally choose a significant portion of their own reading material.* Self-selection allows commitment and involvement. Since they are investing time and effort, individuals will have a stake in the outcome. But self-selection is not a natural gift. It must be learned. Readers have to learn how to judge their own needs, interests, and abilities; where to seek reading material; and how to judge the intents and abilities of authors.

One elementary-school student writing a report for social studies wastes hours seeking the population of a small African country because she does not know about the use of an atlas. Your next-door neighbor invests $7000 in a new car solely on the basis of the salesperson's advice because he does not know about a consumer's guide. A high-school student, fulfilling an English assignment to read a piece of literature focusing on the Civil War period, reads a dull novel, while a classmate reads *Gone with the Wind* for the same assignment. One of those students did not know how to make use of the cross-referencing in the library's card catalogue.

All efforts at producing effective readers will go to waste if they are taught in an atmosphere in which the teacher usually selects the readers' materials. Many people with the facility to learn through reading fail to make use of self-selection because they never learn how to do so.

To summarize the focus on the reading element of the curriculum it is important to remember that reading occurs within a context created by the knowledge and background that both reader and author bring to the situation and the reader must be as actively involved in communication as the author. For this to occur the reader must usually be reading silently, independent in searching for meaning and personally involved in the selection of reading materials.

Reading Evaluation

We have described reading as a private process that can function fully only when it is uninterrupted. At the same time, we believe that reading instruction can be planned and relevant only when it is based on identified needs emerging from reading experiences. It becomes important then to find means of *preserving* reading experiences in order to evaluate them; but these means must maintain the private and ongoing nature of the reading process as much as possible and must reflect the variety of reading experiences students have. The evaluation procedures must measure the cueing systems, the reading strategies, and their relationships as they operate within the reading process.

There are two purposes for evaluating reading. First, there is the need to be aware of (a) the variety of materials that students are reading and (b) their success in working with them. This

[2]*The American Heritage Dictionary of the Language*, ed. Peter Davis (New York: Dell Publishing Co., Inc., 1970), p. 167.

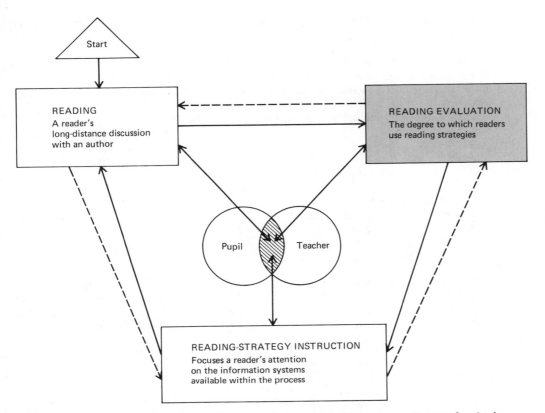

Fig. 2–4   Comprehension-Centered Reading Curriculum (focus on reading evaluation)

evaluation can involve a fairly gross or general examination, since it is meant to determine whether the individual reader is involved with expanded reading experiences, can cope with various materials, and is treating reading as a meaning-gaining experience.

The second purpose for evaluating is to facilitate reading development through instruction. The interest here is to identify a reader's strength and to specify problems and gauge their relative significance. Specificity is needed because the information will determine the content or selection of reading-strategy lessons.

Reading permeates the classroom just as it permeates our society. Even as we engage in reading instruction, we make use of reading as a major means of instruction and communication. The schedule for the day is written on the board, the assignment is prefaced by a set of written directions, a library book is used to change the pace, a school-sponsored bake sale is advertised by signs posted in the halls, the words to a new song are distributed in mimeographed form.

Although reading and reading instruction must be considered separately in planning curriculum, these two functions in fact occur simultaneously and continuously throughout the school experience. There must be an ongoing program of evaluation to make sure that communication is occurring—that students are gaining meaning from both their reading and the reading instruction. Examination of the productive aspects of language in response to reading experiences offers students opportunities to

1. Answer open-ended comprehension questions about a reading experience, or write or tell about a reading experience
2. Create a play, piece of art, or experiment as a result of reading
3. Participate in a discussion on the basis of information gained in reading
4. Follow directions for building, cooking, or experimenting

Such writing and speaking experiences can reveal whether or not the readers

1. Constructed a general theme for what was read
2. Incorporated or related the information to their own construct of knowledge
3. Developed some meaning for new concepts presented by the material
4. Related the theme, concepts, or information gained to any other situtions or circumstances
5. Perceived some underlying relationship involving the events

This aspect of evaluation focuses on the outcome of the students' reading, not on the reading itself. Indications that students are not able to handle the reading meaningfully call for the teacher to use varying combinations of the following responses:

1. Eliminate the need for the reading
2. Provide more oral language support for the reading
3. Alter the materials to be read
4. Plan for a specific evaluation of the reading situation in preparation for offering reading-strategy instruction

Detail and perspective become important in planning for reading instruction. We need to know what specific problems individual readers faced in a text and what strategies they used to handle those problems. Then we need to consider the relative significance of each problem and the strength the readers have in responding to them. We must determine which problems will be

1. Repeatedly faced in varying texts
2. Limited to specific kinds of reading material
3. Most disruptive to gaining meaning
4. Easily amenable to instruction

And we must do all this without disrupting the reading process.

SAMPLING ORAL READING

We have described reading as a discussion between reader and author. Both of the participants bring their language, their knowledge, and their thought processes to this discussion. As in any discussion, there are points where the two discussants do not share a common experience—points where perspective or knowledge differ. At these points readers are not always able to cope, in an expected manner, with the material the author has prepared, and they will not anticipate the author exactly.

Because readers are making use of the available cueing systems but miss producing the expected response, we say that readers make *miscues*. Because readers' concerns are not accuracy but meaning, and because no two people can ever have exactly the same experiences, storehouses of knowledge, schemata or perspectives, miscues are natural to the reading process. All readers make miscues, and because those miscues result from the use of the same cueing systems that expected reading responses use, they reflect the strategies readers apply. We can evaluate readers' use of strategies by examining their miscues.

Miscues must be collected under natural reading conditions:

1. The reading material must be new to the readers. In this way there can be no possibility that the readers' responses are based on expectations from previous reading. The miscues will indicate ability to anticipate the author.
2. The reading must be uninterrupted. Interruptions disrupt readers' search for meaning, for the selected cues held in short-term memory are lost. At the same time, any help supplied by the teacher reflects what the teacher knows, not what the individual readers know.
3. Readers must view the gaining of meaning as the purpose of the reading. There should be no concern with performing for an audience or with producing an exact rendition.

Readers should be focused not on the reading itself but on the use of information, or the enjoyment gained from the reading.

These conditions are met when readers are given an unfamiliar but complete story or article to read and are informed that they will be totally dependent upon their own resources, that they must continue reading past any problems, and that after the reading they will be responsible for retelling the material. The whole process can be preserved for evaluation purposes by tape-recording the reading. Readers' miscues are then available for evaluation by replaying the tape and comparing the reading with the printed text.

EVALUATING READING MISCUES

Evaluation, as an integral part of the reading curriculum, must reflect both the model of the reading process and the instructional procedures that are being used. Only when the three components of the curriculum (reading, reading evaluation, and reading-strategy instruction) are synchronized will evaluation techniques indicate whether students are profiting from the instructional procedures and whether those procedures actually encourage the development of successful reading strategies.

The view of reading and instruction presented in this text is based on, and owes much to, research in miscue analysis. Miscue analysis can provide an insight into how people learn and develop as language users. It can indicate the degree to which the individual reader makes use of available language cues and maintains the integrity of the integrated language systems. It can also aid in examining the relative complexity and predictability of reading materials.

Later in the text, as each strategy lesson is introduced, the evaluation of the readers intended to benefit from a particular lesson will include a description of the miscue profile of those readers. At this point we will provide an informal miscue procedure composed of three questions.[3]

Miscue analysis attaches major significance not to any one miscue or the quantity of miscues but to the general pattern of miscues made throughout a text. Readers who are gaining meaning will produce a large percentage of sentences that remain semantically acceptable regardless of the number of miscues in the sentence. A semantically acceptable sentence makes sense within the text. Insight into the most significant aspects of miscue analysis can be gained by asking three questions in an informal miscue procedure:

1. Does the sentence the reader finally produces make sense in the context of the whole story?
2. What is the degree of meaning change caused by the miscues as finally produced by the reader?
3. In word-for-word-substitution miscues, what is the degree of graphic similarity between the word in the text and the word produced?

Compare the following two readings:

Leslie's Reading

	Accept.	Change
1.	Y	N
2.	Y	N
3.	Y	P
4.	Y	N
5.	Y	N

---

[3]Readers unfamiliar with miscue procedures may refer to the sources suggested in the Bibliography, especially Yetta M. Goodman and Carolyn Burke, *The Reading Miscue Inventory* (New York: Macmillan Company, 1973).

Karen's Reading

^{1}One day Sue was ~~taking~~ *talking* ^{H} a picture in the garden.

^{2}She suddenly ~~wanted~~ *should* *twisted* ^{H} a drink and ran into the

house. ^{3} She left the camera on the grass.

^{4}Kitten had been playing in the ~~rose~~ *nose* ^{H} vines. ^{5} Now

she walked over to the camera.

	Accept.	Change
1.	N	Y
2.	N	Y
3.	Y	N
4.	N	P
5.	Y	N

In their readings of the same story segment, Leslie makes seven miscues, and Karen, only four. The numbers are not as significant as are the kinds of strategies each reader is using.

The most significant strategies to evaluate are those concerned with the degree to which a reader's miscue produces a semantically and syntactically acceptable sentence while reading is taking place, or the degree to which self-correction occurs if the miscue is unacceptable.

1. Does the sentence the reader finally produces make sense in the context of the whole story?

Yes *(Y)* When the sentence, read as finally produced by the reader, is acceptable
No *(N)* When the sentence, read as finally produced by the reader, is unacceptable

To read for acceptability, consider each sentence as the reader finally produced it. All corrected miscues or attempts at correction should be read as finally resolved by the reader. When there are no attempts at correction, the miscues should be read as produced. Miscues that are acceptable within the reader's dialect should be considered acceptable. For this type of informal procedure the coding for each sentence can be tallied in the margin of a copy of the material to be read as shown in the example.

Every sentence Leslie produces results in semantically and syntactically acceptable sentences. Sentences 1 and 5 are acceptable as they are initially produced. She intones sentences 2 and 3 in such a way as to produce acceptable sentence structures. She makes the first clause of sentence 2 into a complete sentence and connects the second clause with sentence 3. She substitutes *she* for *and* and then *and* for both the period and *she* appropriately. She makes no attempts to correct these fully acceptable miscues. Although the substitutions of *glasses* and *on* in sentences 3 and 4 produce syntactically acceptable sentences, they do not make sense in the context of the whole story. Leslie self-corrects to produce fully acceptable sentences.

Although Karen's miscues often retain similar grammatical function, they do not result in fully acceptable sentences in this story.

Additional insight can be gained into a reader's focus on comprehension by asking the second question in the miscue procedure, which concerns the degree of meaning change:

2. What is the degree of meaning change caused by the miscues as finally produced by the reader?

No *(N)* When the sentence, read as finally produced by the reader, does not change the intended meaning of the story
Partial *(P)* When the sentence, read as finally produced by the reader, changes, is consistent with, or loses *minor* incidents, characters, or sequences in, the story
Yes *(Y)* When the sentence, read as finally produced by the reader, changes, is inconsistent with, or loses *major* incidents, characters, or sequences in the story

If the story is between 600 and 1000 words in length, each sentence should be coded. If the story is longer, code all the sentences through the nearest 600 words. A typical pattern of the reader's concern for meaning is usually provided by this point in the reading. This is a rule of thumb and may be varied depending on the reader, the purpose for the evaluation, and the material.

3. In word-for-word substitution miscues, what is the degree of graphic similarity between the word in the text and the word produced?

The third question provides information about the degree to which graphic information is being used by readers. When we evaluate miscues for use of graphic information, we are concerned with the extent to which the miscue (the observed response) produced by the reader looks like the text word. Adequate information about graphic similarity can be obtained from an evaluation of the first twenty-five word-for-word, nonidentical substitution miscues:[4]

High	(*H*)	When there is a high degree of similarity, two out of three parts of the words are similar: the beginning and middle; the beginning and end; or the middle and end
Some	(*S*)	When there is some degree of similarity; one of the three parts of the words is similar: the beginning or general configuration; the middle; or the end
None	(*N*)	When there is no degree of similarity; nothing is similar in the two words

As shown in the samples, the substitutions *glasses* for *grass*, *on* for *in*, *talking* for *taking*, *$winted* for *wanted*, and *nose* for *rose*—all of which show high similarity—are marked right on the worksheet with an H. *Susan* for *Sue* and *should* for *suddenly* involve words having initial consonants, in addition to other cues, in common; and *garden* and its substitution *yard* have medial letters in common. These miscues are marked with an S, for in each case there is some degree of similarity.

The remaining miscues in Leslie's reading have no similarity at all; therefore an N is placed above each of these substitution miscues. Leslie's miscue of *and*, which substitutes for both the period at the end of sentence 2 as well as *she* at the beginning of sentence 3, is not marked at all. This is a complex miscue, since it involves more than a word-for-word substitution. It is not possible to determine whether *and* is substituted for the period, for *she*, or for both. In such instances graphic similarity is not coded. Graphic similarity would not be marked for omission or insertion miscues.

Graphs like those in Figure 2–5 may be developed for each student's reading.

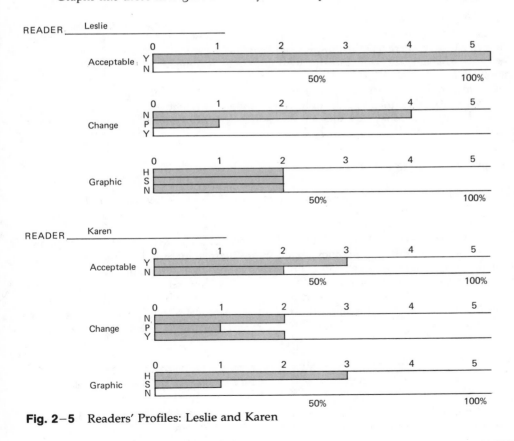

Fig. 2–5   Readers' Profiles: Leslie and Karen

---

[4]Graphic shape should be considered in responding to this question.

As the graph clearly shows, 100 percent of Leslie's sentences retain semantic and syntactic acceptability with only a small degree of meaning change, but Karen's patterns are more mixed. Both readers' miscues show use of graphic cues to various degrees. The biggest differences between the two readers is that Leslie is concerned with having her reading make sense as she reads, and Karen is more willing to stick with look-alike equivalents that have grammatical relationships but do not usually make sense. Leslie produces sentences that are fully acceptable and that in most cases hardly change the meaning of the story. In the three places where there is meaning change, she disconfirms her predictions and self-corrects. During her reading she actually reads "on the glasses" and then says, "no, I mean grass." She transforms sentences but retains their acceptability.

On the other hand, only 60 percent of Karen's sentences are semantically acceptable and sound like language, and all her miscues show at least some graphic similarity. If this pattern continues throughout her reading, then Karen will need help to integrate her reading strategies.

The strategy lessons introduced in Part Two provide suggestions to help readers like Leslie continue good use of reading strategies and to expand reading experience and reading effectiveness. There are also suggestions for readers like Karen who need to be helped to integrate the reading strategies that they use well with a focus on making sense out of the reading material.

We recommend that these procedures be followed in order to produce a protocol ready for miscue marking on a worksheet:[5]

1. Ask readers to read *without aid* a story that they have never seen.
2. Audiotape the reading session.
3. Mark every miscue on a reproduced copy of the story being read.
4. Code the miscues by relistening to the tape at a convenient time and place.
5. Produce a profile for each reader.

Selection of material is important. The story selected should have sufficient theme and plot, or if it is an informational piece, it should provide a complete concept or event. The story line must be of some interest to the prospective reader and be at least 600 words in length. The material must be at a level of difficulty that will cause some reading problems but will not cause frustration to the point of task rejection.

Readers should be informed of the purposes and procedures of the taping session. They must know ahead of time that no aid will be forthcoming during the session. They should also be informed at this time that after they finish reading they will be asked to retell the story or article in their own words.

READER-SELECTED MISCUES

Dorothy Watson has developed an evaluation technique for miscue analysis that involves the students. This procedure known as Reader Selected Miscues calls for the conscious participation of readers in the evaluation process.[6] Readers are given a supply of bookmarks. They are asked to read silently any self-selected piece of material and, as they do so, to insert a bookmark at any point where they have difficulty, without interrupting the reading process. The reading continues for approximately twenty minutes. Following the reading period the reader returns to each marked page, records complete sentences involved in any reading difficulties, and underlines that specific segment of each sentence that proved troublesome. These miscues are then available for analysis by *informally* subjecting them to the reading miscue questions described in the preceding section.

---

[5]Kenneth S. Goodman and Carolyn Burke, *Studies of Children's Behavior while Reading Orally* (Washington, D.C.: U.S. Dept. of HEW, Office of Education, Project No. 425, 1968).

[6]Dorothy J. Harper Watson, "A Psycholinguistic Description of the Oral Reading Miscues Generated by Selected Readers Prior to and Following Exposure to a Saturated Book Program" (Ph.D. dissertation, Wayne State University, 1973).

This procedure can be used with either an individual student or a group of students. When a group has read from a number of varied materials, they then share their miscues. They can identify categories of miscues—that is, unknown names, foreign words and phrases, unfamiliar sentence structure, or any other aspect of written language similar to those treated in the strategy lessons in this volume.

The use of Reader Selected Miscues serves two equally important functions: (1) It provides the teacher with an informal group procedure. It takes little time to administer, and the depth of the evaluation of miscues can vary according to need and time. (2) It provides students with a way of evaluating their own reading without interrupting the reading process. They can read with minimal disruption and still preserve aspects of the process for later scrutiny. By being able to evaluate their own reading, students are in a position to take part in planning instruction. (This procedure is more fully described in the strategy lesson entitled "Identifying Hard-to-Predict Structures.")

Reading-Strategy Instruction

The purpose of reading-strategy instruction is to make students consciously aware of the language and thought cues available to them as readers and to support their developing use of reading strategies. This does not mean that reading instruction becomes an academic naming of parts of speech, systems, or set procedures. The readers' only need is to become aware of the alternate information systems available within the process.

In a previous section reading was described as a private, independent, uninterrupted, and usually silent process in which the focus is upon meaning-gaining. Not only are the language systems on which the readers depend intermeshed but they are also interdependent.

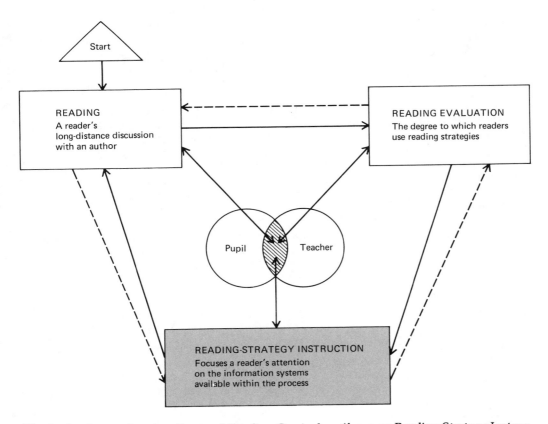

Fig. 2–6 Comprehension-Centered Reading Curriculum (focus on Reading Strategy Instruction)

Consider this sentence:

The *grebe* is a waterfowl, which I have heard about but never seen.

Assuming that the italicized word in the sentence is unfamiliar to the readers, they can develop a pronunciation through use of the letter/sound relationships of the graphophonic system, recognize it as a noun by perceiving it in structural relationship to other items in the sentence, and endow it with meaning through information gained either from past experience or sentence context.

Evaluation of the reading process determines which of the available cues the readers are using. Reading-strategy instruction is intended to strengthen the cueing systems already in use, to legitimize efficent strategies that readers have sometimes been taught to believe are inappropriate, and to develop awareness of those strategies and cueing systems not being sufficiently exploited by the readers. Like reading itself, reading-strategy instruction has three basic attributes, although the focuses are very different: It is public, it highlights the component systems within the reading process, and it limits the responsibilities of the reader.

The first visible distinction between reading and reading instruction is that reading instruction involves participants in addition to the author and the reader. The process of instruction requires at least three people: reader, author, and teacher. In many instances it includes a number of readers who have similar strategy needs. *Instruction is public* and shared with others. The teacher is a necessary third party for two reasons, the first of which we have already discussed. The whole instructional experience is based on evaluative procedures the teacher has conducted, and is carried out through carefully selected and focused materials. The second reason has to do with facilitating learning. Conscious awareness of process is enhanced when a learning experience is shared. Learners provoke insight in one another as they share both their attempts at processing and their partially formulated ideas. The teacher acts as a sounding board against which ideas are played and from which insightful questions are fed back into the discussion. A significant aspect of knowing is not only acting on ideas—a function that is essentially incorporated in the reading process—but being able to put ideas into language. Once something has been communicated, it is available for examination, for further development, and for future use. Language offers some permanency to thought. It increases the likelihood that what was thoughtfully conceived of on one occasion can be retrieved and implemented on another.

During reading all readers intuitively and automatically process needed cues. Their focus is on the meaning that results from the reading process and not on the process itself. When all goes well, readers do not concern themselves with how meaning was obtained—with what cues were derived from what language systems. The person who determines a *grebe* is a bird as a result of reading the earlier example is likely to explain that he or she knew that fact "because the sentence says so." No thought will be given to the complexity of cues necessary to such a development. As long as reading goes as expected, there is no need to consider the process. There is only the need to make use of it. It is only when reading does not go as expected that the reader has a need to shift the focus from ends to means.

When things do not go as planned, readers need to be able to select and consider available cues in order to determine alternative strategies. They need to focus or *highlight the language systems* and reading strategies they use. They need to ask themselves:

How important is this word or phrase?
(Does it look as if the missing information is significant enough to the message to expend effort in seeking it?)

How can I find it?
(Which language cues are generally available in the text?)

What do I know?
(Which cues have I been able to process?)

What is my best guess now?
(What components of a tentative concept or meaning have I distilled?)

These questions may never be overtly formulated by the reader but they are part of the intuitive search for sense that readers engage in as they try to comprehend their reading. With the answers to these questions in mind, readers determine whether any other cues are available and whether they are able to make use of them. Even in instances where readers are unable to process further, they have outlined the limits of their problems and salvaged some cues for possible later use.

Readers could recognize *grebe* as a noun and know that the sentence structure

The *something* is a *something* . . .

denotes a synonym relationship between grebe and *waterfowl*, even if they have no idea what a waterfowl is. If readers are able to consciously highlight the available cues and determine which ones they can process, their search for further information will be more focused than would be the case if they just have a general feeling that they have not understood the sentence.

They will know, for instance, that what they learn about waterfowl can be applied to their developing concept of *grebes*.

The surface of the lake was spotted with waterfowl. All of them were in constant motion, busily diving for food, chattering at each other and preening their feathers.

If waterfowl float on water and have feathers, and *grebes* are waterfowl, then grebes probably float on water and have feathers. Such information will not be available to readers who do not salvage partial cues from the reading of the first sentence. On the other hand, readers may be aware that this reference to *grebe* is of little importance to comprehending the whole text—a fleeting reference not worth much time or effort.

Reading proficiency is based on readers' ability to proceed at full speed with interest focused on the developing meaning but with the flexibility to reprocess, shift focus, or jump ahead when difficulty is encountered. In this respect readers must be like drivers who proceed along the highway in high gear, shift into low to make the grade up a mountain, and then shift back into high gear. The car engine will be overworked if it is in low gear all of the time; the reading process will bog down if readers focus too constantly on the process of reading or become sidetracked by unimportant details.

Not only must readers become aware of alternate available processing cues but they must learn to use them with discretion. They must develop flexibility in determining and applying appropriate reading strategies. Reading-strategy instruction can support both the awareness of the cueing systems and the development of flexibility by *limiting readers' responsibilities* during the learning process. One way this is accomplished is through thoughtful selection of reading material used for instruction. When evaluation procedures indicate a need for specific strategies, reading material is written or selected to highlight the operation of that strategy.

The reading-strategy lesson is constructed to help readers gain information from a cueing system that they may not be using adequately or that they may believe they should not use. It makes readers aware of the reading process. In other words, it raises to a conscious level how reading works. The very structure of the material moves readers back into "low gear." They focus on the process as well as on the meaning. The material must present the highlighted strategy in its most complete and direct form. The strategy is within a language context complete with all the cueing systems, including those with which readers are most successful. Therefore readers approach the new learning with all possible cues available and within structures they already control. The structure of the material allows the readers to discover the significance of the highlighted strategy.

The meaning carried by the material usually involves information and concepts familiar to the readers. The material should be aimed at guaranteeing the gaining of meaning. In this way readers can afford to focus their attention on an aspect of the reading process without losing sight of the very purpose of reading—communication of ideas. Because the highlighted strategy is embedded in a context that has familiar meaning and language structure, readers' responsibilities are both limited and focused.

Reading-strategy instruction operates at a critical moment. It is the planned interaction of language systems and experience to support an insightful event for a reader.

A reading curriculum is a way of organizing language and thought systems for instructional purposes. No curriculum accurately or completely encompasses all the elements and relationships that operate in the reality of reading and reading instruction. Rather, a curriculum offers to the teacher what reading-strategy instruction offers to students—that is, an opportunity to move thought into language and to make it manageable and available for implementation and experimentation. What is down on paper at any one moment should represent the current culmination of ideas about the teaching and learning of reading. What is down on paper should metaphorically be written in pencil, not in ink. It should be amenable to change as our thoughts and our experiences dictate.

Chapter 3

Reading-Strategy Lessons

Our basic model of the reading process incorporates the interrelationship of the reader and the author, and that of the reading cueing systems. Our model of reading curriculum indicates the interrelationship of reading, evaluation, and instruction. The reading-strategy lessons in Part Two exploit these interrelationships.

A strategy lesson is a plan for instruction that focuses on aspects of written language for which students need support. The lessons may grow out of reading experiences that students are not processing effectively or the need for expanded reading experiences from which most students can benefit. Strategy lessons are to be used by individuals or groups who, through evaluation, indicate that they need the specific support emphasized in the lesson. The material for each strategy lesson is carefully constructed or selected to provide a *real, whole* language context while focusing on a selected reading strategy. Materials written or chosen especially for the strategy lessons make it possible for students to use their language competence to the fullest as they continuously develop reading proficiency.

SIGNIFICANCE OF CONTEXT

In written language, readers have available a semantic and syntactic as well as a graphophonic system. A reading *context* is never as ambiguous as are isolated units of language. Only in context is the reader able to make use of syntax and semantics in order to decide on the most appropriate of the possible meanings of a linguistic unit, and therefore approach the meaning of the author. There is no interaction between author and reader when isolated bits of information are being read. For example, you may be able to assign meaning to some of the following words: *if, myself, for, me, will, I, am, who, be, not,* but not until these words have a syntactic and semantic context—*If I am not for myself, who will be for me?*—can you begin to gain some understanding.

When learning takes place in context, learners are able to build on and expand the structures that organize their experiences. Some psychologists call these structures *schemata*.[1] These structures are built through interactions with the environment; the learner then uses the

---

[1] Ulric Neisser, *Cognition and Reality* (San Francisco: W. H. Freeman and Co., Publishers, 1976).

schema to categorize certain items, notice how they operate differently in different contextual settings, and organize their developing concepts.

Life provides situational contexts. It is from these natural, ordinary, everyday contexts that infants from the very beginning of their learning try to make sense out of their world and build their schemata. They use a variety of strategies to discover relationships about language and thinking. Out of such complex situational contexts they learn to select those things that are significant to learn from those things that are unimportant. They find ways to distinguish the sounds of language from the sounds of cars, cats, and fire engines. They do not have to isolate each of these things in order to learn. They learn to identify and classify through years of experience involving talking and thinking. They know when someone they live with is sad or angry from a tone of voice. They have used many strategies in learning prior to their first school experience. As a consequence of developing their language and concepts, they have learned to predict, confirm, and integrate this information into their schemata about the world around them.

These same strategies will be used in their reading if they are permitted to capitalize on them in the classroom; and if significant written context is available, they can be helped to apply them to learning to read. *A student's own strategies are the strengths that a reading program must build on.*

CRITERIA FOR SELECTING AND WRITING MATERIALS FOR STRATEGY LESSONS

Context is a significant aspect of any learning situation. In the writing or selection of materials for reading-strategy lessons, at least seven criteria must be considered to insure that the context of the material will be as supportive as possible of the reading strategies the student is developing. These criteria must indicate concern for the reader, the language, and the content of the written material.

Concern for the Reader

Strategy lessons are most effective when they are used with students who need them.[2] Learners are often confused when they either "learn" something they already know or are "taught" something beyond their understanding. Many students are quick to apply to reading the strategies they use in oral language activities. If you try to teach them what they are already doing well, they may become insecure and believe that they have been doing things wrong. This will interfere with the confidence they need to develop in order to use strategies effectively. At the same time, if aspects of reading are presented and students are not integrating these concepts, they begin to focus on isolated aspects of language rather than learn from the total language context.

Strategy lessons are most effective when they are used at the critical moment. When you become aware of a student's problem, you can select appropriate material for the strategy lesson that will support that student. Through various evaluation techniques, you can decide what will benefit the student most at a particular time. Not all problems can be solved at once. The decision about which problem to focus on can depend on the material being read, the most significant problem of the student, or the particular interest of the student. Strategy lessons are meant to be used when and as they are needed. There is, then, no preferable sequence to the use of the lessons. Moreover, the material for strategy lessons can be used as a model to help teachers develop even more personalized strategy lessons than strangers could ever write.

---

[2]Primary teachers may want to incorporate strategy lessons into their reading program in order to encourage the development of good reading strategies in beginning readers. These activities can be carried out with groups of children in an informal, fun atmosphere. Materials and discussions should be appropriate to the children's backgrounds and experiences.

Concern for Language

The language of material in the strategy lessons is similar to the language of the learners. Most of the material to be read by the students has been written in common sentence patterns, unless a strategy lesson calls for a unique pattern. Common syntax provides students with opportunities to use their language strengths in order to predict and confirm as they read. However, the material has a variety of common sentence patterns so that students learn to predict more than a limited number of sentence structures. As they learn to cope with those structures familiar to them, they expand their use of reading strategies to reading materials that also contain less common sentence structures.

The language of material in the strategy lesson shows concern for literary quality. All written material for reading instruction should take into consideration literary quality. Value judgments on the part of both readers and writers make it difficult to set up criteria for high-quality literature. What should be avoided is the stilted, boring language that sometimes characterizes reading-instruction materials.

The language of material in the strategy lesson minimizes ambiguity and uses appropriately redundant information. Written language that does not provide enough information for the reader can cause the reader to misunderstand. For example, the sentence

They were bouncing balls.

is ambiguous and can easily be misunderstood. There is not enough redundant information for the reader to know what the author is really talking about. However, provided with additional information, the reader may have enough cues to make some judgments about the author's intent:

As John walked into the toy store, some unusual movements caught his attention. They were bouncing balls.

For meaning to be achieved, adding just one sentence may not always provide sufficient cues to the reader. Often a greater amount of context is necessary.

As John walked into the toy store, the movement of colored spheres caught his attention. As he moved closer to look at the spheres moving up and down in a steady motion, he realized that they were bouncing balls although he didn't understand what caused them to move.

Because of the significance of minimizing ambiguity and using appropriate redundant information, instructional material should be a complete story or article of at least 400 words whenever possible. By *complete* we mean material that carries its message through to an appropriate conclusion. We believe that comprehension is aided when the reader has sufficient context to read. One of our assumptions is that a story is easier to read than a page, a page is easier to read than a paragraph, a paragraph is easier to read than a sentence, and a sentence is easier to read than a word.

Concern for Content

The content of material in the strategy lessons is interesting to the readers. When reading material is interesting to students, it helps provide them with both purpose and motivation, which are necessary if they are to enjoy the reading experience. In order to be in a position to satisfy this criterion, the teacher will need to know the interests of particular students—their personal likes and dislikes. In preparing our selections, we have tried to consider student interests, but each teacher must accept the responsibility for gathering the information needed to personalize the program for students. Keeping track of the kind of written material students select when they read on their own will provide additional evidence of their interests.

The content of material in the strategy lessons is significant to the readers. Significance and interest go hand in hand; each supports the other. Readers prefer reading about things important to their lives, and these are the things they tend to be most interested in. Relevancy is often individual, since it relates to things important in the individual reader's life, such as family, hobbies, dreams, or culture. Such relevancy needs no support from the teacher to provide purpose and motivation for reading experience. When the teacher finds exciting ways to show students why certain experiences are important to them, then what is relevant to students can be expanded. Nonreading experiences may need to be provided in order to build the relevant relationship to the readers' lives prior to providing the reading experience.

The materials provided in the strategy lessons in this book have been selected for general appeal. They can be used for a wide range of ages and student interests. For some lessons the materials can be read aloud to students if it appears that the students will have difficulty with the readings.

We have used the strategy lessons in this book with readers of all ages, from five through adulthood. The basic reading strategies remain the same. The materials can often remain the same as well; however, they may be adapted depending upon students' ages and interests. When we have written materials or adapted materials written by others, they have been most successful when they were related to real experiences which we or our students have had.

Remember the materials included in this text are meant to be prototypes. They are examples for you to use and adapt. The best materials will be written or selected by you for specific students with specified needs.

GRID OF COMPREHENDING STRATEGIES

Each strategy lesson in part two highlights one significant reading strategy—predicting, confirming, or integrating—as well as one of the three language systems—graphophonic, syntactic, or semantic. The strategy lessons in the Grid of Comprehending Strategies have been selected because, based on our research, we have discovered that these are the most common aspects of reading that students need help in developing. The grid categorizes the strategy lessons. The horizontal columns list the strategy lessons most related to predicting, confirming, and integrating. Each lesson is placed in the vertical column that identifies its primary focus: the semantic, syntactic, or graphophonic language systems. However, during any lesson all strategies and language systems will occur because of their interrelationship in the reading process. No strategy lessons are listed under integrating for the graphophonic and syntactic language systems, since we believe that semantics must always be involved for integration to take place. There is no meaning in letters and sounds per se and only limited meaning to be gained from syntax.

The grid is not all-inclusive. There is no attempt made to exhaust the possible lessons that can be generated. Rather, we have selected lessons that seem to support the developing strategies of many readers.

STRATEGY LESSONS

In writing the strategy lessons, we kept in mind both how the reading process works and the criteria for writing good strategy lessons. We were also concerned to present each reading strategy in a way that would facilitate learning. The presentation of each reading-strategy lesson is organized as follows:

General Rationale
Strategy-Lesson Plan
1. Specific Rationale
2. Evaluation
3. Reading-Strategy Instruction
   a. Initiating
   b. Interacting
   c. Applying
   d. Expanding

In the General Rationale, we discuss the significance of the reading-strategy lesson and indicate how it interrelates with the language systems. Most of this background information comes from our own or related research. The more teachers understand about why these strategies have been chosen, the more flexible they will be in tailoring the strategies to fit

GRID OF COMPREHENDING STRATEGIES

	Semantic	Syntactic	Graphophonic
Predicting	Content and Organization Focus on Meaning Fiction and Nonfiction Plot or Sequence of Events Pronouns Relational Words and Phrases Negatives Negatives and Meaning Negative Contractions	Grammatical Function Nouns as Names for People Nouns as Place Names Varieties of Grammatical Functions Indicators of Direct Speech Dialogue Carriers—Word Level Dialogue Carriers—Phrase Level Hard-to-Predict Grammatical Structures Hard-to-Predict Phrases and Clauses Identifying Hard-to-Predict Structures	Uncommon Spelling Patterns Eye Dialect Foreign-Language Words and Phrases Graphic Variations Print Variations Format Variations
Confirming	Rethink/Reread Developing Meaning through Context	Punctuation Repeated Substitutions	Initial, Medial, and Final Graphic Cues Spelling Patterns through Language Experience Meaning without Graphophonic Cues Synonym Substitutions
Integrating	Concepts Informational Material Story Material Characterization and Setting Relating of Characterization and Setting to Action Getting To Know the Time and Place Determining Who Is Telling the Story Exploring Plot and Theme Plot Story Schema Theme Generalizations Point of View Propaganda Humor		

students' needs. The specific reason for writing a particular strategy lesson is presented under the Specific Rationale.

The strategy lessons are not meant to be used with all students, nor are they to be presented in a particular sequence. They are to be used for those individuals or small groups who show that they need the particular strategy, and they should be used when a reader will benefit most from the instruction. The Evaluation section of the Strategy-Lesson Plan describes those students who will benefit most from a particular strategy. Whenever appropriate, we present examples of the miscues of such readers. Other appropriate evidence will also provide help in identifying students.

To facilitate learning, we have suggested a teacher-learner organization that has proved successful in the presentation of the reading strategies. It has four distinct phases: Initiating, Interacting, Applying, and Expanding. Each lesson usually provides opportunity for both reading instruction and silent independent reading.

Initiating

The first step in the Reading-Strategy Instruction must catch the learners' interest so it will seem important to them to want to read. Initiating provides specific suggestions for presenting or initiating each lesson in ways that heighten students' interest. However, the teacher knows the students better than anyone else. It is the teacher's responsibility to implement or change the lesson presentations so they are appealing. Teachers should feel free to make decisions about necessary changes as well as to be creative in adapting the lessons.

When readers have particular purposes for reading, they are often highly motivated and eager to get on with the learning. Whenever appropriate, teachers are encouraged to change the names on the material in the strategy lessons to make the characters seem more familiar to the students.

Whenever possible, students should be involved in evaluating and planning their own reading experiences. They can be involved in helping to select appropriate lessons, as well as writing similar and additional lessons. If students are aware of their strengths as learners, they do not mind facing the weaknesses they need to overcome. In an honest, nonthreatening setting they will have this opportunity.

The materials for initiating the lesson often include a selection for the student or students to read. Such reading materials provide the stimulus for a discussion about the strategy to be examined. These materials may be photocopied for use with a small group or whole class. Then the photocopy may be made into a duplicating master or an overhead transparency to fit the style of teaching or the situation most feasible in the classroom.

Interacting

Learning is heightened when students have the opportunity to talk with peers, in nonthreatening or nonjudgmental settings, about what they are doing and learning. We all know that we have learned many concepts best when we have had to teach them, or present them, to others. When we present ideas to others, we get reaction to our ideas. We are then put in the position of having to think about what we are saying and doing. This is the significance of interacting with peers and teachers. It stimulates thought, language, and learning. All students need to develop expertise in discussion techniques. This is at the heart of the Interacting phase of the lesson.

Appropriate discussion experiences are important to all learning, and reading is no exception. The Interacting phase of the lesson must provide opportunities for students to learn by presenting their thoughts to others and by receiving responses that will cause them to rethink or expand their original ideas.

Whether the discussion is about how reading works, or about the content or concepts of the material being read, there should be much opportunity for the students to explore what is happening and why. Students learn to accept the ideas of their peers, examine them carefully, and reach decisions about their reading experiences based on their interactions with one another.

A teacher may be a participant in such discussions as long as he or she can remain a member of the discussion group and not the final resource from which comes all correct answers. It is only in the atmosphere of the explorations of "let's see," "try it out," "how do you know," "where can we go to find out," that learning is encouraged and extended. Right answers need as much challenging as do wrong answers. That is how progress is made—through challenges to "great truths." This kind of approach will stimulate learning in all students, too. We are not advocating a laissez faire approach to teaching. On the contrary, the approach we are suggesting demands careful planning efforts by the teacher. This approach is one that challenges students to think and to push ahead at the frontiers of their knowledge system.

Applying

In addition to having a purpose for reading and interacting with others about reading, students should have opportunities for applying their developing strategies to additional reading materials. Such opportunities are developed in the Applying phase of the lesson. This section sometimes provides additional materials that may be copied and used in the manner suggested in the Interacting phase. The Annotated Bibliography for Children (pages 236 – 243) lists books that can help support the specific strategies considered in this text and, at the same time, provide opportunities for silent, independent reading.

Expanding

Reading is not an end in itself. It is one medium through which learning can take place. The reading curriculum must be organized to help students see the relationship of reading to other learning experiences. The Expanding phase extends reading to other aspects of the language curriculum as well as to other areas of the general curriculum. Suggestions are offered to enhance the integration of reading with the content areas. Writing experiences that offer strong support in developing reading proficiency are also suggested.

There is much written material available for students in libraries, on book stands, in homes. To facilitate the bridging of reading instruction into silent, independent, and self-selected reading, the teacher should be aware of the wide range of reading material to which students should be introduced and which should be readily available to them to help them develop proficient use of reading strategies.

The Grid of Reading Materials on page 38 may be used by the teacher as a guide in setting up or enriching a comprehension-centered reading program.

SELECT BIBLIOGRAPHY FOR TEACHERS

We list here selected references for teachers on language and thought, and their relationship to the reading process, which teachers can use to supplement the information presented in the preceding chapters.

Reading and Reading Strategies

Goodman, Kenneth S., and Olive S. Niles. *Reading: Process and Program*. Champaign, IL: National Council of Teachers of English, 1970.

Goodman, Yetta, and Dorothy J. Watson. "A Reading Program to Live With: Focus on Comprehension," *Language Arts*, Nov.-Dec. 1977, pp. 868–879.

Read, Charles, *Children's Categorization of Speech Sounds in English*. Urbana, IL: Eric Clearing House and National Council of Teachers of English, 1975.

Roseblatt, Louise M. *The Reader, the Text, the Poem*. Carbondale, IL: Southern Illinois University Press, 1978.

Smith, Frank. *Comprehension and Learning*. New York: Holt, Rinehart and Winston, 1977.

Smith, Frank. *Understanding Reading*, second edition. New York: Holt, Rinehart and Winston, 1978.

Reading Curriculum

Britton, James. *Language and Learning*. Miami, Fla: University of Miami Press, 1970.

Destefano, Johanna S., and Sharon E. Fox (eds.). *Language and the Language Arts*. Boston: Little, Brown, 1974.

GRID OF READING MATERIALS

	A. Newspapers and Magazines	B. Research Materials	C. Symbolic Materials Other Than Books	D. Problem-Solving Materials	E. Trade Books	F. Primary Sources
I. Social Studies	Current events Controversial issues Feature articles Political news	Encyclopedias Biographies Texts Journals Research reports Histories	Globes Maps Morse code Photographs Fine art Music sheets Political records Cartoons Ballots	Building models Making clothes from patterns Reconstructing human culture from artifacts	Nonfiction books Biographies History Poetry Anthropology Geography Political Science Economics Human Relations	Family documents Letters Government documents Reports of interviews
II. Science	Weather Science editor Science news	Encyclopedias Texts Journals Histories Logs	Graphs Chemical symbols Films Thermometers Scales	Experiments Cooking recipes Computer printout	Biographies Physical science Natural science Nonfiction Poetry	Conservation records Notes of original scientific records Prescriptions
III. Mathematics	Business news Wants ads Stock-market reports Financial section	Technical journals Histories	Films Formulas Expanded notations Scales Number systems	Solving problems Computation	Biographies Nonfiction Poetry	Written problems Business ledgers
IV. Literature	Book, play, and movie reviews Narratives in magazines	Bibliographies Biographies Texts Histories	Text illustrations Format (book, play, script) Music Works of art	Theme and plot analysis	Fiction Poetry Nonfiction	Creative writing by students in class

Goodman, Kenneth, Yetta Goodman, and Barbara Flores. *Reading in the Bilingual Classroom: Literacy and Biliteracy*. Virginia: National Clearinghouse for Bilingual Education, 1979.

Goodman, Yetta M., and Carolyn Burke. *The Reading Miscue Inventory*. New York: Macmillan, 1973.

Lee, Dorris M., and Joseph B. Rubin. *Children and Language*. Belmont, CA: Wadsworth, 1979.

Moffett, James. *Teaching the Universe of Discourse*. Boston: Houghton Mifflin, 1968.

Moffett, James. *A Student-Centered Language Arts Curriculum, Grades K-13: A Handbook for Teachers*. Boston: Houghton Mifflin, 1973.

Neisser, Ulric. *Cognition and Reality*. San Francisco: Freeman, 1976.

Smith, E. Brooks, Kenneth S. Goodman, and Robert Meredith. *Language and Thinking*, second edition. New York: Holt, Rinehart and Winston, 1976.

Taylor, Joy. *Organizing the Open Classroom: A Teacher's Guide to the Integrated Day*. New York: Schocken, 1972.

Williams, Frederick, Robert Hopper, and Diana S. Natalicio. *The Sounds of Children*. Englewood Cliffs, NJ: Prentice-Hall, 1977.

Reading Strategies Lessons

Allen, Roach Van. *Language Experiences in Communication*. Boston: Houghton Mifflin, 1976.

Goodman, Yetta. "Reading Strategy Lessons: Expanding Reading Effectiveness," in *Help for the Reading Teacher: New Directions in Research*, William D. Page (ed.), ERIC Clearing House, 1975.

Goodman, Yetta. "Using Children's Miscues for New Teaching Strategies," *The Reading Teacher*, Vol. 23, No. 5, February 1970.

Goodman, Yetta, and Carolyn Burke. "Do They Read What They Speak?, *Grade Teacher*, March 1969.

Hittleman, Daniel R. *Developmental Reading: A Psycholinguistic Perspective*. Skokie, IL.: Rand McNally, 1978.

Huck, Charlotte. *Children's Literature in the Elementary School*. New York: Holt, Rinehart and Winston, 1968.

Martin, Bill. *Teacher's Editions: Sounds of Language Readers*. New York: Holt, Rinehart and Winston, 1972, 1974.

O'Hare, Frank. *Sentencecraft*. Lexington, MA: Ginn, 1975.

Stauffer, Russell G. *The Language Experience Approach to the Teaching of Reading*. New York: Harper & Row, 1970.

Tway, Eileen (ed.). *Reading Ladders for Human Relations*. Urbana, IL: ERIC Clearing House and National Council of Teachers of English, in press.

(See professional journals such as *Language Arts* and *English Journal*, published by National Council of Teachers of English, 1111 Kenyon Road, Urbana, Illinois; *Reading Teacher* and *Reading Journal*, published by International Reading Association, Newark, Delaware; and *Horn Book*, for critiques of books written for children and youth.)

Selected Miscue Research

Allen, D., and D. Watson. *Research Findings in Miscue Analysis*. Urbana, IL: National Council of Teachers of English, 1977.

Goodman, Kenneth, and Carolyn Burke. *Theoretically Based Studies of Patterns of Miscues in Oral Reading Performance*. Washington, D.C.: U.S. Dept. of Health, Education, and Welfare, Office of Education, Project No. 9-0375, 1973.

Goodman, Kenneth, and Carolyn Burke. *Studies of Children's Behavior while Reading Orally*. Washington, D.C.: U.S. Dept. of Health, Education, and Welfare, Office of Education, Project No. S425, 1968.

Goodman, Kenneth S., and Yetta M. Goodman, Final Report Project NIE-C-00-3-0087, *Reading of American Children Whose Language is a Stable Rural Dialect of English or a Language Other than English*, August 1978.

Watson, D.J. A psycholinguistic description of the oral reading miscues generated by selected readers prior to and following exposure to a saturated book program. Unpublished dissertation, Wayne State University, 1973.

Part II

Reading-Strategy Lessons

Chapter 4
Predicting Semantic Cues

CONTENT AND ORGANIZATION

General Rationale

The semantic system is at the heart of written communication. The references to ideas, emotions, and objects in a shared environment that language users produce through graphophonic and syntactic rules are what makes communication comprehensible. Understanding the semantic system is a complex and overwhelming task. Although philosophers have been concerned with semantics and meaning for centuries, scientists studying language and thinking have not examined the rules of the semantic system as it relates to comprehension, to the same degree that the graphophonic or syntactic systems have been studied. Only recently have linguists and others begun to explore the interrelationship of the semantic and syntactic systems scientifically. As questions related to the study of semantics are answered, teachers will be provided with significant information to understand how the semantic system functions in reading.

Nevertheless, there are many aspects of semantics that can be exploited for instructional purposes. The meaning that authors believe they present through written language does not correspond directly to what readers claim they have understood. An overview of the information presented by the author, and the ways in which the author presents it, may serve as a basis for understanding the disparity between authors and readers.

1. *What the author intends to say:*
   a. *Purpose.* The author's purpose is often reflected through an abstraction of the main ideas, ethical statements, or knowledge that the author hopes to convey to readers. This abstraction is often referred to as the author's theme or generalization.
   b. *Point of view or motive.* All writing expresses a bias or an opinion that the author holds about the knowledge or ideas being presented to the readers.
   c. *Area of content.* The specific information or knowledge that the author wishes to present emerges from many fields of study, such as science, math, home arts. An author may or may not be sophisticated about the most up-to-date knowledge in the field. The author's point of view, knowledge, and purpose will all be reflected in the degree of accuracy and objectivity of the content.

2. *How the author intends to say it:*
   a. *Form.* The author selects a form that he or she is most successful with or would like to explore. These forms include, among others, drama, prose, poetry, journalistic writing, instructional materials. The form an author chooses depends on the purpose for writing. The author also decides whether to present the material as fiction or nonfiction. In most cases, only in the last analysis does the author become concerned with the specific medium through which the writing will be presented: books, newspapers, magazines, comics, cereal boxes, television.
   b. *Style.* The author's knowledge of language is reflected in the style of writing. The author often makes conscious choices concerning the use of vocabulary, syntax, and semantics, although much of his or her style may be reflected in intuitive use of language. That is to say, the author may make choices about language use without consciously thinking through uses of specific vocabulary or syntactic structures.
   c. *Organization.* The written material is organized around an overall question, problem, or concept that is of central concern to the author. In fiction this is often called the plot. The author has a plan of events through which the plot, or major concept, will emerge and either be resolved or be left unresolved. Included in the organization is the setting—the time and place to be described—and characterization—the people, the animals, used to convey the author's ideas.
   d. *Contract between author and reader.* The author makes many assumptions about the reader's knowledge, background, and experience. The author assumes that the reader will understand what he or she is writing. It is as if the author had a contract signed by the reader, stating, "I the reader will make every effort to understand what you are saying and why you are saying it the way you chose." In reality such contracts rarely exist but the assumption is there nonetheless.

In each section of this overview it is obvious how much of the author's individuality is expressed in the written material. The writing reflects the author's schema of language, background, knowledge, experiences, values, points of view—in other words, his or her very particular world view. Readers bring the same individuality to their long-distance discussion with the author. Readers' comprehension reflects their schemata, background, knowledge, experiences, values, points of view—their own world view. Therefore, there is no great mystery in understanding why interpretations vary from author to reader, from reader to reader, among even the most proficient readers.

Readers approach written material as language users and thinkers. Their thoughts and language are actively involved in processing what they read. Readers' use of predictions and other reading strategies depends not only on their point of view, knowledge of content, and awareness of form, style, and organization of material but also on their purposes.

Since purposes are so intrinsically and basically involved in what kinds of predictions readers make as they search for meaning, we want to expand here on the significance of reader's purposes.

PURPOSE FOR READING

The purpose readers have in mind as they read, often controls what they are reading for, the strategies they will use in their reading, and what they will remember from their reading. *No reading takes place without a purpose.* Proficient readers, even though they may not be consciously aware they are doing so, set their own purposes, and decisions they make about their reading strategies are based on those purposes. For example, your reading of a movie critic's review of a film playing at a local theater will differ depending on whether you read the review before or after seeing the movie. If your purpose is to find out whether you want to see the movie, you will (based on your values and experiences) select and predict specific aspects of the review. You may search for answers to the questions *Who is in the film? Is there much violence? Can I take my eight-year-old nephew to see it?* Once you find answers to such questions, you may be able to predict other points in the article if you decide to continue reading it. If, however, you have already seen the film, you will not pay much attention to information about the cast or the degree of violence because you will already know this information. Instead you will read to see the degree to which the critic agrees with your own point of view. If you often read movie reviews and know the orientation of the particular critic well, you can, based on this prior knowledge, predict how the critic will respond to certain actors or to the use of violence, or the degree to which the critic will like the film. Then you will read to confirm your prediction.

Although all reading has a purpose, teachers often assign specific purposes for students without considering whether the students need to have purposes set for them. Setting purposes for students is an attempt to determine what the students will predict as they read. For example, if a teacher says, "I want you to read this story to find out how the boys got away from the monster," the students not only have been given a specific purpose but can predict that the story is probably fanciful fiction and that the author will describe a method of escape. If, on the other hand, the teacher says, "Read the 'Cross of Gold' speech and write a newspaper article as if you were at the convention and heard the speech given," the students' predictions about the content of the material to be read will be very different from those made about the first reading assignment.

It is important to allow students to set their own purposes and make their own predictions. Consider the following:

1. Set purposes for readers *only* when you have an educationally sound reason to do so.
2. Involve students in discussing the importance of setting their own purposes for their reading.
3. State the purpose in such a way that there will be a number of appropriate, acceptable responses. For example: "When you read this story, see if you can find in what ways it is similar to, and different from, the story we read last week."
4. Set purposes that go beyond reading for facts and surface detail. Avoid this type of instruction: "Read to find out how many boats Columbus led to the New World and how many men were on each of the boats."

Proficient readers exploit to the fullest their own knowledge, experience, and language, which they bring to their reading to help them set appropriate purposes as they read. Most readers are not consciously aware of these strategies. They have become proficient readers because they have learned to interrelate their purposes with their knowledge of language, and their experiences and are able to make predictions about what the author wants to say, how it is likely to be said, and the medium through which the message might be presented. As they read widely, their proficiency in using these various strategies grows.

However, there are some readers who are not confident about their reading and who tend not to use their own language strengths effectively. They tend to let their teachers set their purposes for them and read only to gain the minimum required information for a particular assignment. In addition, there are some readers who are not fully aware that gaining meaning should even be a serious consideration. They do not think of reading as a form of pleasure, or an activity for personal gain. Often their instructional programs have concentrated on narrow aspects of sounding out graphic symbols, recognizing a certain number of words, reading to fill in slots on a worksheet or to answer specific questions about the reading. For such readers reading has no intrinsic purposes; it is simply viewed as instructional. These readers generally view themselves as *learning to read*—and not very successfully at that. For these readers the purpose for reading is seldom *reading to learn*.

The strategy lessons that follow are designed to help students predict semantic information; they also focus on helping students set their own reading purposes.

FOCUS ON MEANING: STRATEGY-LESSON PLAN

Specific Rationale

One initial procedure that can help your students focus on comprehension is to discuss with them the major purposes for reading.

Too often students view reading as something that will help them learn specific skills related to school instruction, but that is unrelated to their own need to comprehend the written language that surrounds them. They may not even recognize that many of their daily contacts with written language outside the classroom (reading TV Guide, comic books, the Bible, bubble-gum cards) are legitimate reading experiences that help them develop reading strategies. Beginning readers sometimes respond to queries about why they read with such answers as "To learn the alphabet," or "To learn to read words." When asked why they think an author wrote a particular story, some older students often state, "To teach you letters and words," or "To teach you to read."

The main objective of the discussion of purposes is to help students become aware that (a) reading must be for them and (b) learning to read enables them to read whatever they want for whatever purpose they have in mind. This lesson departs from the usual strategy-lesson procedure, since it involves students in discussion of the reading process without interaction with written material.

If you become aware early in the discussion that your students understand that the major goal of reading and reading instruction is comprehension, then you need not pursue the questioning further. However, for those students who respond with answers similar to those mentioned earlier or who seem uncertain about their purposes for reading, we suggest the following interaction:

1. What *do you read outside school? Why do you read those things? Do you ever reread them and why?*

    At first the students may focus on school-related reasons because they may be anticipating answers they think *you* are looking for. When any students suggest a self-directed reason for reading—such as to build a model, to follow a recipe, to find the time of a TV program, to find out about other people, to locate the appropriate restroom, or to purchase a favorite candy—expand and support their answers with examples taken from your own experiences that parallel those of the students.

2. *Why do you read anything?*

    As you help the students consider a variety of reasons, remind them of the specific reasons they mentioned in response to the first set of questions and help them realize that reading must be for their own personal learning or personal enjoyment.

3. *Why do other people read? Do you know adults who read? What do they read, and why do they read those things? If you don't know, how can you find out?*

    If the students are not too sure of the answers to these questions, you may want to postpone further discussion for a few days. Ask the students to interview their parents, older siblings, neighbors, other teachers, and continue the discussion in a few days when the students have gathered some answers.

4. *Based on your investigation, what did you find out? What are the* main reasons *people read?*

    Help your students generalize that reading is for gaining information, responding to forms or questionnaires, and gaining self-enjoyment and pleasure. For all these purposes they must understand what they are reading. That is the only goal of reading. Begin to use the words *purpose* and *reasons* as synonyms where they are appropriate. You may enhance the discussion by having copies of various reading materials available—an encyclopedia, a newspaper, a comic book, directions for building a model car, a recipe, a telephone book, a TV directory, a pill bottle, a ticket stub. Discuss each item separately.

5. *When would you use this reading material?* [Hold up the specific reading material.] *Why would you read it? What would you want to know?*

    Through the discussion the students should understand that readers always have reasons for reading and that those purposes depend on the individual and what he or she wants to know. At a later date you can expand on this discussion by using the same materials and deciding how different types of reading materials are read in different ways depending on the purpose of the reader.

NOTE   Students may raise the issue that often they read things that they do not understand because they are assigned to do so. Discussions of this issue must be taken seriously because they concern a major problem for many readers. Help students learn how to ask questions of teachers when they do not understand an assigned reading. Show them ways to get through some of these assignments. Most important, help them realize that if they become good readers for their own purposes, it will help them handle with a little more proficiency the more difficult assignments. Teach them how to play the game.

FICTION AND NON-FICTION: STRATEGY-LESSON PLAN

Specific Rationale

The distinction between fiction and nonfiction is not intrinsically clear. Although authors may know for sure whether what they have written really occurred, even sophisticated adult readers are often uncertain whether or not what they have read is fiction. For example, in Eleanor Roosevelt's autobiography, written late in her life, she reported a dialogue word for word that took place when she was seven years old. Is it possible that fictionalizing takes place in the writing of such a dialogue in an autobiography?

Another example of the fuzziness of the distinction between fiction and nonfiction occurs with satire. Readers can believe that a particular column is factual if they are unaware that the newspaper columnist to whom it is credited regularly writes satire. A spoof on research, appearing in a professional journal such as *Reading Teacher*, can often be taken seriously by readers who do not recognize the author's intent and do not expect to find satire or comedy in a professional journal. Doctorow explores the thin line between fiction and history in his book *Ragtime*.

Readers should be aware that the distinction between fiction and nonfiction may not be easy to discover. The line separating the nonfiction of a feature article in a newspaper from the fiction of well-researched historical or realistic works are difficult for a reader to determine. For elementary-school students it is easier to introduce the distinction between fiction and nonfiction by contrasting fantasy and reality. The question for these students thus becomes, Could this story really happen? In helping students begin to explore this question, it is important to examine the cues available in written language that help formulate predictions about whether something is fiction or nonfiction. Readers use a variety of cues to predict fiction and fact: (1) the title of the work, and the table of contents; (2) previous experience with the author's work; (3) the language of the material. We shall consider how each of these helps readers to formulate and focus predictions.

Title of the work, and the table of contents. Often predictions can be made by looking at the cover of the material. The cover designs on paperbacks, dictionaries, newsweeklies, or sports magazines provide the initial information about what a reader can or cannot expect in the writing. Knowing what will not be in a particular piece of writing narrows the scope of what the reader can predict.

In addition, titles provide additional cues that help in predicting whether the subject matter is fiction or nonfiction. Consider the titles *The Secret of Childhood, The Disenchanted,* and *A Journey to the Center of the Earth.* What cues in those titles help you determine that the works are fiction or nonfiction?

Once a reader has made initial predictions about the title, the preface and table of contents, or their lack, can be used to confirm these predictions and to provide additional information from which the reader can make new predictions. Although it is not necessary to use the table of contents all the time, you may want to explore with your students instances when it is most helpful to use such additional information and how it helps them know what to expect as they continue to read.

Previous experience with the author's work. Familiarity with the author also focuses the scope of the predictions that can be made about the reality of subject matter and whether it is fiction or nonfiction. Consider these examples: *The Secret of Childhood,* by Maria Montessori; *The Disenchanted,* by Budd Schulberg; and *A Journey to the Center of the Earth,* by Jules Verne. If you know anything about Jules Verne, you are more likely to make appropriate predictions than if you have never heard of him. If you are aware of the sophistication Maria Montessori has about children, you will be better able to judge the quality of information and you may know what to expect in terms of the age of the child she writes about and her point of view. Of course, knowing the author is more than simply memorizing a name. It means having read the author's work, being aware of whether he or she usually writes fiction or nonfiction, having some familiarity with the author's writing style. Even hearsay evidence can be very helpful in the process.

Language of the material. The first paragraph from each of the books listed earlier provides language cues that will confirm or disconfirm your earlier predictions and help you make new predictions about the material.

From *The Secret of Childhood:*

For some years childhood has been the object of intense social interest. Like other great movements this interest has not been aroused by any single individual but it has burst forth like a volcano shooting forth fires in all directions. Science provides the incentive for this new movement by drastically reducing the rate of infant mortality. Then it came to be realized that children were frequently worn out from the drudgery of their school work.[1]

From *The Disenchanted:*

It's waiting, Shep was thinking. You wait to get inside the gate, you wait outside the great man's office, you wait for your agent to make a deal, you wait for instructions on how to write and then when you finish your treatment and turn it in, you wait for that unique contribution to art, the story conference.[2]

From *A Journey to the Center of the Earth:*

Looking back at all that has occurred to me since that eventful day, I am scarcely able to believe in the reality of my adventures. They were truly so wonderful that even now I am bewildered when I think of them.[3]

What are the language cues that you used to help you confirm your predictions about the subject matter of the material and whether it was fiction or nonfiction? Some of the language cues might include

1. The degree of formality and/or figurative use of language
2. How the language refers to people, places, or events
3. How the language indicates whether the characters are real or fictitious
4. The kind of mood the language choices convey

Through the following strategy lesson you and your students will explore these aspects of written language, which provide cues for appropriate predictions about the subject matter of written material, and for consideration of whether or not it really did happen. Such an exploration enables readers to make the best use of their initial contact with a selection. Good predicting strategies facilitate the task of gaining meaning from reading.

EVALUATION

The strategy lesson for Fiction and Nonfiction will benefit

1. Students who make it clear through their retellings or discussions of events that they do not distinguish between fact and fiction, or between fantasy and reality.
2. Students whose retellings focus on surface events and recall of characters but who do not begin to suggest inferences about the different nature and intents of varying reading materials.
3. Students who read only one kind of reading material, such as horse stories or motorcycle stories, and make little or no effort to expand their reading.
4. Students whose miscue-analysis profile shows that 60 percent or more of their sentences have no syntactic and semantic acceptability.

---

[1]Maria Montessori, *The Secret of Childhood* (New York: Ballantine Books, Inc., 1966), p. 1.
[2]Budd Schulberg, *The Disenchanted* (New York: Bantam Books, Inc., 1968), p. 1.
[3]Jules Verne, *A Journey to the Center of the Earth* (New York: Scholastic Book Services, 1965), p. 1.

Reading-Strategy Instruction

INITIATING

MATERIALS   "How the Whale Got His Throat," from *Just So Stories* by Rudyard Kipling
The World Book Encyclopedia, under the word "whale"

How the Whale Got His Throat

In the sea, once upon a time, O my Best Beloved, there was a whale, and he ate fishes. He ate the starfish and the garfish, and the crab and the dab, and the plaice and the dace, and the skate and his mate, and the macereel and the pickereel, and the really truly twirly-whirly eel. All the fishes he could find in all the sea he ate with his mouth so!

RUDYARD KIPLING

Whales

Whale is the largest animal that has ever lived. Whales are much bigger than elephants or even prehistoric dinosaurs.

Whales live in oceans and look much like fish. But they are not fish. Whales are mammals as are dogs, cats, horses, and human beings.

There are two main types of whales: (1) whales that have teeth, and (2) whales that do not have teeth.

THE WORLD BOOK ENCYCLOPEDIA

Start the discussion by viewing the two titles: "Whales" and "How the Whale Got His Throat." These can be placed on the board or on a transparency. (For each section of this discussion you may follow the guideline questions used in the Interacting phase of this lesson.)

If you have the appropriate books, show them as you point out the titles, telling the students which passage comes from which book. (Copies of both an encyclopedia that has an article on whales, and Kipling's *Just So Stories* will enhance this lesson.)

After discussing the cues provided by the titles of the passages (and the books if you have them), show the students the titles with the authors' names included. This information could be placed at the bottom half of the transparency or you may add the names next to the titles on the board. Discuss any additional cues the students do get from the authors' names. (If you have the books, you may also explore with students the ways illustrations provide additional cues.)

Provide each student with a copy of the first paragraph of each piece of writing. After the students have had a chance to read the paragraphs silently, you should read both selections to them. Allow your voice to suggest the discursive style of the article as opposed to the literary language of the story. The students will probably feel the need to reread portions silently as you discuss the cues provided by the language in these first paragraphs.

INTERACTING

QUESTIONS FOR DISCUSSION

1. [Show only the titles.] *What do you think will be the subject discussed in each of these titles?*
2. *How will the selections be different, and how do you know?*
3. [Show the books if you have them.] *How do the books help you know that the subject matter will be different?*
   Explore similarity of subject matter, and differences in how the subject matter will be presented.
4. [Show titles with authors' names added.] *Do you know the author? What can you tell us about him?*
   Students should know that having such information may help them. Not having such information is not a disgrace. They are meeting someone new and need strategies to help them get to know the new author. Explore with the students that an author always exists even if no name is listed. Does not having a stated author supply them with cues?
5. *What effect does knowing or not knowing the authors have upon your predictions of what the writing might be about?*
   Do not spend too much time on this. Simply help students understand that when they do know authors or have heard about them, they also know more about the material they are going to read.
6. [Ask students to read the first paragraph of each piece, then read the selections to them.] *In what ways are the two pieces of writing similar?*
   Explore the subject matter and how both authors decided to write about whales. Explore other similarities.
7. *In what ways are the two pieces of writing different?*
   Discuss the different ways in which the authors handle the same subject.
8. *Do you think each author has different purposes for writing? What are they?*
9. *Is there something in the way the author uses language that makes you believe that one of the selections is more factual or true to life than the other?*
   Explore the students' ideas, encouraging them to support their hypotheses with examples from their reading. You might explore the following:
   a. How the author talks to the reader
   b. The use of real as opposed to unreal creatures (*Are there garfish? How would you find out?*)
   c. Strange spellings, and the like
   d. Style ("Ate with his mouth so!" as opposed to "There are two main types of whales . . .")
   e. The terms *article* and *story* as ways to differentiate between fact and fiction

10. *How do references to people, places, and animals help you decide that one selection may be more true to life than the other?*
    If you have the books' illustrations available, examine how these help the reader to know fact from fiction.
11. *In what kind of materials would you find articles, and in what kind, stories?*

APPLYING

MATERIALS   Select two pieces of material on the same subject or concept. One should be fiction and the other nonfiction. An article on baseball from an encyclopedia or newspaper and a short story or poem about a baseball hero would provide a good contrast for the lesson.

Have the students work in small groups or in pairs. (Use the questions suggested in the Interacting phase, following the procedure recommended there.) As students become sophisticated in the use of this technique, they can compare the two texts to note differences between fiction and nonfiction. They can list cues that tell them

1. What subject matter the author is talking about
2. How the author says it
   a. Whether it could be real or not
   b. What cues there are that tell whether it could be real or not

Encourage similar discussions about other material students read. Permit oral discussions about these things in conferences with individual students or in small groups.

EXPANDING

READING   Have the students (a) select a favorite animal and (b) find an encyclopedia article, a newspaper article, and a poem about it. The students can share with the class the different ways in which different authors handle the same content.
    The students can look for (a) feature articles about favorite sports figures, TV stars, or movie stars and (b) a review of a game, TV show, or movie in which the person they chose appears. They can then compare the language differences in these two pieces of written material, following a procedure similar to the one used in the Interacting and Applying phases.

WRITING   Have the students take an interesting feature or news article from the newspaper and write it as a story. Or have them select a comic strip or a favorite TV show and rewrite it as if they were newspaper reporters and the incident described had really happened at the corner of the street where they live.

PLOT OR SEQUENCE OF EVENTS: STRATEGY-LESSON PLAN

Specific Rationale

The overall question, or the central problem, of a story generally determines the author's organizational plan or the sequence of events. In fiction this problem and its solution is generally referred to as a *plot*. In nonfiction the sequence of events, ideas, or information is similar to the plot. However, an article that has a story line can also be referred to as having a plot.
    Even poor readers are often able to provide the cast of characters and surface events from a story. They can usually tell what has happened and who was involved. However, they are not always certain of how the events and the characters are related, why the events took place, or that there was a problem to be solved in the story. When readers become aware that there are reasons why stories take place in certain ways, they begin to look for plot, main ideas, and the relationship among events in a story.

In this strategy lesson students will predict events in a story and identify the problems and the solutions presented to the reader through the course of the story.

It is important to remember that sequence of events should only be emphasized when it is significant to the plot. In a descriptive part of a story it is usually unimportant if, for example, the boy sees the tree or the ground first. However, in a story where first comes the little billy goat, then the middle-sized goat, and last the big billy goat, the order in which the characters are introduced in the story is related to the plot, and the sequence is important.

Reading-Strategy Instruction

EVALUATION

The strategy lesson for Plot or Sequence of Events will benefit

1. Students who cannot predict endings of stories.
2. Students who cannot identify a central problem in a story.
3. Students who find it difficult to interrelate features of a story that are important to the plot.

INITIATING

MATERIALS   Select a cartoon with a simple plot. *Peanuts, Nancy, The Ryatts* are some that can usually be used. Make a Ditto of the selection, or an overhead transparency. If you use transparencies, show the group one frame of the cartoon strip at a time; or if it is on a Ditto, have them expose one frame of the comic strip at a time. Begin by asking the students to look at the first frame.

INTERACTING

QUESTIONS FOR DISCUSSION   (Use similar questions after each frame is presented.)

1. *What do you think is going to be pictured in the next frame of the cartoon? Why do you think so?*
   Encourage each student to make suggestions and encourage different types of responses.
2. *Are there any other alternatives that might occur besides the ones you've mentioned? Why do you think so?*
   The students may not be able to limit their discussions to only the very next segment and may provide more information. Do not discourage this. After each response, ask why they chose that idea. Once you have explored the various possibilities, then present the next cartoon sequence. Do not focus on which of the students was right. Rather, go on to ask question 3.
3. *Do you like any of our ideas better than the ones the cartoonist came up with? Which ones? Why?*
   If the students suggest appropriate or inappropriate solutions based on partial information, they need to understand that this is the way the reading process operates. After you have shown the first three frames in order, using questions similar to the ones suggested above, then prepare for the conclusion.
4. *How do you think the cartoonist will end this story?*
   Again allow for variability. Remember that if the students have not had experience with the problem presented by the author, they may be unable to consider the cartoonist's solution and may also not even understand why it is a possible solution. It is also possible the cartoon may provide an unpredictable surprise.
5. *Do you think that there will be something funny about the ending? Why or why not?*
   Not all cartoons are necessarily humorous, and your students' responses will depend on what kinds of cartoons they read. Some of them may have little experience with

cartoons, and this will be evident in their answers as well. Once you have explored all the possible solutions presented by the class, show them the last frame.

6. *Which of our solutions do you like as well as, or even better than, the cartoonist's solutions and why?*

Encourage cross-discussion among the students so they explain or support their own opinions.

7. *Do you think the cartoonist's solution is funny? Which of our solutions were funny and which were not?*

What is considered humorous depends on age and experience. Do not be surprised (a) if your students are amused by things that you did not expect them to find humorous or (b) if they do not see what is funny the way you do. In order to legitimize the students' own plot suggestions as well as their own solutions, encourage them at the close of the lesson either to make their own cartoon sequence using their own ideas or to write out their ideas in story form. Students who generate the same idea can work together.

APPLYING

MATERIALS   "Jane Accepts a Dare," by Barry Sherman

Jane Accepts a Dare

Jane was very sorry that she said yes when the other kids dared her to go into the old house at the end of the road. Everyone in town said that the house was haunted, and some people even said they had seen ghosts. Why did she agree to do it? Was it just to show off to the other kids? Was it to prove that she was as brave as any other girl or boy in town? Or was it to prove to herself that she could go into the house even if she was afraid?

Now it was time to go ahead with it. She was standing in front of the gate to the house. The other kids were waiting half-way down the road. Jane looked at the old, rusted iron gate and at the tall grass in front of the yard. It was very strange. Every time she passed this house, she noticed that it was always gloomy, as if the sun didn't shine here. Today it was the same way. Everywhere else it was late afternoon, and the sun was shining. Here it looked dark, as if it was already sunset. Jane decided she had better get moving if she was going to be in and out of the old house before the sun really did set.

Slowly, she pushed the gate in. The gate was tall and heavy. Jane had to use both hands to push it in. The gate squeaked and groaned as it moved, as if it didn't like being awakened after all those years.

"I bet nobody has come here in years," Jane said to herself. The path to the house was almost covered by grasses that no one ever cut anymore. Jane tripped twice as her feet got tangled in the long grass. But finally, she was standing in front of the house. She looked up. The house was three stories high. Many of the windows were broken. Others were boarded up.

Jane wondered if she should go through the front door or if she should look through one of the windows first. Would the kids think she was a coward if she looked through the window first?

No, she decided, she would go straight up to the front door and take her chances. Secretly, she hoped that the door would be locked. She turned to see if the other kids were looking at her. Yes, there they were, waiting at the gate. She could see that they were surprised that she had come this far. Well, she would show them just how far she could go!

Jane took a deep breath and knocked on the door. She could hear the sound of her knocking echoing in the big house. She reached for the door knob and found that it turned. The door was not locked. Jane pushed in on the door and it creaked open slowly. As the door opened, a blast of ice-cold air hit her in the face. Jane felt like running away, but she forced her legs to move forward into the house.

Inside the house it was very dark. Cobwebs covered the walls and furniture. But except for cobwebs and dust, the house looked ready for people to live in it. None of the furniture was covered with sheets, and there were lots of candlesticks in the front hall. Jane kept her hand firmly on the door holding it open. She was not going to let herself get trapped in that house. It looked like a great place for ghosts.

She was trying to see how far inside she could step without letting go of the door, when she heard a noise. It was a creaking sound, as if someone—or something—were stepping on the floor and trying not to make noise. And the creaking sound was coming from the dark hallway in front of her! It was getting closer, but Jane couldn't see anything.

THE CONCLUSION FOLLOWS

Then Jane made up her mind: she turned and ran out of the house, slamming the door shut behind her. As she jumped off the front porch, she thought she heard the sound of laughing behind her, but she couldn't be sure. She ran through the grass without stopping or tripping until she came to the front gate.

"What happened?" asked the other kids. "Did you see anything? Did you see a ghost?"

"I don't know what was in the house," Jane said. "I didn't see any ghosts or any people, but I sure did hear something. I guess I should have stayed around to see what it was." She felt a little ashamed that she had been afraid.

But the other kids didn't agree. They said she had been very brave to go into the old house alone. They all wondered what had made that noise in the hallway of the old house. But they never found out because that summer the house was hit by lightning during a storm and it burned to the ground.

That was the end of the old haunted house. But Jane never forgot the time she accepted the dare to go inside the house. She always remembered the ice-cold blast of air and the soft creaking sound from the dark hallway.

BARRY SHERMAN

After you demonstrate the following procedure once or twice, groups of students can work with different stories at the same time. You may then divide your students into groups, put one of the students in charge of each group, and suggest that they use the procedure that you have demonstrated.

First, have the students examine only the title of the selection. Keep the rest of the story covered until after your discussion about the title. Consider the following questions to stimulate discussion:

1. *What will the story be about?*
2. *Can you tell?*
3. *Will it be a true-to-life story or not?*
4. *Do you think it could really happen or not?*
5. *What are the reasons that you might want to read the story?*
6. *How will we find out which of our predictions are most like the author's?*
    Help students realize that their answers can be solved by continued reading and their own interaction with the author.

The students should read the story silently, stopping where a line of space separates the first section from the section that follows. Ask the questions above again in the light of their additional reading and add the following questions:

7. *Were your original predictions appropriate?*
8. *Why did you think you were right in your predictions?*
9. *Do you like what the author is doing with the story?*
10. *Do you like your idea as well?*
    Have them write down their ideas and save them. Suggest that they may wish to make up a cartoon or write a story using those ideas.
11. *What do you think will be the main problem that the author will want to solve?*
    Remember that students may know the word *problem* only in relation to arithmetic. You may have to rephrase the question, but keep using the word *problem* so that the students expand their understanding of the concept of *problem*. Alternate rephrasing of this question might include: *Was there a conflict that was happening in the story that the author had to work out? At what part of the story did you begin wondering how things would work out? Did you think* that *was a worry, concern, or problem for the characters in the story?*

Have the students continue reading to the next blank line. Then have them stop and ask the questions above once again.

Have the students continue reading each story segment in turn, and then reexploring the set of questions. The last section of the story is marked "The Conclusion Follows." At this point the students should be asked to predict how the problem will be solved in the story.[4]

EXPANDING

This phase does not apply to this lesson.

PRONOUNS

General Rationale

It is not uncommon for readers to miscue on pronouns, making such substitutions as *he* for *we*, or *her* for *him*. Careful examination of these miscues can reveal whether the readers are

---

[4]Russell Stauffer has written a great deal about strategy lessons similar to this procedure, which he calls Directed Reading-Thinking Activity (DRTA). See bibliography at end of Chapter 3.

comprehending and predicting appropriate pronoun substitutions or whether they are confused about characterizations and are not integrating meaning as they read. Substitutions, omissions, or insertions of pronouns may be produced for a variety of reasons:

1. *Using context for appropriate predictions.*

    George was lying face down on the grass with his bicycle all bent out of shape beside him. The doctor and I stood over him. "Let's lift him carefully," he said to me. He placed the board under George's body and we began to lift George into the car.

    Miscues of the type illustrated in the passage indicate that the reader is concerned with meaning. The sentence starting *"Let's lift him"* cues the reader to expect both characters to be involved in the subsequent action. The substitution of *we* for *he* in the first instance indicates the reader's prediction about what might occur subsequently. The reader self-corrects, indicating an awareness of the dialogue carrier subject. The second *we*-for-*he* substitution does not change the meaning of the sentence very much and is acceptable in the story. Both miscues indicate the reader's awareness of the author's intent.

2. *Using conceptual understanding to produce pronoun substitutions.*

    The dog was a big, brown police dog and was ready to protect the chickens from any harm. When the coyotes came in to attack the chickens, the dog stood her ground. She was ready for a fight.

    In this case, the substitution of *it* for *her* and *she* reveals the reader's concept about animals. (Even a substitution of *he* for *she* would have provided conceptual insight.) Animals of all kinds can be considered neuter if no name or personification is provided to help identify gender. In addition there are conceptual differences about animals and gender often based on the cultural view of the reader. Many people think of dogs as "he" and cats as "she" unless the context provides additional cues about the animal that would establish a concept of maleness or femaleness for that animal. In this case you should deal with the concepts of gender *only* if they interfere with understanding. The problem is not in and of itself related to reading.

3. *Having insufficient or confusing cues from the context to predict appropriately.* The readers may have had experiences that would help them expect another pronoun:

    Mr. Rudy paid the babysitter. "Does that seem right?" He smiled and nodded. "That's fine, I usually charge only 75¢ an hour."

    If readers think of babysitters as girls, and there are insufficient prior cues provided by the text, a confusion of character may result. Such miscues are produced even by proficient readers. The writer did not provide enough redundant information to give the reader appropriate cues. Even though this could cause a problem in developing appropriate characterization, especially if the confusion is not resolved through the reading, the teacher needs to view this as a problem complicated by the author. Subsequent cues in most cases provide the reader with enough information so that the confusion can be resolved. In this case the appropriate pronoun will probably be supplied by the reader later in the reading.

4. *Overusing the graphic cueing system*

    Persia has just had a family of five little kittens. All the children in the neighborhood had come to watch the mother cat take care of her kittens. She licked them all the time with her rough tongue. She really knew how to take care of her babies.

    Although the kind of miscues coded in the above example occurs rarely as a consistent problem, there are some readers who produce miscue substitutions that are neither semantically nor syntactically acceptable. Such readers are paying too much attention to graphic information, substituting look-alike words, and seem unconcerned that meaning is being disrupted.

The strategy lesson that follows will focus on pronoun substitutions that disrupt meaning.

PRONOUNS: STRATEGY-LESSON PLAN

Specific Rationale

A selected-slotting procedure will be used to encourage students to make use of context clues as a means of predicting appropriate pronouns for the blanks. The materials provided deal with *he* and *she* pronoun slots. If your students have problems with other pronoun substitutions that interfere with meaning, you can use these materials as models for writing or selecting materials with the appropriate pronoun focus. Be sure that the content contains enough cues to maleness or femaleness so that the reader is forced to deal with meaning.

EVALUATION

The strategy lesson for Pronouns will benefit

1. Readers who overuse graphic information and usually provide inappropriate pronoun substitutions that interfere with or disrupt comprehension.
2. Readers who indicate through their retelling or discussion of stories that they have confused characters because they misunderstood pronoun references.

Reading-Strategy Instruction

INITIATING

MATERIALS   "The Family Group," by Yetta Goodman

The Family Group

A girl named Judy
Eleven years old
Long brown hair in a pony tail
Taller than the boy
Blue jeans, a white shirt and barefoot.

A boy called Matt
Twelve years old
Dark long hair
The shortest in his family
Blue jeans, a striped tee shirt and brown shoes

The boy and girl's mother called Mama
Thirty years old
Dark short hair
Taller than the boy and the girl as tall as Papa
A green pants suit.

The boy and girl's father called Papa
Thirty years old
Brown short hair and a mustache
Taller than the boy and the girl as tall as Mama
A yellow sport shirt and blue slacks.

Their dog named Ginger
A big Collie
Long yellow, orange and white hair
A collar

YETTA GOODMAN

Show the students a copy of The Family Group. Tell them that together you are going to write a short sketch or story about one of the members of this family. Read aloud each member's characteristics so the students can decide which character you will write about first. After you work together on the first short story, the students should write their own sketch focusing on another member of the family. They can work alone or in groups of two or three. In writing each sketch, use all the facts listed about the character. Each sketch should describe a family member participating in an activity and should include another member of the family and the dog. The sketches should be at least five sentences in length but no longer than a page. After the group has decided which character to focus on for the first example, let them each dictate a sentence as you act as the scribe, writing on the chalkboard or on an overhead transparency. When any student uses a pronoun in the story, begin to raise questions.

INTERACTING

QUESTIONS FOR DISCUSSION

1. *Why did you use this particular word or pronoun?* [Use *he, it, she, them, they* as appropriate.]

   Students will recognize that when they know the people or animals being described in a story, they also know how to refer to them. Explore the notion that information comes from what they know about the characters in the story and not from the words themselves. They might explore the idea that repeating the proper noun all the time is not quite appropriate in language.

2. *Why did you decide to call the dog "he" instead of "she" or "it"? Why do we sometimes call animals "it" and other times, "she" or "he"?*

   Raise this question only when a student describes the dog. Refer to the pronoun used by the student. Explore the notion that *it* is often used, unless the author knows whether the animal is male or female. There are usually more cues in a story indicating whether people are male or female than there are cues indicating the gender of animals.

After the group story has been written, ask a volunteer to read it aloud to the class. Now they are to write their own stories focusing on a different character and incident.

After your students have finished their writing, take each of the sketches, including the one that you wrote as a group, and either duplicate them or prepare them for use on an overhead projector. When you write them up, omit all references to pronouns, replacing them with a five-space blank. Select one of those stories (one that a student has produced) and ask the students to read the entire short story to themselves once through. Tell them that they are to mentally place an appropriate word in the blank as they read. If they cannot decide what to put in the blank, they are to continue reading. Later, they can return to the blanks they are not sure about and decide which words fit appropriately. When they have finished reading the story to themselves, you read the story aloud. Stop at each blank and continue interacting.

MORE QUESTIONS FOR DISCUSSION

1. *Why do you believe this is the appropriate pronoun for this slot? Who does or does not agree?*

   The students should suggest the cues in the rest of the written material that support their answer. Permit the students to discuss any disagreement that they might have with each other.

2. *Whom do the words in these blanks seem to be referring to? How do you know?*

   You want the students to be aware that the words in the blanks relate to the people in the story. You want to help them generalize that they can find cues to different characters in the stories that they read that will help them predict the appropriate pronouns.

APPLYING

MATERIALS "My Little Brother and My Big Sister," by Dorothy Watson
"A Pet for Franklin," by Dorothy Watson and Carolyn Graves

My Little Brother and My Big Sister

Sometimes I get so mad at _____ little brother and _____ older sister! They bug _____ to death! Last night _____ brother took _____ crayons and scribbled all over _____ homework paper. Because _____ messed it up _____ had to do the whole thing over again. _____ is always getting into my things. _____ big sister is just as bad. _____ thinks the whole house belongs to _____ . _____ washes out _____ clothes and hangs them all over the bathroom. Between the two of _____ I think I'm going nuts. Sometimes _____ wish I had never heard of brothers and sisters. Look! Someone has been in my room again. I can tell because my sweater isn't on the floor where I left it. What nerve! What's this? _____ left me a note.

Hi,

Billy and I have gone for a walk. _____ cried all afternoon because _____ thought you were mad at him about the homework paper. _____ is really sorry.

We made some cookies and left them for you in the kitchen.

We love you.

Helen

Gosh, I've got a nice brother and a neat sister.

DOROTHY WATSON

A Pet for Franklin

The morning was bright and sunny as Franklin and _____ mother walked down the street to the pet store. Franklin was very excited. _____ was going to have a pet of _____ own. In a few minutes _____ would get to pick out the pet _____ wanted.

They entered the store and began to look around. Franklin did not know what to choose. _____ saw so many wonderful pets to pick from. How would he ever choose just one? _____ mother smiled as _____ watched _____ face. _____ understood _____ problem and was waiting quietly.

Suddenly _____ heard a whistling noise that sounded like music. _____ looked up over _____ head into a cage filled with feathers going in every direction. "Mother, what are those birds?" _____ asked.

"Parakeets," _____ answered.

"I want a parakeet!" _____ said. "I can teach it to talk."

_____ mother smiled. "Are you sure you want a parakeet?" _____ asked.

"Oh, yes," _____ answered.

"Okay, let's talk to the man at the counter," said Franklin's mother. _____ and _____ mother crossed the pet store to the counter where a man was putting away some pet food.

The man looked up and smiled when Franklin said, " _____ want to buy a parakeet."

The man asked, "What color bird do _____ want?"

Franklin answered, "I want one that can talk."

"Then you want a male parakeet," said the man.

"Male parakeets learn to talk better than the females do."

Franklin waited while his mother paid for _____ bird. _____ also bought a cage and some food.

_____ was very happy as _____ walked home with _____ mother and _____ new pet. "What a wonderful day," thought Franklin. _____ mother smiled at _____ .

DOROTHY WATSON AND CAROLYN GRAVES

Indicate to the students that "My Little Brother and My Big Sister" and "A Pet for Franklin" are similar to their own stories. They are to read through the whole story, and if they come to a blank they are uncertain about they are to continue to read and search for cues that indicate the person, persons, or animals being referred to.

Help the students understand that whenever they read it is most important to know who is being discussed in the story. They will then be more sure about the pronouns than if they concentrate on only the pronouns themselves.

EXPANDING

LANGUAGE DISCUSSION   Discuss with the students what pronouns they tend to use when they refer to animals. When they think of a dog, cat, horse, or cow, do they usually think of *he*, *she*, or *it*?

Have them keep track in their reading of how different animals are referred to by different authors. Have them interview several people to find out if different people have different notions about why a cat is often referred to as "she" and a dog is more often "he."

Explore with the class the different personal pronouns used to refer to inanimate objects such as ships, cars, or hurricanes. Consider how such conventions develop.

RELATIONAL WORDS AND PHRASES

General Rationale

Paragraphs, sentences, and clauses frequently deal with complex relationships between people, events, places, things, or ideas. These relationships are often indicated by a clause marker, an adverb, or a conjunction. The relationships that these words indicate include

Cause
Since my mother spilled coffee on it, I didn't do my homework.
I fell on my head and hit the edge of the step. *Consequently*, I had to go to the hospital.

Contrast
I like my brother; *nevertheless*, I feel like breaking his neck every once in a while.
I have very bad teeth and the dentist frightens me. *However*, I do go for a checkup every six months.

Time
The pot boiled over. *Subsequently*, the odor of burned food filled the room.
When the boys got home from school, the wind began to blow. *Then* the rain started to fall rapidly and hard.

Purpose
I want you to stop playing the piano *so* that I can go to sleep.
He went to the hospital *in order* to get the stitches removed from his hand.

Even students who do not miscue on the relational words or phrases in complex clauses or sentences sometimes show, through their retelling, that they did not understand the relationships. There are several possible reasons for reader difficulty in understanding relational words or phrases.

In some cases there is a difference between the oral and written terms used for the clause relationships. Sometimes the relational word is seldom used in oral English. In other cases the relational word is not common to the dialect of certain speakers. These terms may therefore be unpredictable for readers. Each *written* sentence below is similar to an example found in a basal text or trade book for elementary-school children; and the *oral* sentence represents a form that is used by some speakers:

Oral: He walked *like* he *was* hurt.
Written: He walked *as though* he *were* hurt.

Oral:	He finally paid his book fine *so* it was possible for him to take books out of the library again.
Written:	He finally paid his book fine *thus* making it possible for him to take books out of the library again.
Oral:	I asked her *did* she want to help me.
Written:	I asked her *if* she wanted to help me.
Oral:	She's the one *what* gave me a penny, Or: She's the one *that* gave me a penny;
Written:	She's the one *who* gave me a penny.

In other cases it is possible to predict more than one relational word in a certain slot, and it is not until much later in the sentence that it becomes obvious that the relational word or phrase predicted is not appropriate. The reader's sentence is syntactically and semantically acceptable even after the miscue is produced (see slash[/]), and it is sometimes difficult for readers to self-correct because they may be unaware at what point the miscue was made:

Text:	He went to the store *when* he was not hungry in order to purchase his food with greater objectivity.
Reader:	He went to the store *then* he was not hungry/in order to purchase his food with greater objectivity.
Text:	I used to share a place with two girls, but *when* I went to work downtown about a year and a half ago, I moved.
Reader:	I used to share a place with two girls but *then* I went to work downtown/about a year and a half ago, I moved.
Text:	It all happened so fast that I could not for the life of me remember *that* I was supposed to be at the doctor's office at three o'clock.
Reader:	It all happened so fast that I could not for the life of me remember *what* I was supposed to be/at the doctor's office at three o'clock.

Sometimes a perfectly acceptable sentence can be produced with an alternate relational word. However, when the acceptable sentence produces a change of meaning, problems in understanding may occur:

Text:	He didn't know *that* the boy wanted to be brave or dead.
Reader:	He didn't know *what* the boy wanted to be—brave or dead.

Often the relationship exceeds clause or sentence boundaries. The reader must be concerned with the meaning of a whole paragraph in order to understand how the relationship is operating in the story. The less knowledge readers have about the content of the materials, the more difficulty they have understanding such relationships.

Preventive dental care of teeth is very important for all children. The most important aspect in dental care is the regular visit to the dentist. *Unfortunately*, this regular practice can occasionally be accompanied by pain.

All you have to do to get a loan is flash a credit card or write a check. For more substantial amounts of money, *though, or* if you haven't yet established credit, you still have to take out an installment loan.

The teacher must help students deal with relational words by helping the students focus on how the events, the characters, and the setting interrelate with each other to construct the plot, theme, concepts, or generalizations of written material, rather than concentrating on the words themselves. Comprehending the message will be the greatest help in predicting the appropriate relational word or an appropriate synonym substitution. This focus on understanding is also most important in providing the reader with the appropriate cues to confirm and self-correct if the predicted relational word happens not to fit the syntactic pattern of the sentence.

RELATIONAL WORDS AND PHRASES: STRATEGY-LESSON PLAN

Specific Rationale

All readers are familiar with many relational words. Children use *and, but, so,* and *because* appropriately in oral language from the time they are four or five years of age. They do understand that events, characters, and settings have relationships to each other. They need to be helped to expand both their knowledge of the variety of relationships, and the ways in which they can be expressed in writing. In order to help students, some relational words and phrases may need to become the object of a strategy lesson. For example, *though* can cause problems for a number of reasons:

Though is seldom used in oral language, and students must begin to realize that it is not uncommon in written language. Although relationships expressed through phrases that include *though* are found in materials aimed at readers as young as seven or eight years old, most speakers do not begin to use such relational terms in their oral language until they are older.

Even though, as though, although, and *though* have different meaning relationships in different contexts, although they often seem to express contrastive relationships:

It seemed as *though* I would never get there.
The odds were against him. He went, *though*.
Although (*though*) older than his brother, he was much shorter.

The various forms of *though* can appear in different places in a sentence. It is therefore not easy to predict the syntax of such a sentence, since more than one prediction is often available to the reader:

He walked *even though* he was crippled.
Even though he was crippled, he walked.

Since the various words and phrases incorporating *though* are movable within the sentence, students often predict the words *thought* or *through* in certain grammatical slots. Because *thought* and *through* look so much like *though*, and since they can occur more often in language than *though*, readers are likely to predict either *thought* or *through* in the *though* slot:

Text: I left *though* John was happy.
Reader: "I left," *thought* John/was happy.

Text: He left quietly *though* the door had hurt his foot.
Reader: He left quietly *through* the door/had hurt his foot.

Of course, if readers are concerned with integrating meaning rather than simply dealing with surface graphic input, they will become aware that their prediction is not acceptable and make efforts to regress and correct.

Some students, however, are so tied to graphic information that they may consistently substitute *thought* or *through* for *though*. For these students you may want to present a strategy lesson for repeated substitution before you use this lesson (see chapter 8).

The focus of this strategy will be on helping readers understand the relationship expressed by *as though, even though, although,* and *though.* Once they are able to do this, they will in turn be able to predict the most likely clause markers or meaning equivalents as they read and then confirm the information through subsequent reading of the text.

EVALUATION

The strategy lesson for Relational Words and Phrases will benefit

1. Students whose retelling of stories they have read indicates that they lose the relationships suggested through the use of *though, even though, although,* and *as though*.
2. Students who frequently miscue on those words or frequently regress to reread them.

Reading-Strategy Instruction

Two Initiating and Interacting sequences are presented. One provides suggestions for the use of *even though* and the other incorporates the use of other forms of *though*.

The materials included in the Applying phase of this section incorporate all forms of *though* in order to avoid producing written material that might seem artificial. Selections can be dittoed or made into overhead transparencies.

INITIATING 1

MATERIALS   "As Though" Comprehending Sentences

"As Though" Comprehending Sentences

SELECTION 1

The Blue Stars hockey team is the best team in the league. The captain of the team is Leonard Thomas. He is tall and very strong. Leonard plays hockey very well. He always acts as though he is the only good player on the team. He acts as though he is the best hockey player in the world.

SELECTION 2

Julie and Marcia are my best friends. We are in the same class in school. We live on the same street. The three of us get along pretty well most of the time. Every afternoon we all go to one of our houses. Sometimes we do homework. Most of the time we talk about our teacher or other kids in the class. I like Julie and Marcia a lot but sometimes they make fun of me and that really hurts my feelings. Julie and Marcia sometimes act as though they were my enemies instead of my friends.

SELECTION 3

Bob and Sally walked down the narrow street. Bob tried to look as though he were not scared. He smiled at Sally and said, "We will be home very soon." He walked slowly looking back every once in a while. Then Bob said to Sally, "How was school today?" He was trying to act like everything was the same as always. But all he could think about was that strange noise and the blue light that came out of nowhere when they passed Betty's house.

Begin with one of the selections you think might be most interesting to the students. After completing the discussion of that selection go on to discuss another. If the students are interested in the process, use a third selection or write similar selections that are related to the particular experiences of your students.

In each case you should read the paragraph aloud to your students on the assumption that they do not often use *as though* in their oral language. They may have occasionally heard the words or seen them in print. However, they do have a synonym substitution—*like*—which helps them understand the meaning of the paragraph if they understand the relationship within the sentence.

INTERACTING 1

QUESTIONS FOR DISCUSSION OF SELECTION 1

1. *Tell me about Leonard. What do you think about him? Do you like him? Would you like to have him on your team? Do you know any people like Leonard?*

   In this case you are concentrating on Leonard's character to give the students an opportunity to understand how *as though* functions in the paragraph. From the discussion you will gain information about how much the students comprehend. An open discussion might also provide an opportunity for the students to use *like* as an appropriate synonym for *as though*. (Make note of this so that you can refer to it later in the lesson.)

2. *Is Leonard a good hockey player? Is he the only good hockey player on the team? How do you know? Why do you think so, or why don't you think so? What helps you to know whether or not he is a good hockey player?*

   Again you help the students to concentrate on the meaning of the sentences and their relationships with each other—and not simply on the words.

3. [Point to the sentences in which the *as though* phrase appears.] *How might you write these sentences differently without changing the meaning?*

   Help the students understand that authors always have choices and that some authors might actually use *like* or one of the other substitutions that they suggest. You might want to explore with the students the notion that authors sometimes use some words that seem more formal than those they might use in oral language. Emphasize the differences between written and oral language. Note, too, that when writing dialogue for characters or when representing the speech of young people, authors may choose to use *like*. The point should be that just as authors have options, readers have the option of restating sentences in order to understand them for themselves.

Throughout the discussion ask the students (whether you agree with their response or not), *Why do you think so?* Have other students give their opinions in response to another student's answer. If the students suggest possibilities that do change the meaning, and you provide opportunity for peer interaction, the students will begin to understand better where their thinking went astray.

QUESTIONS FOR DISCUSSION OF SELECTION 2

1. *Are Julie and Marcia the author's friends? How do you know?*
2. *Are they the author's enemies? How do you know?*
3. *What is the difference between acting in a certain way and being that way in reality?*

QUESTIONS FOR DISCUSSION OF SELECTION 3

Use questions similar to those suggested for the first two selections. Change the questions on characters and story line to fit the context of Selection 3. In this selection *like* has been used where *even though* or *as if* can be used. This was done to show the students that authors can also choose to use *like*.

INITIATING 2

MATERIALS   Transform Sentences for "Although"
Selected-Slotting Procedure for "Although"

Transform Sentences for "Although"

1. The boys and girls in our class do not like to go on trips together most of the time.
2. The day they went to the zoo they really enjoyed the trip.

1. The pool was small and crowded with swimmers.
2. Phillip put his inflated air mattress in the pool.

1. Wendy jumped into the pool and swam across.
2. The water in the pool was icy cold.

Selected-Slotting Procedure for "Although"

1. Pat did not like to drink milk. Her mother said that milk was good for her and that she should drink it.
   Restatement: Pat's mother said that milk was good for her and she should drink it _____ Pat did not like milk.
2. Most of the time Sally doesn't play well during a baseball game. She tries to be a good player, but usually she strikes out or flies out to an outfielder. Today Sally hit some really good balls. She got a single and was hit home. She almost made it to third the second time she came up to bat, but she was tagged out.
   Restatement: Today Sally played ball very well _____ she isn't usually a good ball player.

3. Karen always asked questions. She wanted answers to so many things that she didn't understand. She knew she might get into trouble, but she kept asking questions anyway.
   Restatement: Karen kept asking questions _____ she might get into trouble for asking them all the time.

4. Danny had worked very hard to get enough money to buy very expensive skis. Both of his parents worked, but they were not a rich family. His parents told Danny they didn't think he should spend too much money on skis. But he bought the skis anyway because it was his own money and he had worked for it.
   Restatement: Danny bought expensive skis _____ his parents told him not to spend too much money on them.

Read to your students each pair of sentences in Transform Sentences for "Although." After a discussion that gives the students an opportunity to rewrite the sentences, proceed with Selected-Slotting Procedure for "Although." Have the students read silently. You may suggest that they think the word *blank* wherever a blank appears. Both of these techniques provide the students with a variety of ways to transform and rearrange sentences without changing the meaning. If you decide to write your own sentences, use names of your students and events they are interested in. You might do this in any case for students who are not very effective in most of their reading or for those just developing reading.

INTERACTING 2

QUESTIONS FOR DISCUSSION OF TRANSFORM SENTENCES FOR "ALTHOUGH"

1. *How could you rewrite the events of the first pair of sentences into one single sentence without changing the meaning?*
   You can carry out this activity by having the class dictate to you while you write on the board. After this activity, students can work on the next two selections in pairs or individually.
2. *Can you now write* one *acceptable sentence by combining the two sentences? This time place sentence 2 at the beginning of the sentence without changing the meaning.*
   Any meaningful transformation of the sentences into a single sentence should be accepted. Ask the students to share their sentences with the rest of the class. Students can write them on the board or on a Ditto sheet to be reproduced for another day.
3. [Direct students' attention to a sentence written by a classmate.] *Did this sentence keep the meaning? How do you know?*
   If none of the sentences include *although, even though,* or *though* as possible relational words, add some samples of your own to the class' list. This should be considered simply as another alternative.
   Example: The day they went to the zoo the class really enjoyed the trip even though they do not like to go on trips together most of the time.

QUESTIONS FOR DISCUSSION OF SELECTED-SLOTTING PROCEDURE FOR "AL-THOUGH"

1. *What words or phrases go into the blank of the restated sentence without changing the meaning of the original?*
   Have the students share their choices and indicate why they think those choices retain the original meaning.
2. *What other words or phrases can be used without changing the meaning?*
   Again they can share their choices with others and discuss the meanings of the sentences. If the students do not use some form of *though* in the sentences, again provide *even though, though,* or *although* where appropriate as another alternative equal to theirs.

APPLYING

MATERIALS   "Bikes," by Yetta Goodman
"The Stormy Night," by Barry Sherman

Bikes

Tom and Danny were very good friends. The two boys would go everywhere together. When Tom wanted to go to the movies, Danny would go, too. When Danny wanted to go bike riding, Tom would go, too. One day Tom said to Danny, "I want to get some books to read. Let's go to the library."

Danny didn't like to read books very much but he wanted to be with his friend. So, he went to the library even though he didn't like libraries very much.

When the boys got to the library, Tom took books from the shelves and began to read parts of them. Danny looked around for something to do. He saw a sign on a table that said Books on Bikes. Danny loved anything about bikes so he went over to the table with the sign on it.

There were so many different books and magazines about bikes! Danny couldn't believe that there could be so many books about bikes. There were some books that told how to fix bikes. Other books showed how bikes looked a long time ago. Some of the magazines showed what changes have taken place in different parts of the bicycle over the years.

Danny was still looking at the books and magazines when someone said, "Come on, Danny, it's getting late." Danny looked at his watch. He and Tom had been in the library for an hour. Even though he didn't like libraries, he had found something to do and had enjoyed himself.

"Maybe we'll come back here again sometime," Danny said to Tom.

"You act as though you like libraries," Tom said smiling.

YETTA GOODMAN

The Stormy Night

Linda walked over to the window, where her brother Jud was standing. He was looking at the rain hitting the windowpane.

"What a terrible storm," he said as lightning flashed and a loud clap of thunder sounded outside.

"I hope Mom and Dad are all right," said Linda, joining her brother at the window. "I hope they stay at the restaurant. I don't want them to drive home in this thunderstorm, even though I wish they were here."

"Me too," her brother whispered, but he was feeling a little uneasy alone in the house with his sister on a dark, stormy night. Linda went back to her reading in the next room. Jud still watched the storm.

It began to rain harder, the lightning became brighter, and the thunder much louder. It seemed as though the storm was right on top of them. Suddenly, after a very loud thunderclap, the lights went out. Now, Linda and Jud were in total darkness.

"Where are you?" asked Jud. "I can't see you."

"I'm over here, in the next room," answered Linda. "I can't see you either."

"Keep talking," Jud said. "Even though I can't see you, I can hear you."

"OK, I'll keep talking, and you do the same thing. We'll both try to get closer to each other. But be careful not to hit your head or stub your toe."

So Linda and Jud began to walk slowly toward each other, even though they couldn't see anything in the darkness. They slid their feet along the floor so they wouldn't stub their toes. And they kept talking. Outside the storm was still raging. The rain was falling as hard as ever, even though the sound of thunder seemed to be getting lower. It seemed as though the main part of the storm were moving away.

"We're getting closer," said Jud. "I can tell because I hear your voice getting louder. I can even hear the sound of your breathing."

"Just keep on moving," said his sister.

"Ouch!" Jud screeched. "I just hit my toe against the table."

"You must be moving too fast. Slow down."

"Where are you now?" asked Jud.

Linda thought a moment, then laughed and said, "I think I passed you, although if I did, we should have bumped together."

Just then the lights went on again. Both Jud and Linda laughed when they saw that they had passed each other. In fact, Jud had almost walked into the next room.

A while later, their parents arrived. The storm had let up, and they had driven home. They were happy to see that Jud and Linda were not afraid and were even having a good time.

"I thought you would be upset when the lights went out," said Dad. "What did you do?"

"Oh, nothing much," said Linda, winking at her brother. "It was nothing to get excited about."

"I'm glad to hear that," her father answered. And they all went to bed.

BARRY SHERMAN

The repetition of any one relational word or phrase more than a few times seldom occurs in any story. It is therefore most important for students to read widely in order to encounter a wide variety of such words or phrases.

Before the students read the selections in the material available for the Applying phase of the lesson, discuss with them the purposes of the lessons they used during the Initiating and Interacting phases. Remind them that the strategies they have been using include

1. Concentrating on what the sentence means in relationship to other sentences
2. Rearranging or transforming the sentences (they can do it in their heads when they are reading) so the sentences are easier to understand
3. Substituting a known word or phrase that retains the meaning of the sentence when encountering an unfamiliar word or phrase.
4. Using the term *blank* when unable to make appropriate substitutions

As they read the selections provided, ask the students to write down any example from their reading where they were aware that they used one of the strategies. These they will later share with the class along with a description of how they discovered the meaning. Have the students continue to collect similar examples every once in a while for purposes of general discussion and for legitimizing such strategies for readers. *Do not force* this assignment if it appears to interfere with the students' reading.

EXPANDING

CREATIVE WRITING   Have the students take any of the sentences used during the Initiating phases of this lesson and ask them to write a story embedding the sentences. Get students started by asking them to make up some experiences that would cause the things described in the sentences to occur. Then ask them to think of a way to end the story. They should try to use relational words similar to the ones in the sentences whenever it is appropriate to do so.

Encourage the students to write their own humorous picture books that have relational terms as their themes. For example, a student can write a book called "Even Though" with one page that says, "Even though an elephant weighs a ton . . ." (accompanied by an illustration of an elephant), followed by a page that says, "It can dance on the head of this pin" (again accompanied by a humorous illustration). A book called "Except" might start with one page that says, "I flew around the world in my own super jet last night . . ." followed by, ". . . *except* I was dreaming at the time" (accompanied by illustrations). Students can read each other's books, or read their own books to others, allowing listeners to predict based on the term used.[5]

LANGUAGE DISCUSSION   Have the students begin to collect from their reading any new relational words that are interesting to them. They should write down the sentence in which the word or phrase appears; as well as other sentences that help define the relationship. Interested students may categorize the words according to whether they suggest cause, contrast, time, or purpose. However, let the students develop their own categories and labels.

If your students are developing their own personal dictionary, they may wish to put some of these words in it.

NEGATIVES

General Rationale

It is not only the presence of negative words, such as *not, no, never, none,* and the like, that indicates negation in English. Usually the meaning that readers have already accumulated from a story provides them with cues to any negative that occurs. As we consider the next two examples we will explore some of the cues which help language users predict negatives. (Use the verb "waste" in the first sentence, and "know" in the second sentence.)

---

[5]For patterns, see *What Good Luck, What Bad Luck* by Remy Charlip (New York: Scholastic Book Services, 1972).

John's eyes opened wide when he saw two of the biggest animal tracks he had ever seen. It was already getting dark, so he _____ any time getting home.

Bob looked dazed. "What happened?" I asked. "I really do _____ ," he answered.

Often relational words like *although*, *yet*, *but*, and *nevertheless* support the developing semantic cues and help the reader predict negatives. Words like *do* and *any* tend to be used differently in sentences that contain a negative than in those that do not.

Miscues in relation to negatives can arise for a variety of reasons:

1. *Negatives causing little or no change of meaning.* When the statement is not significant to the major plot of the story, whether it is negative or positive can often be unimportant.

    He *was* a little bit sleepy so he continued to sing loudly.

    He *wasn't* a little bit sleepy so he continued to sing loudly.

    In dialogue, questions can be asked that cause no difference in meaning regardless of whether the negative or positive statement is used.

    "You can't hold a hammer right! *Don't* you know you have to hold it at the end?"

    "You can't hold a hammer right! *Do* you know you have to hold it at the end?"

    In such cases the insertion or omission of negatives makes little difference to the story and therefore should *not* be considered a problem.

2. *Misconceptions or misunderstandings.* For students who are focused on meaning, the strategy of predicting negatives will only cause problems when those readers do not fully understand the events of the story because of their own misconceptions about or unfamiliarity with those events.

    The children always set the table before dinner. They placed the napkins carefully and set the large bowls in place. During the roundup, when the men were out on the range, the tables were not set carefully.

    If the students do not understand the social behavior at the ranch described in the preceding excerpt, and if that behavior is not carefully developed through the story, they may then easily omit the *not* in reading the last sentence.

    Each evening they made a wide circuit of the bedding grounds and built fires on high points, where they could be seen for miles around.[6]

    If students are unaware that fires scare away animals (which is the reason the fires were to be built in the story excerpt) and assume that "they" would prefer to hide, it would be reasonable for them to insert a negative in the verb phrase *could be seen*. In this case the negative results in a logical and possible, although changed, meaning.

3. *Negative contractions.* Occasionally readers predict a negative contraction as they read, produce the contraction (*can't*) and then realizing that the negative is in its full form (*can not*) produce what sounds like "I *can't* not go." Such readers are overemphasizing graphic information and are unaware that producing *can't* for *can not* or vice versa is appropriate for proficient reading.

The strategy lessons that follow are designed to help students focus on meaning; these lessons are concerned with problems of negation that result from misconceptions or misunderstandings, and misreading of negative contractions.

NEGATIVES AND MEANING: STRATEGY-LESSON PLAN

Specific Rationale

The best way to help students predict aspects of negation in their reading is to help them focus on the meaning being developed in the story.

In addition to the context which provides clues to negation, certain words or phrases

---

[6]James C. Stovall, "Sheep Dog," in *Widening Views*, ed. William D. Sheldon and Robert A. McCracken, Sheldon Basic Reading Series, 8th ed. (Boston: Allyn and Bacon, Inc., 1965).

provide redundant information indicating that a negative may occur or has occurred. Words like *although*, *yet*, *but*, *any*, and *do* function in different ways in negative and positive sentences.

The auxiliary *do*, for example, is only used in positive sentences to indicate emphasis, but it is often obligatory in negative sentences:

> I don't want to go.
> I want to go.

Any is used in sentences with negatives, but in a related positive statement *some* is used more frequently.

> I don't want any.
> I want some.
> I won't give you any.
> I will give you some.

The double negative was common in English at an earlier historical period. Many languages in the world today have an obligatory double-negative form. Although some dialects of oral English still retain the double negative, most forms of written English use the negative only once in a sentence, except for dialogue representing dialects that retain the double negative. Double negatives have the advantage of providing redundant information for the reader or listener on the syntactic level. If the language receiver misses the first negative, there is a second or third cue available to confirm or disconfirm the earlier prediction of a negative or positive statement:

> He *can't* do *nothing nohow*.

However, since the redundancy of the multiple negative is not available in most written English, the reader must rely on other cues to understand fully what is happening and to appropriately predict negation.

The lesson that follows concentrates on helping the reader to think of the developing meaning of the story as well as to explore the language cues that signal negation.

EVALUATION

The strategy lesson for Negatives and Meaning will benefit

1. Readers who omit or insert negatives with resulting loss of meaning.
2. Readers who omit or insert negatives in materials because of misconceptions or limited experience.

Reading-Strategy Instruction

INITIATING

MATERIALS   Scenes for Negatives and Positives

Scenes for Negatives and Positives

Scene description: Four young people are going fishing. Each brings along different bait but enough for all the others. One brings *artificial* bait (you decide what kind); another *live worms;* a third, *cheese;* and a fourth, _____ (your favorite bait).

1. What would their dialogue be like if they all decide to use the same bait and not to use any of the other three?
2. What would their dialogue be like if each likes his own bait best and rejects the other three?
3. What would their dialogue be like if they decide all the baits are equally good and each will use some of the bait brought by others?

Scene description: A young person has a brand new bicycle. Two friends come over and want to ride the bike together. They suggest that one will ride while the other sits on the handle bars.

1. What would the dialogue be like if the owner refuses to allow the friends to ride the bike?
2. What would the dialogue be like if the owner says only one of them can ride at a time?
3. What would the dialogue be like if the owner permits them both to ride after the owner rides the bike first?

Scene description: Two children in the family have a large dog. Father has asked them to wash the dog.

1. What would the dialogue be like if the children refuse to wash the dog?
2. What would the dialogue be like if the children agree to wash the dog?
3. What would the dialogue be like if one child agrees to wash the dog and the other child refuses?
4. What would the dialogue be like if one child agrees to wash the front end of the dog and the other child agrees to wash the back end of the dog?

Provide the students with a copy of Scenes for Negatives and Positives. The questions accompanying each scene provide students with various ideas for dialogues of short stories that they will write, dictate, or have dictated to them. Some of the stories will elicit language that includes negatives and others will not.

Here is an overview of the procedure:

1. Have a group of students choose the one scene from Scenes for Negatives and Positives that they are most interested in.
2. Have each member of the group choose a different question from the three or four choices listed under each scene. (If more students are involved than there are questions, you may have two or three students work together.) The alternate choices are so stated that some will elicit negatives as they are written or dictated and others will probably produce few if any negatives.
3. After the writing or dictating of the scene and its description, the students will use these stories to discover the language cues that help to predict negatives in written language.

A more detailed explanation of this procedure follows:

Explain the purpose of the dialogues to the students and decide (depending on the students' age and ability, and equipment available) whether you want them to write the scenes themselves; dictate to you; dictate to a selected student; or dictate into a tape recorder. Tell the students they will choose which of the scene descriptions they want to work on. Read all the scenes to them so that they can make their own choice.

When the scenes have been selected, have each group name characters and describe the settings that they will use. This is done so that the whole group will have the same images of the people and places in the scene. Using names and places with which they are familiar makes the writing process more relevant and more fun. Read aloud the question choices for each scene and have each student (or students) select the one he or she wishes to write. Explain to the students that after each has written a story that goes with a particular dialogue, together the class will compare them to determine how the language of each story differs depending on whether it describes a negative or positive incident.

Reproduce the written stories so that each student can have a copy. Then, as a group, compare the three or more dialogues that go with each scene, and begin to note the language, mood, and plot development that suggest the negative and the positive. After you have done one together as a class, those who wish can choose a second scene to do in small groups or individually and can again explore the similarities and differences in language that provide cues for negatives or positives in written language.

INTERACTING

QUESTIONS FOR DISCUSSION

1. *In what ways does the sequence of the dialogue suggest that there might be a negative statement or incident? In what ways does the sequence suggest that it will be positive?*
   Try to have the students look at the story line itself. Then ask the same question about the other dialogues and compare the language. On the chalkboard make two columns labeling one Negative Characteristics and the other Positive Characteristics. List the characteristics suggested by the students in the appropriate column. Then, in the adjoining column, indicate how the language differs. List a sentence from the story as an example when appropriate. Have the students check the characteristics as you proceed through each dialogue to see if they find additional support for their decisions or information that may lead to a change of mind.
2. *In what ways does the mood of the characters suggest whether incidents will be stated in a negative or positive fashion?*
   Again follow the same procedure of listing the characteristics in the appropriate columns. Use the other dialogues to make comparisons and to support the categories being developed.

3. *What words or phrases are used with negatives that are either not used, or used in different ways, in positive statements?*

Try to get the students to look at phrases or whole sentences as well as words. It is not possible to suggest what examples you may encounter in this line of questioning, since there is no way to predict which of the scenes your students will select or what language they will use in their writing. An example might be: When *but* is in a sentence with a *not* in the first part or clause, there will not be a *not* in the second part, as in *He's not big but he's smart*. You and your students will have the excitement of discovering these aspects of language together. Continue to add to your list of negative and positive characteristics. Reproduce these columns for your students and encourage them to keep adding to the list that will become the basis for the Applying phase of this lesson. Do not insist that the students include *each* statement that has a negative. If the process becomes too analytical, the students will lose interest. Follow their lead by using their suggestions, and stop the discussion when interest wanes.

APPLYING

MATERIALS   Any material chosen by a student or material from a collection of old basal-reader stories that have been set aside.

Encourage pairs of students to work with their lists of negative and positive characteristics, developed during the writing of the dialogues. They are to add to the lists and confirm statements that are already on the lists, indicating the name of the story they are reading, the sentence example, and the page number; or they can reject something that is listed, writing down the sentence examples that suggest that the characteristic is not consistently representative of negative or positive statements. After they have worked together for a reasonable length of time allow the students to present their findings to others, and discuss the findings using questions similar to those in the Interacting phase:

Negative Characteristics	Positive Characteristics
1. *Beth and Friends*	1. *Beth and Friends*
When a character shakes her head, that means no.	When a character nods, it usually means he agrees.
"I don't agree," Beth commented, shaking her head. (p. 43)	"Jimmy's right," Tom nodded in agreement. (p. 22)

EXPANDING

CREATIVE WRITING   Take a scene from any story that includes negatives and rewrite it removing all negatives. Rewrite the context to fit the positive statements. Underline the aspects of the story that are changed because of the rewriting. Next, take a scene that does not include any negatives. Rewrite it to include negatives and make the rest of the story consistent with the negatives. Underline changed aspects. Discuss what happens to the language surrounding negative and positive words or phrases when such changes are made.

NEGATIVE CONTRACTIONS: STRATEGY-LESSON PLAN

Specific Rationale

There are some readers who have limited reading experiences. They may have spent too much of their time working with highly controlled easy-to-read or basal materials and may not be used to seeing negative contractions in print. When they encounter such contractions, they are often confused about how to handle them. These readers can predict the negative and may orally read *can not*; but on becoming aware of *can't* in the print, they may correct. Once they are used to seeing contractions in written language, these students will begin to predict them. However, if the author chooses to use the full form for the contraction (*can not* for *can't*), again the reader may become confused and either correct or read orally the *not* following the miscue *can't*. Although these strategies do not usually interfere with gaining meaning, they are inefficient, since the reader is focused on surface information and is not aware that reading should sound like language. The main focus of this strategy lesson is to make students aware

1. That written language and oral language have many things in common
2. That it is acceptable to read a contraction for a full form, or vice versa, and that such miscues need not be corrected

EVALUATION

The strategy lesson on Negative Contractions will benefit

1. Students who tend to substitute look-alike words for negative contractions when those words are not in fact appropriate substitutions for those contractions—as in *want* substituted for *won't*—and who do not correct such miscues.
2. Students who orally read a contraction for a full form, or vice versa, and almost always correct such high-quality miscues:

   I should not be in this room.

   They haven't had breakfast yet.

3. Readers who predict a negative contraction in their oral reading but, when they encounter the full form in print, say *not* following the contraction and do not correct:

   I will not go to his house.

   He can not be in six places at one time.

4. Readers who are just beginning to encounter contractions in print either because of limited reading experiences or because they are beginning readers.

Reading-Strategy Instruction

INITIATING

The purpose of this lesson is to help students become aware that contractions are alternate options in oral and written language and that reading either a negative contraction (*won't, can't, don't, wouldn't*) for the full form, or a helping verb plus negative (*will not, cannot, do not, would not*) doesn't produce a change in meaning.

Think of some activity in your local area that your students are often involved in: going downtown or to the closest shopping center; going to a local baseball or football game; taking a bus to some local recreation spot; or going to a school dance or party. Then on the chalkboard write both a negative and a positive reaction to the activity:

I like to go downtown.   I do not like to go downtown.

These sentences are the headings under which you will list the responses to questions asked in the Interacting phase.

INTERACTING

QUESTIONS FOR DISCUSSION

1. [Use the activity that interests the students most.] *Why do you like to go downtown?* Ask any person in the group to provide one reason. List the response, being careful to record any negative contraction or full form exactly as the student produces it, although for this question you will receive few if any negatives.
2. *Why don't you like to go downtown?* Follow the earlier procedure and record exactly what the students say. When you have at least five or six examples in each list underline the *do not* in the heading sentence and all other negative full forms that appear in the students' sentences.
3. *What other ways can you write* do not? *Or what other ways can you write [any of the negative forms in the sentences]?* If the students do not respond easily, ask them how they might say "I do not go," another way without changing the meaning. Write the sentence on the board as you say it. Write the contraction form if a student responds appropriately. If not, say, "I can say *'I do not go.'* " Point to it on the board. Then: "And I can say, *'I don't go.'* " Write this form on the board as you say it. Give the students an opportunity to respond using the other full forms on the board. Record their responses on the board as they say them. Now point to any of the contractions that are in the students' sentences.
4. *How could you write this in a different way without changing the meaning?* Again give the students an opportunity to provide four or five examples, recording their responses on the board as they say them.
5. *What difference does it make whether you use* do not *or* don't *when you are reading or writing?* You should ask this question each time the students respond with a form equivalent to the one you have pointed to. You want the students to realize that the different forms do not make for a difference in meaning. They represent an option that a speaker or an author uses. Some of your students may say that you are not supposed to use contractions in writing. The activities in the Expanding phase help the students explore when and where contractions are used, and if any student raises this question, this would be a good time to introduce the suggested activity.

APPLYING

Write several times the beginning words of a positive statement at the top of a sheet of paper. Then, halfway down the page, write the negative, or opposite, forms of that statement. Leave room for the students to finish the statements:

Tomorrow I will _____
Tomorrow I will _____
Tomorrow I will _____
Tomorrow I will _____

Tomorrow I will not _____
Tomorrow I won't _____
Tomorrow I will not _____
Tomorrow I won't _____

When I am in the kitchen I can _____
When I am in the kitchen I can _____
When I am in the kitchen I can _____

When I am in the kitchen I can't   _____

When I am in the kitchen I can't   _____

When I am in the kitchen I can not   _____

When I am in the kitchen I can not   _____

I like to   _____

I like to   _____

I like to   _____

I don't like to _____

I don't like to _____

I do not like to _____

I do not like to _____

Point out to the students that in the negative form you have used both the full form and the contraction so they can see them both in use and decide if they prefer one over the other and why. Start them off doing the first one together.

When the students finish, have them share their responses. Ask if there is any difference in meaning when they use *will not* or *won't, can not* or *can't, do not* or *don't*. Discuss any preference they have for one form over the other and why. Encourage the students to add their own sentences to those you have given them. Relate sentences to significant events or holidays taking place at the time you are using the lesson:

On Thanksgiving I like to eat _____

On Thanksgiving I don't like to eat _____

For my birthday I would like _____

For my birthday I wouldn't like _____

EXPANDING

LANGUAGE DISCUSSION   Divide the students into teams. Have each group of students record, in a complete sentence whenever possible, all the negative contractions or full-form equivalents that they hear in one of the following:

1. Fifteen minutes of a comedy show on television
2. Fifteen minutes of a mystery show
3. Fifteen minutes of a news broadcast
4. Fifteen minutes of a social-studies discussion in class
5. Fifteen minutes of an address by the president

Have another group of students record all the negative contractions or full-form equivalents that they find in the following:

1. Four pages of their favorite book
2. One page of the comics in the newspaper
3. The front page of the newspaper
4. Two pages of a news magazine
5. Two pages of the Bible

Add your own or your students' suggestions regarding what could be investigated. Using the results of their investigations, discuss with the students whether contractions or full forms are used more in oral language or in written language. Also discuss which forms seem to be used more in some functions of writing or speaking than in others.

Chapter 5

Predicting Syntactic Cues

GRAMMATICAL FUNCTION

General Rationale

Readers use syntax or grammar all the time when they read. They use their own knowledge of syntax to predict the author's syntax. This is equally true of words, phrases, and clauses:

The boys ran around the _____ .

Every speaker of English knows there are only a few possibilities that can fit the blank following the second *the*. If there is only one more word in the sentence, it will be a noun, such as *circle*, *corner*, or *block*. If there is more than a single word, it will be a noun phrase, such as *next street corner*, *big circle*, or *first block*.

One of the major purposes of the strategy lessons that follow is to build confidence in readers by making them aware of their language competence and helping them apply this competence to their reading so they will feel secure about predicting syntactic structures.

You can discover this strength in your students and at the same time make them aware of their own language competence by using a selected-slotting procedure. This procedure involves leaving a blank in sentences for specific language slots selected for specific instructional purposes.

Through oral discussion, present the following sentences, one at a time, to your students:

_____ boys went to the store.
The boys _____ to the store.

Ask students to suggest what word or words can be put in the blank so that the sentence makes sense. Encourage them to think of more than one word that can be placed before *boys* in the first sentence or after *boys* in the second sentence. Keep asking if they can think of any more possibilities until they no longer respond. The students will be able to do this task fairly easily. They will provide a variety of adjectives or determiners in the first sentence and a variety of verbs with adverbs in the second sentence. Let the students know that they can do this task well because they are using their knowledge of their language. They will need this confidence both when they apply these ideas to independent reading and when they are working with strategy lessons.

People who study how children learn language have not reached agreement on how children develop and learn the complex syntax of their language during their preschool years. But linguists all agree that children do learn it. We believe that understanding syntax is more difficult for the scientists studying it than it is for children learning to use it. Although meaning is derived from the semantic relationships in language, these relationships are carried through the syntactic structure.

In English the only way you know who is doing what to whom is through the order of words in the sentence. This is one of the ways that syntax provides a vehicle for meaning to take place:

Mary tickled Betty.
Betty tickled Mary.

Syntax also provides cues to the number of things in a story and the time the story takes place. In English this is often indicated through inflected word endings:

The boys jumped and landed on their feet.

Questions are often predicted through the use of markers at the beginning of sentences, like *what, why, who,* or through inverted sentence order, as in *Is she? Did you? Can he?* The order of words in sentences also helps the reader predict whether the sentence will be a statement or an imperative.

I will go.
Come here, Sally.

There has been a great deal of change in the way linguists interested in grammar have looked at language in recent years. No one views grammar prescriptively, believing that there are absolute ways to say, read, or write things. Language is a medium for human communication. Like all other aspects of culture, language changes and has variations from group to group and from place to place. That is why there are language differences and dialect differences within each language group.

There *are* language rules, but these rules *cannot* be imposed on language users by grammar books or teachers. Linguists have discovered the rules by studying the way people talk or write and then categorizing the system people use.

Language users *know* these rules intuitively by virtue of having grown up in a society that uses language. Different dialect groups use different rule systems just as different language groups use different sets of rules to communicate. We could not communicate if we did not *know* and use the rule system of our language. These rules do not have to be taught. They are learned tacitly by all speaking and hearing children before they come to school through normal interaction with their culture.

It is important that you know about language so that you do not impose inappropriate rules on your students simply because they know and use languages or dialects different from the one or ones you use.

In English words may be categorized into five grammatical functions: nouns, verbs, adjectives, adverbs, and function words. The more linguists learn about language, the more complex they realize their categories must be, and so they have created many subcategories and overlapping categories. There is often controversy about which categories should be used and what words should be placed in each category. We will therefore be oversimplifying to some degree as we make use of the five major grammatical functions.

Linguists prefer not to define categories of grammatical function; rather, they indicate the function of a word based on how the word is used in the sentence. Function depends on how words relate to each other, their order in the sentence, and how the words are inflected.

For example: *The* is a noun in this sentence because it is the subject of the sentence—it refers to an abstract idea and is followed by a verb phrase. It can be inflected like a noun, too, as in "There are three *the*'s in the first sentence of this paragraph."

In summary, the significant aspects about syntax and grammatical function that apply to reading include the following:

1. Syntax is the vehicle through which language can be understood.

2. Syntax can only have meaning, and grammatical function can only be assigned, within the context of language.
3. Children are proficient language users by the time they come to school.
4. Every language user tacitly knows how to use the syntax of language.
5. Reading demands the application of a language user's knowledge of syntax.

NOUNS AS NAMES FOR PEOPLE: STRATEGY-LESSON PLAN

Specific Rationale

Nouns are words that refer to concrete or abstract things or ideas and are subjects and objects of phrases and clauses. Nouns are usually predictable, and readers generally have little problem predicting most nouns. However, there are nouns that do cause some problems in reading.

Proper nouns frequently have spellings that are not common to English, like *Sato*, *Papazian*, *Wyche*. That the proper noun refers to a person and not to an animal or a geographic unit or a brand name can be determined by the information in the surrounding context:

Stanislaw Zychiewicz's family has lived in Chicago for three generations.

Yaityopya Niguisa Nagast Manguist is a country in Africa. It is known to Americans by the name Ethiopia.

The family name of the common squid is Loliginidae, the genus is Loligo, and the species is *pealil*.

If readers concentrate on trying to pronounce or sound out proper names, they are apt to disrupt efficiency in reading. Such readers must be helped to rely on their sophisticated use of syntax and to concentrate on searching for meaning. Proficient readers use the following strategies to understand nouns as names (you might verify these by trying to remember how you handled the proper names when you read the examples above):

1. Predicting a proper name slot (since a pronoun can often appropriately be predicted for the same slot, pronouns are often categorized as a type of noun)
2. Omitting the name or preferably substituting another name, nickname, or initials for the proper name
3. Trying to determine some characteristics of the person, which would include physical, occupational, and personal characteristics
4. Determining the significance of the name to the written material, and not concentrating on those names that they predict they will never meet again in their reading and thus will not need to remember.

EVALUATION

The strategy lesson for Nouns as Names for People will benefit

1. Students who are not able to provide information about characters in a story during a discussion about the story.
2. Students whose miscue pattern on names might look like the following (examples taken from different points in the story):

We had just never had any pets until Sven Olsen wanted one.

Sven's pet was everybody's pet.

"Where's Sven," I asked.

Just then Sven appeared at the door.

"I don't know," said Sven sadly.

Many readers may have predicted *seven* for the first occurrence of *Sven* in the examples, but by the second time the name appeared, they would have substituted a namelike word such as *Steve* or *Seever*. Intonation helps you know whether students consider what they are reading to be a name. The reader represented in the example never indicated that he was aware that *Sven* was a name. He tried all types of nonwords, omitted in the fourth occurrence, and finally went back to *seven*. His retelling confirmed his confusion over this character in the story. Students like this one often have miscues that look very much like the text but do not make much sense.

3. Students who are so concerned about not having the right name that they keep changing the substitutions each time the word appears in the text, or sometimes they omit the name throughout the entire story. If they provide evidence during the retelling that they *do* understand the role of the character in the story, they have not disrupted comprehension. However, such students will become more efficient in their reading if they learn to consistently substitute one name for another.

4. Students whose miscue profile shows a high graphic similarity score of more than 75 percent and a semantic and syntactic acceptability score under 60 percent.

Reading-Strategy Instruction

INITIATING

MATERIALS   Two or three local phone books
"My Friend Larry," by Barry Sherman

My Friend Larry

I want to tell you a story about my friend Larry. When Larry was as old as you are, something always gave him trouble in school. His full name was very long. Everybody thought it was hard to say Larry's name when they saw it written down. That was because Larry's full name was Lawrence Annicchiarico. You can imagine the problems that such a long name caused.

Every September, at the beginning of school, Larry's new teacher would try to say his full name: "Lawrence Anni—,Lawrence Annic—, Lawrence, how do you say your name?" And Larry would tell his teacher how to say his name. Of course, by that time, everyone in the class was laughing. Even his friends would laugh. Luckily for Larry, the fun only lasted a day or two. And as he grew up, the laughing over his name bothered him less and less. But then, when he was eighteen, a new problem began.

A few months after his eighteenth birthday, Larry was drafted into the U.S. Army. In the Army, soldiers are called by their last names. But "Annicchiarico" was a hard name to say. It was also very long; so the officers shortened the name to "Anni." And this is how Larry became known as Anni to his fellow soldiers.

You can imagine that Larry was not too happy about the name. It sounded just like the girl's name "Annie." Sometimes, when Larry and a few friends visited a new town or city, people would laugh when they heard his friends call him Anni. In one way, Larry was lucky. Nobody would laugh too long because he was tall and strong, and people did not want to make him angry.

After Larry left the Army, he decided to become a teacher. His long name helped him to teach his students an important lesson. That lesson may help you, too.

The first day of school, Larry began by saying, "Hello. My name is Mr. Annicchiarico." He looked at the class and saw that the children were going to have problems with his name. He had to shorten it to make it easy for the class, and for the other students in the school. So he wrote his name on the board and said, "This is how my name looks when it is written down. It is a very long name and hard to say. O.K. From now on, whenever you want to speak to me, instead of 'Mr. Annicchiarico,' say 'Mr. A.' And when you read my name, instead of trying to sound out all of the letters, read 'Mr. A.' "

And so, Larry became known as Mr. A. in his school. And he taught all his students that they could do the same thing whenever they came to a hard name in a story. If they came to a hard Russian name such as "Svidrigailov," they could read "Sam" or "Sid" instead. The French name "Jean-Pierre" could be read as "John or Jim." The name Mr. Zychiewicwz could be changed to "Mr. Z." You try it the next time you come to a hard name in a story you are reading.

BARRY SHERMAN

Provide each reader with a copy of the story "My Friend Larry." Tell them that they are to read the story silently and that after the reading there will be a discussion about the people in the story. Since the story is somewhat long, students will finish at different times. As students finish reading, ask them to look through the phone book and find names that they think no one in the class, including the teacher, will be able to pronounce. Have them make a list of the names, which will be used later in the lesson. Two or three students could do this together quietly.

INTERACTING

QUESTIONS FOR DISCUSSION

1. *Who was in the story? What do you know about them* [or *him* as appropriate]?
   Any information that the students remember or infer can be accepted. Whether or not they make appropriate responses, it always helps them to be more responsible for their answers if you ask, *How do you know that?*
2. *What kinds of things do you know about Mr. A.? When you read a story, what kinds of things should you find out about the characters in the story? Should you know as much as possible about every single character in the story?*
   You might list on the board the kinds of things the students think they should know about any characters in the story and compare the list to what they know about Mr. A.
3. *In this story why does the author choose to tell you certain things about the main character instead of other things?*
   Help them explore the notion that the significant characters can be set aside from the insignificant characters based on what the author tells the reader about each character. Explore the role of the author in the story in relation to his characters. He tells the reader what he wants the reader to know based on the purpose the character has within the story.
4. *Why do you think it is acceptable to call the character in this story Mr. A.? When you read, is it sometimes acceptable to omit or substitute another name for an unfamiliar one?*
   Try to get students to understand that silent reading is for their own information. What is important is knowing aspects of characterization, not the exact name of the character. Help them see the superiority of substitution over omission.
5. *When might it be important to pronounce someone's name appropriately?*
   Students should realize that this is important only when oral language is required. Even when they are reading about famous people, it is more important that they recognize the historical significance of the character and know what he or she is famous for, the relationship to other famous people, and aspects of personality, rather than be overly concerned with being able to pronounce the name.
6. *How do you find out how to pronounce someone's name?*
   Readers must all be aware of the limitations of asking teachers or looking in dictionaries for this information. Sometimes the only true source for how a name is pronounced is the person who has the name. You might want to take this opportunity to discuss how the same name can be pronounced differently depending on what part of a country the name comes from or from what language. Also explore the notion that most names are Anglicized even by television and radio reporters when they come from languages that are not English.

APPLYING

MATERIALS   "The Mad Russian," by Barry Sherman

The Mad Russian

Alexei Mikhail Feodorovich Lermontov was born in New York City in 1916. Two years earlier, his mother and father had come to America from Russia. That was why they gave him a Russian name. But most of his friends found his Russian name hard to say, so they called him "Al" or "Alex." Al's name wasn't really so unusual. "Alexei" in Russian is the same as the English name "Alex." The name "Mikhail" is the same as "Michael." The name "Feodorovich" means that Al was the son of a man named "Theodore." "Lermontov" was Al's last name, just like the American last names "Smith," "Jones," or "Evans." So his American friends might have thought of him as "Alex-Michael-Son-of-Theodore-Lermontov." But it was a lot easier for them to call him "Al" or "Alex."

When Al grew up, he got a new name. His friends started calling him "The Mad Russian" because he did crazy things from time to time, and "mad" is a word that can sometimes mean crazy.

The first crazy thing Al did was when he was in college. He was playing fullback in an important football game. The score was tied 12−12, and Al had the ball. As he started to run with the ball he lost his sense of direction. He was running the wrong way! All of a sudden, he realized that he was going the wrong way, so he turned around and started back. He ran so well that he scored the touchdown that broke the tie. His team went on to win 22−15. Al's run was amazing because he ran 32 yards the wrong way and 62 yards the right way. He had to run a total of 94 yards before he scored the touchdown! It was after this game that his friends started calling him "The Mad Russian."

Alexei did other "mad" things besides running the wrong way in a football game. He learned to fly an airplane and he became a good pilot. But he also did a few crazy things in the air. Once he tried to fly under a bridge upside down. The plane crashed into the water, and Alexei nearly lost his life. The next crazy thing he did was when he decided to go into the jungles of South America to look for gold and diamonds. His friends didn't see him again for two years. Everyone thought he had died in the jungles. But the Mad Russian was not going to let a jungle stop him. Two years after he started out to look for gold and diamonds, he came back home a rich man.

Al did many crazy things, as if to prove to his friends that "The Mad Russian" really was a good name for him. He would tell his friends that he really should be called "The Mad American" because he was not a Russian at all—he had been born in New York City. But then his friends would say, "Listen, Al, anyone with a name like Alexei Mikhail Feodorovich Lermontov has got to be Russian. And everyone knows you're mad." At this point, Alex and his friends would laugh, and someone would remember one of the crazy things The Mad Russian had done. Al had been everywhere and had tried to do almost everything. But he loved to fly airplanes best. That is why he became a fighter pilot in the U.S. Army during World War II.

Al became part of a new fighter squadron on an island far out in the Pacific Ocean. From this island, Al and his friends flew their planes against the enemy. Al's plane was a new twin-engine fighter called the P-38 or Lockheed "Lightning." He named his plane *The Mad Russian.* The name was painted in big black letters on the plane's nose.

Al and his plane went through many adventures together. Some of them were very crazy. But the last adventure seemed to be the craziest of all. One of the planes in Al's fighter squadron had lost the use of one engine in an air battle.

This damaged airplane was trying to return to the base. The plane was flying very slowly. The Mad Russian reduced speed and was flying alongside to protect the crippled airplane. The other planes in the squadron went on ahead. Al and his friend flew as fast as they could, but it wasn't fast enough. Suddenly, ten enemy fighters came at Al and his friend from out of the clouds. Al had been watching for signs of enemy planes, and saw the ten planes immediately.

"Don't worry," said Al over the intercom as he started to turn his plane around to face the enemy fighters. "With the Mad Russian on your side, you don't have a thing to worry about. You just keep heading for home."

Al's friend wanted to help but he couldn't get his one good engine to produce more power. He could only watch as Al's plane single-handedly took on the ten enemy planes. Because his own plane was too damaged to turn and fight, he had to keep heading for home. He knew that Al didn't have a chance, and he expected to be attacked from behind at any moment. But no plane attacked him, and he returned safely. But the Mad Russian did not come back, and no one ever saw Al again. Alexei was listed as Missing in Action, and he was awarded a medal for bravery above and beyond the call of duty.

Some people said that what Al did was the craziest thing he had ever done. They said that he should have kept heading for home and saved himself. How could he have expected to fight ten planes by himself? But the Mad Russian's friends knew better. They knew that Al never expected to beat the ten enemy fighters. He did what he felt he had to do, even though he had to die.

World War II ended a long time ago. But today, on that lonely island far out in the Pacific Ocean, there are still signs showing that Al's air base had been there. Palm trees grow where P-38 fighters used to take off and land but it still looks like an airfield. At one corner of the old runway, there is a stone with a picture of a P-38 carved into it. Below the picture are these words: In Memory of *The Mad Russian,* Alexei Mikhail Feodorovich Lermontov, Craziest Guy of a Crazy Bunch.

BARRY SHERMAN

Have the students read "The Mad Russian" silently. Using this story as an example, go through the following suggestions with small groups of students so the students can follow the procedure as they read on their own.

Have the students write down difficult names they encounter in their reading over a two-week period. Have them record the whole sentence or sentences in which each name is included so they have enough context for meaning. Also have them write down two or three things they have learned about the person from the story.

At a group meeting or independent reading conference, have the students share their examples. Have them indicate what they did when they came to the name in order to find out more about the character. Always have them focus on understanding character development as a more important objective in reading than proper pronunciation of the name.

EXPANDING

CREATIVE WRITING   Have the students write stories using the unusual names they have collected from the telephone book. They are to build a picture of the character through language by giving information about the character's personality, occupation, actions, role in life, and so on. The students can read one another's stories and tell the student-author what they found out about the character. Emphasize how much a reader can know about a character even though she or he cannot pronounce the name. If there are some well-written stories, you may wish to keep these for other groups of students to use.

LANGUAGE DISCUSSION   Students can discuss the spelling patterns, as well as the ethnic origins, of names (see strategy lesson for Foreign-Language Words and Phrases in Chapter 6). Start with the surnames of the students in the class. Find out the national origin of the names. The phone book may also be useful for this assignment. How many ways is the same name spelled? Can students discover whether the different spellings mean the names come from different parts of a country or from different countries? They might interview parents, grandparents, or neighbors who are new to the United States about how similar names can differ in spelling or pronunciation. Has their family name been changed in the last two generations? Do they know why? The teacher might be able to get phone books from other parts of the country to extend this lesson if the students are interested.

The more interested students can categorize some of the spelling patterns related to certain languages or national origins and develop some rules about the spellings of names as they relate to national origin.

SOCIAL STUDIES AND SCIENCE   As students study famous people in social studies or science, they may want to explore the national origin of their names. An interesting search for some students is to look up famous people's names in the phone book to see how many people are named after famous people and how the names have been altered. One random look through a city telephone directory produced *Mildreda Fillmore,* most likely named after President Millard Fillmore.

When the names of famous people from other countries are encountered on the radio or on television, students might check with people from those countries and see how differently the people who come from those countries pronounce the names as compared with the way local commentators pronounce them.

NOUNS AS PLACE NAMES: STRATEGY-LESSON PLAN

Specific Rationale

Reading nouns that are place names is similar to reading nouns that are people's names. (See General Rationale for "Grammatical Function" or Specific Rationale for "Nouns as Names for People.") The reader of place names must be concerned with searching for the cues to the kind of place being named, such as a body of water or land mass. The focus must be kept on the concepts related to the place—and *not* the oral pronunciation. The place name is usually embedded in language that provides many cues to understanding the type of place being referred to, as in the following examples:

The water in the Oose flowed rapidly.

They reached the peak of Kosciusko after a great deal of hard climbing.

They got on the bus headed for New York. The bus roared out of the rolling hills. They passed farmhouses and suburbs. They rolled along the highway, across the bridge, and into the big city. They came into the heavy traffic. As they found themselves among tall buildings the traffic got heavier and heavier.

The language cues *water, flowed,* and *rapidly* in the first example suggest to the reader that the Oose is a body of water. However, the reader must have a conceptual understanding of how water flows and how its movement is described, to be able to indicate a body of water. Likewise, in the second example, the concept that people can climb mountains to reach a peak must be known by students if they are to use the language cues *reached the peak* and *hard climbing* in determining that Kosciusko is a mountain. The language in the last example provides evidence to those who understand the cues that the bus is headed for New York City and not New York State. The language provides the cues for the place; the cues are seldom in the name itself.

Once students become aware of the need to use a variety of the available language cues to understand the place names in their reading, they can begin to deal with specific words or parts of words that cue meaning. Such language cues include

1. The place name itself containing meaningful words:

   Culver City
   Detroit River
   Mount Rushmore
   Niagara Falls

2. A meaningful word embedded in a common place name or historically derived place name:

   Riverview
   Woodland Hills
   Bloomington
   Petersburg
   Morristown
   Deerfield
   Evansville
   Middleborough
   Williamsport
   Bournemouth

By exploring these names with students as they appear in their reading, or as they are relevant to other curricular studies, the teacher can help the students to develop concepts about how these names came into existence. It is important, however, to stress that often names have only historical significance and may not provide appropriate cues for the place being named. Riverview may not have a view of the river but still carry the name. Highland Park may be an urban area, have no resemblance to a park, and be relatively flat. Kansas City may be a city in Kansas and also a city in Missouri, and Michigan City may be in the state of Indiana.

Students should be aware that even when the name itself has meaningful words, it is necessary to rely on the cues in the total language context in order to build a complete picture of what the author is describing.

Naturally, students must understand prior to their reading that language cues can provide conceptual information that distinguishes a political division, such as a city or state, from a geographic entity, such as a river or mountain. Students must have concepts about such entities before they can recognize appropriate language cues. Such basic concepts cannot be learned simply through reading. Although reading can enhance and broaden concepts, they must be built through many *nonreading* experiences. Trying to learn something completely new from simply reading about it is a frustrating and often unsuccessful experience even for the most proficient readers.

As you plan activities to help students understand new concepts, remember that it is easier for students to distinguish the broader and distinctly different categories of places: for example, bodies of water may be easily distinguished from hills and mountains. Once students have developed concepts to distinguish places that are very different, they can begin to understand the characteristics that distinguish more similar types of geographic or political divisions: for example, seas, as distinguishable from lakes, from rivers, from streams. The more similar the concepts, the greater amount of experience and knowledge is necessary to understand their differences.

Even educated adults continue to have difficulty distinguishing very similar kinds of places unless they have specific knowledge. For example, in Israel, Lake Kinneret and the Sea of Galilee are the same body of water. The characteristics that distinguish a lake from a sea are not as obvious as it might seem when different people at different times can call the same body of water by either term. The possibilities for confusion of the lake and sea are reflected in a dictionary definition of the word *sea*:

> sea (sē) *n*. 1. the continuous body of salt water that covers nearly three-fourths of the earth's surface; the ocean. 2. large portion of this, partly or almost entirely enclosed by land, as the Caribbean Sea or the Aegean Sea. 3. large inland body of water, salt or fresh as the Sea of Galilee or the Dead Sea.[1]

The experience students need to broaden their concepts can be gained through field trips if the real entities are close at hand. Secondary representations, such as films, filmstrips, and pictures can also prove helpful, especially if they supplement students' sharing of their real-life experiences. When they discuss the places in their reading, students should be introduced to the word *setting* and be helped to understand that more important than pronunciation of the names of places in the story is the relevance of the setting to the plot or meaning of the written material.

EVALUATION

The strategy lesson for Nouns as Place Names will benefit

1. Students who do not concentrate on understanding the concept of a place. For example, a student might read a place name without a miscue but later give evidence of not understanding that reference was made to a place or to the characteristics of a place.
2. Students who make miscues on the place name that indicate they are sounding out rather than producing appropriate namelike substitutions:
   "Robin climbed the Apple-a-chain Mountains."
3. Students who need assistance in the strategy lesson for the Nouns as Names for People. (See the Evaluation of that lesson.)

Reading-Strategy Instruction

INITIATING

MATERIALS: "I'd Like To Live in Colorado," by Valerie Gelfat
"Goin' Down the Colorado," by Valerie Gelfat

---

[1]*Macmillan Dictionary*, ed. William D. Halsey (New York: Macmillan Company, 1973), p. 897.

I'd Like To Live in Colorado

I'd like to live in Colorado.
I'd like to live out where it's green.
I'd like to be where mountains, trees,
And rivers are all waitin' to be seen.

I'd like to sit beneath an aspen,
Find a field in which to lie
And watch the Rocky Mountains
Climbing halfway to the sky.

I'd like to live in Colorado.
I'd like to see wildflowers grow,
And smell their perfume in the air
As I wander down dirt roads.

I'd even like the cities there,
Small mining towns that grew
Like Durango, Silverton, Ouray;
Big ones like Denver, too.

VALERIE GELFAT

Goin' Down the Colorado

Get the raft, Sam,
And let's go!
Goin' down the River!

Find a spot
And throw it in!
Headin' down the River!

I got my paddle.
Have you got yours?
Paddle down the River!

See them rapids?
Hold on tight!
Rushing down the River!

Look out for rocks!
Yipes! There's one!
Dangers on the River!

Yes sir, we're goin' down the Colorado,
Going fast and hard.
Feelin' like we're on a tornado.
Feelin' mighty small!

It's a churning, whirling bathtub.
It's a race against the rocks.
It's a muscle-tearing contest
And a challenge to survive.

It's a mighty work of nature
That don't care if you live or die,
Yes sir, we're goin' down the Colorado
And we can't tell you why!!

VALERIE GELFAT

Distribute a copy of each poem to the students. Ask them to read the poems silently to find out what each is describing. Students who finish reading before the others do might look at maps of the United States to locate places they know.

INTERACTING

Have students first discuss the poems separately before comparing them. Ask the first three questions about each poem; then use questions 4 and 5 comparing the two poems.

QUESTIONS FOR DISCUSSION

1. *What is being described in the poem "I'd like to live in Colorado"?*
   Accept answers in generalized terms like "a place out west" or "back east" (depending on where you live), as well as in specific terms like "a state."
2. *What language in the poem helps to tell you what kind of place is being described? What makes you think so?*
   Accept any answers students can justify.
3. *Why do some of you use language cues that are different from those used by others to help decide about the type of place being described?*
   Point out that the students' own personal experiences help them decide what language reminds them of a particular place.
4. *What are the obvious language cues that make the place in one poem so different from the place in the other poem?*
   If the students cannot easily distinguish between the state and the river in the two selections, have them explore other language indicating this difference. Select terms that do not appear in the poem. If you are in or near the state of Colorado or a state through which the Colorado River flows, have the students use their own personal experiences with the river or the state to discuss whether the author of the poems was accurate in her descriptions. If you are not in the state of Colorado or a state near the Colorado River, have the students compare a river and state that they know of with the river and state described in the poems.
5. *What language would you use to make the places in the poems more real to you? Or: What language would you use to change the poems so that they describe the river or state you know best?*
   As students discuss various places, have them locate them on a map.

APPLYING

MATERIALS   "A Bus Ride through Paris," by Barry Sherman

A Bus Ride through Paris

Hello, everybody. Today we will take a bus ride through the city of Paris, France. I will be your guide on this trip. I will tell you all about the interesting places that you will see.

Paris is often called *la belle Paris*—beautiful Paris—because this city is one of the most beautiful and interesting cities in the world. Paris has beautiful streets, beautiful old buildings, and a beautiful river, the Seine. The Seine River cuts the city of Paris into two parts. One is called *la rive gauche*—the Left Bank. The other part is called *la rive droite*—the Right Bank. Each part of the city is interesting in a special way.

We will start our trip through Paris on an island in the middle of the Seine River. Then we will drive over a bridge to the Right Bank. We will end our trip by driving across another bridge to the Left Bank, where we will see the famous Tour Eiffel.

We are now on City Island in the middle of the Seine River. City Island, or *Ile de la Cité,* as it is called in French, is the place where the city of Paris started out a long time ago. All of Paris was on this one little island for a few hundred years before the city began to grow. Today, there are interesting streets and buildings still standing on the island that remind us of what Paris probably looked like six hundred years ago. We will have time to look at only one building while we are on the island, the great church of Paris, the Cathedral of Notre Dame de Paris. This church is one of the most beautiful buildings in the world. It took a long time to build, and it is about seven hundred years old. Look at the wonderful windows made of small pieces of different-colored glass! Look at the carvings all over the outside of the church! *C'est magnifique.* It's wonderful! Wonderful!

Now we drive over the bridge to *la rive droite*—the Right Bank of the Seine River. Here we see the largest palace in the world, the Louvre. This palace is very famous because it is now an art museum.

As we leave the Louvre, we will come to one of the most beautiful streets in Paris—the *Avenue des Champs Elysées.* This wide, tree-lined street is loved by everyone who lives in Paris. When you look down the Avenue des Champs-Elysées, you can see the famous monument called the Arc de Triomphe. This famous Arch of Triumph is the center of many streets called the Place de l'Etoile. The place de l'Etoile looks like a star because twelve streets branch out in all directions from the Arc de Triomphe. Can you imagine the traffic jam when automobiles from twelve streets meet? *C'est terrible!*

Now we will drive across the Seine River to *la rive gauche*—the Left Bank. We will see the famous Tour Eiffel, or Eiffel Tower, as you say in English. When most people think of Paris, the first thing that comes to mind is the Eiffel Tower.

We will end our bus ride through Paris here at the Tour Eiffel. I hope you enjoyed your visit to *la belle Paris.* Maybe you will visit us again someday. Until then, *au revoir*!

BARRY SHERMAN

As students read the materials provided, as well as other selections, they can begin to record, either in chart form or in a log, the following information about place names, which can be used in further discussions or conferences:

1. New concepts they learn about different places whether they are able to pronounce the place names or not.
2. Information about places that does not ring true based on their own knowledge or personal experiences.
3. New places that are adequately described including the various language cues used in the descriptions.
4. New places that have not been adequately described, with a note indicating the significance or insignificance of the place named to the understanding of the material. Students might want to make guesses about the place based on additional reading or research if they are interested.

Have on hand atlases, maps, globes, and travel folders, and encourage students to refer to them for information about any places in which they become interested.

EXPANDING

CREATIVE WRITING   Have students look up additional information about the place, in the materials they read, that interests them most and write a story as if they have visited that place. Suggest that they incorporate in their story language cues that readers can use to understand the setting.

Suggest that students look at maps of places they have traveled to, or would like to travel to, and write descriptions using some of the geographic names they find difficult to pronounce. Have them avoid using giveaway words like *river, ocean,* or *mountain* in their stories. Have other students read these stories to see if they can understand the kind of place that is being described from the language cues provided by the student-author, even if they cannot pronounce the place names.

SOCIAL STUDIES   The concepts of place differences are often related to social studies or science. It is important to integrate social-studies or science lessons with reading.

Encourage younger children to use information based on their own backgrounds to develop strategies for predicting place names. Discuss why places in their own cities have seemingly misleading names. For example, children from New York City may be familiar with residential areas that are urban, yet have such names as Forest Hills, Fresh Meadows, Woodside, Bay Ridge, and Forest Park. Students may also be familiar with places in New York City whose names reflect their historical origins but not what they are today, such as Bowling Green, Wall Street, or Fort Tryon. Students could write about what visitors might expect these places to be, based on their names, and then what they actually are. These student-written materials may later be used with others to develop place-name strategies.

Develop with your students categories of different kinds of places, and begin to list the characteristics necessary to build concepts for them. The following organization may be helpful:

1. *Political entities (land):* city, state, town, country, nation, county, republic, province, township, borough
2. *Geographic entities (land):* mountain, hill, slope, plains, flatland, plateau, desert, valley, mesa, forest, woods, jungle
3. *Water entities:* ocean, sea, river, lake, pond, stream, creek, rill, pool, rapids, falls, swamp
4. *Buildings:* house, school, library, store, office, government building
5. *Monuments:* statue, architectural structure, historical place

Discuss with the students how the language cues about places in social-studies material differ from the cues about settings in fictional material. To establish contrast, you may use the poem "Goin' Down the Colorado" and an encyclopedia article on the Colorado River. Select materials from both social-studies and fictional materials that easily lend themselves to this kind of comparison. Discuss a particular place, comparing and contrasting language cues about that place in the materials selected. You may want to keep lists of differences and similarities, adding to them or changing them as students gain additional evidence from their reading.

Have students examine newspapers to find out how they indicate setting. Students may note that the dateline, which sometimes includes a place name, tells that the material was written in that particular locale or transmitted from that locale. However, the body of the story may indicate that it took place elsewhere. Confusion in understanding datelines is common among readers, so it is worthwhile to clarify their meaning here.

Use stories or articles that provide information about a lot of places, and have students map out the routes described. For example, students could draw maps of the tour through Paris as described in "A Bus Ride through Paris." They may then want to draw maps of their own travel plans. Or they may want to make maps based on a walk around their neighborhood or a field trip. Suggest that students use their maps to make an oral presentation in class and, if possible, enhance their demonstration with pictures or slides.

VARIETIES OF GRAMMATICAL FUNCTION: STRATEGY-LESSON PLAN

Specific Rationale

Except for names used as nouns or noun phrases, no particular grammatical function within a sentence causes consistent problems for readers. More than 70 percent of the time most readers retain the grammatical function of the text word when they produce a substitution miscue on the word level. The following miscues exemplify this phenomenon:

He called his pet Lightfoot. *[her Whitefeet]*

Penny rushed up the front steps. *[reached]*

Even when miscues do not retain the grammatical function of the text, there is evidence that readers predict appropriate or acceptable grammatical structures:

Pulling the kitchen stepladder out into the hall and climbing up on it, he reached the *[to climb]*

light.

It was almost like his own voice speaking to him. *[the owner's]*

Look for my toy, Jimmy.

It is down here. *[do it ?]*

Or if the predicted structure is not confirmed by subsequent language cues, readers will correct the unacceptable grammatical structure:

And so he burst into the apartment. *[© the]*

This is for man and the work he is best able to do. *[© in his abili-]*

These miscues often are syntactically acceptable up to the point of the miscues because the reader has predicted a possible language structure that does not fit the total sentence structure.

Although no word has an identifiable grammatical function outside the context of a sentence, there are distinct variations in the frequency with which individual words fill particular grammatical-function slots. *Circus* and *river* will most frequently occur as nouns; *trained* will most frequently occur as a verb:

The children went to the *circus.*

The boat went up and down the *river*.
They *trained* the parakeet to talk.

Students who do not read widely will tend to predict the most commonly used grammatical function for a word and can become confused by its placement in less frequently used grammatical slots:

He was selling *circus* balloons.
He wanted to be a *river* man.
He has a *trained* parakeet.

Beginning readers may need extra encouragement or support in using their language knowledge to make predictions about grammatical structures. Some beginning readers who are already utilizing their grammatical knowledge may need an OK from you, an affirmation that guessing or risk taking is a legitimate strategy. Such activities as reading patterned literature to and with children, and allowing them to complete predictable sentence patterns and make up new ones, will give them the confidence they need. (See the strategy lesson "Spelling Patterns through Language Experience" in chapter 9.)

Although the evidence suggests that most students do not have difficulty predicting grammatical function as they read, some students are not always confident about their ability to make use of their own grammatical knowledge. They often minimize their language strengths by focusing on less effective strategies, such as "sounding out." It is important to help these readers rebuild their confidence. Many of the strategies that involve both predicting and confirming place responsibility on the reader to take risks, to guess, and, when predictions do not work, to overcome the problem independently by using various confirming strategies.

The materials in this lesson explore two different reading strategies:

1. Using the word *blank* and continuing to read when an unfamiliar word or phrase is encountered for which the reader has no immediate prediction. Additional context provides many cues that enable readers to develop synonyms or definitions for significant units unfamiliar to them. Saying "blank" for the unfamiliar provides a syntactic or grammatical sense that permits the reader to retain the sentence structure until meaning emerges. Readers making use of this technique often begin to say "blanks," "blank*ed*," "blank*ing*," appropriately, revealing their strengths as users of language and their awareness of grammatical structure. This strategy also gives readers independence by allowing them to continue reading even when they are insecure about substituting appropriate synonyms.
2. Substituting an unfamiliar word or phrase with appropriate grammatical function and meaning. As readers begin to justify their own synonym substitutions based on grammatical function and context, their attention will be focused on overall meaning. This strategy not only helps readers concentrate on comprehension but also provides readers with a way to be independent and rely on their strengths as language users. It legitimizes risk taking in the process of learning. (For further development of this point see the strategy lesson "Synonym Substitutions" in Chapter 9.)

Of the two sample materials provided in this strategy lesson, the first uses uncommon words in the adjective position and the second deals with prepositional phrases.

Of course, if evaluation reveals that an individual student is having difficulty with a particular grammatical function not included in this strategy lesson, you will want to write your own strategy-lesson material. In such cases you may find it helpful to refer to the section in Chapter 3 called "Criteria for Selecting and Writing Materials for Strategy Lessons."

EVALUATION

The strategy lesson for Varieties of Grammatical Function will benefit

1. Students who do not do much independent reading.
2. Students who show lack of confidence in making predictions in their reading, who read slowly and haltingly and often look to the teacher for specific help.
3. Students who prefer to omit unknown words or carefully sound them out rather than substitute meaningful alternatives.

4. Students who recognize words in their more frequent grammatical-function position but not when they occur in a less common position. Such readers might be able to read the sentence *He fell into the river* but become confused reading the sentence *He wanted to be a river man*.

Reading-Strategy Instruction

INITIATING

MATERIALS   "Tom's Birds," by Dorothy Watson
"Little Red Riding Hood," adapted by Carolyn Burke

Tom's Birds

Tom loved birds. He became interested in birds when he started to feed the ones that came into his back yard in the winter time. He would put _____ crumbs on the ground behind the house. Soon there were many birds that came. He built two _____ feeders for them and hung them up on some _____ branches so that he could see them from his _____ window.

At first Tom did not know the names of any of the _____ birds he was feeding. After a while he began to look for their names in _____ books. He discovered that there were cardinals, grackles, and sparrows visiting his _____ feeders.

When his mother and father saw how interested Tom was in birds, they decided to buy him some birds that he could keep in the house.

One day they came home with a parakeet. A parakeet can be trained to talk. Tom worked very hard to train his parakeet to talk. He worked with him every day. He would repeat the same words in the same way over and over again. After a long time and a lot of hard work Tom had a _____ bird. His parakeet could say things like "Hello, everybody" and "What's up, doc?"

About a month later his mother and father bought him a _____ bird. It was a canary. Tom was looking at the bird as it hopped from perch to perch in the cage. It turned its head from side to side to look at Tom. It chirped and peeped as it jumped. Tom knew that a canary could be trained to sing. He also knew that he would have to work as hard teaching his canary to sing as he had done teaching his parakeet to talk. But then he would have a _____ bird and a _____ bird.

DOROTHY WATSON

Little Red Riding Hood

One day Little Red Riding Hood's mother sent her to her grandmother's house with a basket of goodies. It was a long walk to her grandmother's house. She went _____1_____ to the path in the forest. As she walked along she saw a rabbit sitting _____2_____ . And she saw a bird's nest high up _____3_____ . It was a nice day and Red Riding Hood was happy to be going to her grandmother's house so she began to play. She ran ___4___ _____ and jumped _____5_____ . She climbed ___6___ _____ and then went skipping on down the forest road. She saw a deer get a drink_____7_____ . She picked some flowers from the side _____8_____ . She was happy because she knew that her grandmother would like the flowers. But then she saw something that really scared her. She saw a wolf hiding_____9_____ . She knew the wolf would want to eat her so she began to run. She ran as fast as she could. She ran right _____10_____ of her grandmother's house.

Adapted by CAROLYN BURKE

Provide the students with a copy of "Tom's Birds" (adjective position) or "Little Red Riding Hood" (prepositional phrases) depending on your evaluation of their needs.

Ask the students to read through the story silently one time.

Tell them to think of a word or phrase that best fits the blanks so that the sentences make good sense to them and good sense in the context of the whole story. If they are not sure what belongs in any blank, suggest that they can think the word *blank* instead and continue reading. Then, after they have gotten additional cues from the story, they can go back to the blank and choose a word or phrase they think fits the slot best. Explain that it is possible to think of more than one word or phrase for some blanks. Allow plenty of time so that the students have a chance to read the whole selection and then reread any section in order to build a complete, meaningful story for themselves. At this point you and the students can read the story aloud. Ask them to fill each blank with their personal response and to listen for the choices of others. (In an alternative procedure, to be used with "Little Red Riding Hood," the teacher reads aloud while the students look at the map and respond with appropriate prepositional phrases.)

INTERACTING

QUESTIONS FOR DISCUSSION

1. *What words or phrases do you think fit in the slot and make the sentence and story make sense?*

   Accept all responses.

2. *What cues in the story helped you decide on each choice?*

   Allow the students to interact, agree, or disagree with each other based on the context of the story. As the students continue to provide choices for each blank, help them realize how appropriate all their choices are. Their ability to fill in the slots appropriately and make meaningful sentences proves their ability to use their language when they are reading. Point out, as well, that they do not need every little bit of information to make sense out of the story. If they are thinking about what they are reading, they can supply a lot of information themselves. Stress that *all* readers replace words they are not sure of with other words that make sense. In that way they can continue to read and understand the overall selection without waiting for help from others. Explore with them the idea that the main purpose of their reading is to gain meaning for *themselves*.

3. *Are there any other words or phrases that you could put here and keep the sense of the story?*

   Try to elicit alternative words or phrases for the slots. If students do not produce any, you might suggest one or two. Your students will begin to see the possibilities of using a variety of words or phrases in the blank slots as they participate in this activity. Their predictions will show increasing flexibility as they recognize that they can supply words and phrases that fit and make sense in the story.

APPLYING

Find materials that are interesting to students, and keep them for use in this phase. Stories from discarded basal readers are a good source for such materials. Any stories used for selected slotting should provide a variety of experiences with different grammatical functions. The students may work in pairs on the different stories and compare the versions each produces. They might discuss which of the versions they think are most appropriate and why they think so.

Point out to students, when appropriate, that as they read, gaining more information about the story, they were often able to figure out what word encountered at an earlier point in their reading filled a particular blank, if that particular word was important enough to the story. Other times they were able to get enough meaning from their reading without knowing a particular word, because any single word is usually not very significant to a story.

Encourage the students to use the strategies of either saying the word *blank* or substituting an appropriate synonym each time they come to a word they think they do not know in their own reading. Suggest these strategies to your students whenever they come to you for help with a particular word or phrase. This helps students become more and more independent as readers.

EXPANDING

CREATIVE WRITING   Have the students take a story they like and change the ending or write an introduction about what happened before the story started. Then have them rewrite these new stories leaving a blank for one type of word, such as all descriptive words or one repeated noun or verb. Then let other students read the additions to the stories and fill in the blanks. The students can compare versions to see how similarly they filled in the blanks and what new stories or plots were developed based on the words they chose.

Cut out unusual or interesting headlines from the newspaper. Have the students write stories to fit the headlines and then follow the selected-slotting procedure described above. Save all good stories for use with other students.

LANGUAGE DISCUSSION   Students may wish to compile their own dictionaries listing the words that were unfamiliar to them when they started reading a selection and that they came to understand through their reading. Suggest they divide a small notebook into alphabetic sections and write the words that *they* select into the appropriate section. Younger children often find it easier to use a file box for this purpose, recording each entry on a separate card. Have them record the sentence from the story where they first noticed the unfamiliar word and then their own definition or concept of it, developed through their reading. After (never before) they have begun to write their own definitions, they may look up the words in the dictionary to confirm their own definitions and to note any differences, if they are interested in doing so.

INDICATORS OF DIRECT SPEECH

General Rationale

Written language makes use of a set of print conventions to indicate direct speech. These written conventions include dialogue carriers, paragraphing, and quotation marks.

Dialogue carriers are the short clauses that indicate who is talking:

I said, "Stop that!"
"Dinner's ready," *yelled Robin*.

Said is the most common verb used in dialogue-carrier clauses; however, other verbs are also used to describe body movements, facial expressions, or feelings that accompany the direct speech. Sometimes such descriptions are expressed in phrases that accompany the dialogue carrier:

"I'm really disturbed," *frowned Mr. Sanders*.
"She hit a home run!" *John yelled with a sob in his voice*.
Mother smiled joyfully, "I'm glad you're home now."

A new *paragraph* is begun each time there is a shift from one speaker to another.
Quotation marks are used to set the spoken message apart from the rest of the text.
The conventions used for indicating direct speech are relatively simple and straightforward. Yet factors exist that cause some readers to experience difficulty in handling them.

1. Most of the conventions that are used to indicate direct speech in writing are seldom represented in oral language. When we report what a third party said, the intonation in our voice and the use of indirect quotes is the oral equivalent to the punctuation and dialogue-carrier phrases used in writing:

   Oral: Mom said that we better come home right now.
   Written: Mother called anxiously, "You better come home right now."

   Oral: He told us all to come over for ice cream.
   Written: Bob included everyone present, when he said sincerely, "I want you all to come over for ice cream."

2. Dialogue carriers with their accompanying written conventions can start a sentence, end a sentence, or be found in the middle of the speaker's utterance:

   "I'll be home late," John answered. "Don't wait for me for supper."

3. Dialogues are often in the present tense while the language in the dialogue-carrier clause and the story is in the past:

"Come and have some cake," Mom called.

4. Authors often do not choose to use dialogue carriers in extended exchanges between characters in a story, and readers must rely on quotation marks and paragraphing as graphic cues indicating direct speech. These cues are supported by the readers' knowledge of the developing story context.

DIALOGUE CARRIERS—WORD LEVEL: STRATEGY-LESSON PLAN

Specific Rationale

The dialogue carrier has one specific function, and that is to identify the speaker. This function can always be fulfilled by the use of a dialogue-carrier clause composed of the verb *said* plus a proper noun representing the speaker. The verb *said* can therefore replace any verb that an author may have chosen to use in the dialogue-carrier clause. If in a dialogue there are two speakers asking questions of each other, *said* can still be used, but *asked* and *answered* can often be as easily predicted. When readers are aware that a character is speaking and can recognize the purpose of the dialogue, they can substitute *said*, *asked*, or *answered* for any unfamiliar verb used by the author and continue to gain meaning. Readers can even omit the dialogue carrier and still retain the meaning of the passage.

This strategy lesson will help students recognize *said* as an all-purpose verb within the dialogue-carrier clause so that they can use one of the following strategies.

1. Filling the verb slot
2. Substituting *said* (or *asked* or *answered*) for an alternate verb in that slot
3. Knowing the speaker and omitting the dialogue carrier

EVALUATION

The strategy lesson for Dialogue Carriers—Word Level will benefit

1. Readers who focus on graphic information only and miss *all* the cues that indicate who is talking. These readers need help in integrating all the cues. Take the following passage as an example:

John was dragging a large tree branch. He saw his friends. "Bob and Mary," said John. "Please come and help me."

Readers who do not integrate the cues might read the last sentence as follows:

a. Bob and Mary and John. "Please come and help me."
b. Bob and Mary said, "John, please come and help me."

In *a*, the reader is unable to handle the dialogue-carrier verb and confuses *and* with *said*. The reader in *b* is confused about who is talking to whom. Both readers need the support of this strategy lesson, especially if they have made no attempt to correct.

This strategy lesson is not designed for readers who appropriately recognize the cues and at the same time produce miscues in sentences that retain the story's meaning:

a. He saw his friends, Bob and Mary.
   John said, "Please come and help me."
b. John said to Bob and Mary, "Please come and help me."
c. "Bob and Mary," John said, "Please come and help me."

2. Readers who are unable to develop a picture of what various characters are like, what they said, and what they did, even though the story has a significant amount of dialogue.
3. Readers who repeatedly substitute the words *said* and *and*. (See also the strategy lesson on "Repeated Substitutions" in chapter 8.)
4. Readers who produce a large number of intonation miscues that relate to dialogue carriers that are not syntactically or semantically acceptable.

Reading-Strategy Instruction

INITIATING

MATERIALS   "The Skating Rink," by Barry Sherman

The Skating Rink

Scene: Saturday afternoon at the roller-skating rink. It is very crowded. Two boys and a girl are standing at the edge of the rink with their skates on. They are talking to each other.

Johnny: It sure is crowded today.

Teresa: I don't think I've ever seen so many people here on a Saturday afternoon.

Mike: I knew we shouldn't have come today. How can you have fun skating when there are so many people around? Let's get out of here and go to the show.

Teresa: No. Not me! I've got my skates on. And besides, we've already paid. Let's skate.

Johnny: Look over there! There's a bunch of guys from school trying to play whip.

Teresa: On this crowded floor? Where?

Johnny: [Pointing] Right over there. See them?

Mike: Yeah, I see them.

Teresa: I see them too. If they don't stop, they'll be thrown out of here. Better keep away from them or we'll be thrown out with them.

Johnny: Do you see those three girls skating with Ben? Aren't they in your class, Mike?

Mike: They sure are. One of them sits next to me. Let's skate over there and break into their group.

Johnny: Good idea. We'll hit them from behind and surprise them.

Teresa: You go first, Mike.

Mike: Heck no. Why should I?

Teresa: It's your idea.

Johnny: Boy, are you brave! All right, I'll go first.

Teresa: I'll go with you.

Mike: OK. Ready, get set, go!

Teresa: Let's hit them hard!

[*They skate off across the floor toward the other group of skaters.*]

BARRY SHERMAN

Distribute copies of *The Skating Rink*, and give students an opportunity to read the play silently. When they have finished, have them look it over a second time to choose the parts they wish to read; then have them read the play aloud.

INTERACTING

QUESTIONS FOR DISCUSSION

1. *If we wanted to rewrite the play* The Skating Rink *as a story, how would we show that the characters are talking to each other and what they are doing? What language is used in a story to show that people are talking to each other?*
   The students should explore the following ideas:
   a. In a story descriptive language tells what is happening in the scene.
   b. The language would have to indicate who is talking by the inclusion of *Johnny said* or *Teresa said*.
   c. The dialogue would be spaced on the page as part of the story.
   d. Quotation marks would be used to show who is talking. (With younger children you might want to use the terms *talking marks* or *speech marks* for *quotation marks*.)

   You can list student responses on the board as they are suggested by the students so you can refer back to them.
2. *If you were writing the story of* The Skating Rink, *how would you start? How would you describe the setting? How would you tell what the children were talking about? How would you tell what a particular child said?*
   As the students talk, begin to write the play in prose form on the board, incorporating the students' suggestions. Write *exactly* what the students dictate. (One of the students may act as scribe.)
   You and the students may rewrite the whole play as a story. If you prefer, get them started and have them complete the rewriting themselves in small groups. When they are finished, have them hand in their stories.

APPLYING

MATERIALS   Selected-Slotting Version of "The Skating Rink"
"The Incubator," by Yetta Goodman

Select a version of "The Skating Rink"—either one of the stories that you and the class wrote together or one that the students themselves wrote—and type it as written, but replace all dialogue-carrier verbs (that is, *said*, *discussed*, *smiled*) with a five-space line.

The Incubator

Dave walked down the three flights of stairs to the second floor. He went up to the door that had the number 24 on it. The name Turner was written under it. He knocked on the door.

Richard's mother opened the door.

"Is Richard home?" Dave _____ Mrs. Turner.

"In his bedroom," _____ Mrs. Turner. She opened the door wide and let Dave in. He walked right to Richard's room. Richard and Dave were good friends. They had lived in the same apartment building since they were in first grade together. They used to be in the same class, but this year they were in separate classrooms.

Dave poked his head into Richard's room and looked around.

"Where are you?" Dave _____ .

"Here I am." Richard's voice came from the bedroom closet.

"What are you doing in there?" Dave _____ .

"Looking through my old animal cards," _____ Richard.

Everyone knew that Richard loved animals. He told everyone that he was going to work in a zoo or be an animal doctor or something like that.

"What do you think I should do for my science project this year?" _____ Dave. "Mr. Grant just told us today that we have to have our project ready in six weeks."

"Why don't you hatch chicks," _____ Richard. "I just saw a TV program, and they said you could hatch eggs in twenty-one days."

"Isn't that hard to do?" _____ Dave.

"Nope," _____ Richard.

"What do you have to do?" _____ Dave.

Richard _____ , "First, you've gotta make an incubator. All you need is a fairly good size box with a cover. You line it with foil to insulate it. Then you put an egg carton in it. You fix up a light socket through a little hole on the side of the box and attach a light bulb of about seventy watts. You'll need to have a small bowl full of water in the box all the time. That keeps the humidity right. Then you'll have to get some fertilized eggs."

Dave _____ , "Where do I find the eggs?"

"Fertilized eggs are not easy to find," _____ Richard. "Sometimes you can get them at a health-food store, a feed store, or a live-poultry store. You should call those places on the phone to make sure they have them before you go."

"OK. If I get the eggs, what will I have to do next?" _____ Dave.

Richard _____ , "You'll have to put a mark on one end of the egg."

"Why?" _____ Dave.

"You have to turn the eggs every day. If you mark them, and keep a written record of which day it is, and what side the mark is on, you won't get mixed up," _____ Richard.

"Is that all I need to know?" _____ Dave.

"Did I tell you about the temperature?" _____ Richard.

"No," _____ Dave.

"Oh, I must've forgot," _____ Richard. "I guess we should look in a book to make sure we don't forget anything."

Dave _____ , "Do you have a book on hatching eggs? It seems like fun. I think I'd like to try it. Will you help me?"

"Sure!" _____ Richard. "I used to have a book on eggs around here. Let's see if I can find it."

Yetta Goodman

Provide each student with a copy of the selected-slotting procedure story that you have prepared. Ask them to read the whole story silently. Explain that they must think of at least one word or phrase that can fit each blank.

QUESTIONS FOR DISCUSSION

1. *Can you think of one word or phrase that will fit all those slots and make sense?*
   Although the word *said* would be the most likely answer, accept any answer that the students can justify, and permit class discussion so that students can determine which possibilities are most appropriate. Help students eventually conclude that *said* can always be a place holder for any word in the dialogue-carrier slot for verbs, although other words make the story more interesting.
2. *What other words or phrases can be placed in each blank to make the story more interesting?*
   A variety of dialogue carriers should be elicited from students. Proceed slot by slot. Depending on time and student interest, ask for additional possibilities that fit and make sense. Help students conclude that no matter which word is in the slot, *said* can always be used and the whole sentence will make sense.

ASK-ANSWER   The Incubator is an *ask-answer* selected-slotting story. Prior to its use, discuss with the students how questions and answers are handled in dialogue. Then, during another strategy-lesson sequence, go through a procedure similar to that used for "The Skating Rink." Encourage substitutions of dialogue carriers, but at the same time help students feel confident about using *said*, *asked*, or *answered* so that reading and understanding can continue uninterrupted. Encourage students to apply this strategy whenever they read.

YOUNGER READERS   For younger readers use questioning techniques similar to those outlined above, but use the following procedure to explore the function of dialogue carriers:

Lesson 1. Make up a short play. Involve the students by letting them dictate the dialogue as you set it out in play form. Have them first read the play as a radio script and then act it out.
Lesson 2. Discuss with the students how a play can be rewritten as a prose passage. Then do so with this play, following the procedure suggested in the Interacting phase.
Lesson 3. Using the prose story prepared in Lesson 2, prepare a selected-slotting story as described in the Applying phase of this strategy lesson. Replace all dialogue-carrier verbs with a five-space line, and follow the rest of the Applying phase procedure using this student-authored story.
Lesson 4. Rewrite the prose story using a variety of dialogue-carrier verbs suggested by the students. Have the students read the story. Whenever they are unsure of the dialogue-carrier verb, help them understand that *said* can be used as an appropriate substitution.

EXPANDING

CREATIVE WRITING   One small group of students may write plays and exchange them with another group who will then turn them into a story format using dialogue carriers. The students might read the stories and plays and discuss which seem best suited to each format and why. They might consider the criteria of action, number of characters, and purpose of writing.

Have the students write an appropriate ending to "The Skating Rink" in story form, making use of dialogue carriers.

Whenever students read (or you read to them), ask that they be aware of dialogue carriers that are new to them. These can be listed on the board for a period of time and students can watch the list grow. Encourage them to use these new dialogue carriers appropriately in their own creative writing.

SOCIAL STUDIES OR SCIENCE   Have students write an interview with the scientist, government official, sports figure, or entertainment personality who interests them most. Articles in current magazines or newspapers will provide information they can use for such interviews. Encourage the use of dialogue carriers. Students might also conduct real interviews with community leaders or speakers invited to class and then write them up.

Tape-record a discussion of a small group of students as they examine an interesting object or are involved in a discovery activity. Then with the students, transcribe the discussion using dialogue carriers and other dialogue conventions, identifying the speakers and describing their speaking manner and tone.

LISTENING   Immerse students in listening to stories that contain a great deal of dialogue. Read them aloud to the whole class regularly. Read them to very small groups or to individual students so that they can follow along and see the conventions of dialogue carriers as they occur in print; they will also see how an efficient reader interacts with such print. Paraprofessionals, or older or more proficient readers, may serve as readers as well. Read-along books with taped recordings would be especially helpful in this lesson.

DIALOGUE CARRIERS—PHRASE LEVEL: STRATEGY-LESSON PLAN

Specific Rationale

Authors make their dialogues more interesting, as well as more complex, to read by moving the dialogue carrier to different places within the sentence and by adding descriptive phrases or clauses to indicate the body movement, facial expressions, and condition of the speaker's voice. These phrases or clauses are used to give added dimension to the characters and to their relationships with others in the story:

Mr. Roberts said *as his face was turning red*, "That isn't true."

"Cut the kidding," Gert said *with her fist clenched in anger*.

"Don't you ever do that again," Chuck cried *loudly*, "never again!"

Although such phrases are not always easily predictable, proficient readers develop a variety of strategies to deal with them. Usually, readers who handle such phrases effectively read, or are read to, a great deal and are used to the idea that dialogue carriers may include descriptive information as well as serve the basic function of identifying the speaker. By focusing on meaning, and using the context to predict the mood or posture of the person who is talking in the story, these readers are able to predict variable dialogue-carrier phrases. If they predict inappropriately, they usually know enough about the story to rethink or reread and self-correct when necessary.

Readers need experiences with variations in language in order to be able to make use of appropriate strategies when unpredictable phrases or clauses occur. This strategy lesson will provide such experiences with dialogue-carrier phrases.

EVALUATION

The strategy lesson for Dialogue Carriers—Phrase Level will benefit

1. Students who need help with dialogue carriers in general (see Evaluation section of the preceding strategy lesson, "Dialogue Carriers—Word Level").
2. Students who can retell events about dialogues but who often miss the tone of the story; the characters' feelings about the happenings, and toward the other people in the story; and the personality of the characters.
3. Students who tell you they do not like to read stories in which people talk to each other a lot.

Reading-Strategy Instruction

INITIATING

Before introducing this lesson, read to the children from books heavy with dialogue and descriptive dialogue-carrier phrases.

Write the following sentences on the board *one at a time;*

1. *"Watch out for that car,"* _____ *said.* (Use the name of someone in the class.)
2. *"Get in your seat right now,"* _____ *said.* (Use the name of a teacher or administrator in the school.)
3. *"It was nice of you to stand up for me that way,"* _____ *said.* (Use the name of someone in the class.)
4. *"What flavor ice cream do you have?"* _____ *asked.* (Use the name of someone in the class.)

As each sentence is presented, use the procedures outlined in the Interacting phase which follows.

INTERACTING

QUESTIONS FOR DISCUSSION

1. *If you were reading this sentence in a story* [point to the sentence], *how could you show the way* _____ [use appropriate name] *was feeling while he* [or she] *talked?*
   Select a student to read the sentence with an appropriate intonation.
2. *How could you write what you said so that a reader could understand how you felt as you said the sentence?*
   The students should be encouraged to move the dialogue-carrier phrase to the beginning of the sentence or to interrupt the sentence in the middle, if it is appropriate to do so, and then change punctuation:

   "Watch out!" _____ said, "for that car!"

   The students may wish to use substitutions for *asked* and *said:*

   "Watch out for that car," _____ screamed.
3. *How could you let the reader know the tone of voice that* _____ [use appropriate name for the sentence] *was using when he* [or she] *ds?*
   "Watch out for that car," _____ said with a controlled tone.
4. *How could you let the reader know what the speaker was doing with his* [or her] *body while talking? What words might you add without changing any of the other words?*
   "Watch out for that car," _____ said as he pushed me out of the way.
5. *How might each sentence be written if the speakers were joking, crying, angry, sad?*
   "Watch out for that car," _____ said looking down the empty street.

If the students enjoy this lesson segment, continue with additional sentences about experiences with which they are familiar and which will provide a variety of reactions. If you believe the sentences above have little appeal for the students you are working with because of their age or interest, feel free to make any appropriate changes.

APPLYING

MATERIALS   "Angie's Glasses," by Debra Goodman

Angie's Glasses

Angela ran into the house screaming angrily, "Carol! Carol!"

She found her sister in the kitchen talking on the phone.

"Carol," she said, "Johnny stole my glasses and won't give them back, and every time I chase him he gives them to Eddie and Eddie rides off with them on his bike—"

"Listen, will you stop running to me to tattle all the time." Carol's voice was filled with exasperation. "Why don't you just stay away from the boys and take care of your own business?"

"But Carol—" Angela began in protest.

"I'm trying to talk on the phone Angie," Carol interrupted. "Will you please leave me alone?"

Angela stormed out of the house to find her brothers.

"Angie, Angie, can't catch me!" Johnny jeered.

Angela ran as fast as she could, but just as she was about to catch up with him he tossed the glasses to Matthew.

"Run, Matthew," Johnny and Eddie shouted at their younger brother.

Angela laughed because she knew she could catch Matthew.

"Boy, just wait till I catch you," she threatened.

But Eddie on his bicycle was faster than Angela, and he took the glasses from Matthew just before Angela caught up with him. Twelve-year-old Patty looked out the window just in time to see Angela angrily hitting her little brother.

"Angie," she demanded, "you leave Matt alone."

Completely discouraged, Angela sat down on the front porch steps and let the tears fall down her cheeks.

"Angie, Angie, can't catch me," her brothers teased her, holding the glasses nearby until she grabbed at them, then running out of her reach.

Then Bethy came up the steps and sat down at Angela's side.

"What's wrong with you?" she looked questioningly at her sister.

"Everybody hates me" was Angela's tearful reply. "Patty and Carol keep yelling at me and Matthew gets to do anything he wants, 'cause he's youngest, and Johnny and Eddie stole my glasses—"

"Angie, Angie, can't catch me," Eddie screamed from across the street.

"Well," Bethy announced. "We don't care about those silly boys. "We're going to sit here and play cards and enjoy ourselves."

Angela ran to get the cards, and she and Bethy started a game of war. Attracted by all the talking and laughing, soon their brothers came and sat nearby.

"Can I play?" Matthew asked in a pleading tone.

"Well," Bethy thoughtfully replied, "I suppose so, we're not selfish, right, Angie?"

"Right," Angela agreed.

"Can I play?"

"Can I play?" almost at the same time Johnny and Eddie begged.

Soon the five brothers and sisters were involved in an exciting game of war.

"Oh, I almost forgot," Johnny remarked offhandedly. "Here's your glasses, Angie."

"I don't need them right now," Angela replied. "Will you hold on to them for me, Johnny?"

DEBRA GOODMAN

117

Have students read "Angie's Glasses."

Encourage them to discuss the cues in the dialogue-carrier clauses, as well as cues in the story as a whole, that tell them about the emotional state, the stance, and the voice quality of the various speakers. Use questions similar to those in the Interacting phase, but rephrase them for reading rather than for writing purposes. The first two questions might be rephrased as follows:

1. *How does the author let you know how the character feels?*
2. *How does the author let you know the character's tone of voice?*

EXPANDING

CREATIVE WRITING   Write a short story in which the dialogue is carried *only* by a noun or pronoun plus *said*, *asked*, or *answered* (as in *mother said*, *he asked*); or select from various materials (basal readers are good sources) stories written in this style. Have students rewrite this material enhancing the story by adding to the dialogue-carrier phrases.

Use "The Skating Rink" or "The Incubator" (if the students liked those stories), presented in the strategy lesson "Dialogue Carrier—Word Level," adding a variety of dialogue-carrier phrases and clauses. Or you may want to use stories the students themselves wrote for that strategy lesson, again adding dialogue-carrier phrases.

Provide the students with several sentences that, if spoken by different characters in different situations, would take on different meanings. For each sentence, give students information about various speakers and situations. Have them write dialogues for each situation, using the sentence and the information about the situation that is provided:

"I'm going to kill you."

1. A big sister talking to a younger brother
   who just broke her pearls
2. A robber without a gun
3. A soldier to a civilian enemy

Have students, one at a time, think of a sentence and say it orally. Direct the others to write the sentence with a dialogue-carrier phrase that describes the way it was said. This activity can be done in small groups.

HARD-TO-PREDICT GRAMMATICAL STRUCTURES

General Rationale

Readers can handle grammatical structures that are familiar to them with greater ease and confidence than they can handle those structures that are less familiar. Familiar structures are predictable. When most of the language structures are familiar to the reader, few syntactic unknowns disrupt the reader's ability to predict the language of the author. Even beginning readers can handle such sentences as *John hit Mary* or *The girl gave an apple to her teacher* with greater facility than they can a sentence such as *See Rover jump*. The subject-verb-object structure of the first two examples is more common in the language of a five- or six-year-old than is the imperative form of the last sentence. This is especially true when the sentence includes a verb like *see* which is rarely used to convey the meaning it is supposed to have in the example. The meaning is more appropriate with terms like *watch* or look at. The ability to predict familiar structures explains why so many beginning readers transform a sentence like *Father! See Maria* into *Father sees Maria* when they encounter it in their reading.

Unpredictable structures can surprise even the most proficient reader for reasons that we outline below.

1. *Style*. Authors have distinctive styles because of their own language background as well as the conscious choice of grammatical structures that they use to enhance their

writing. It is this style that makes each author's writing unique. Depending on the mood that they want to construct for their audience, the personality they want to develop for their characters, or the image they want to project for the story's setting, authors may choose a variety of grammatical structures to carry their message. They may purposely choose short, clipped sentences or long, rolling run-ons in the same way an oil painter chooses stroke, color, and texture, or a composer uses tempo, key, or volume, to convey a mood or feeling. These structures may often be unpredictable especially for the reader who is not familiar with a particular author's other works.

2. *Differences between written and oral language.* Structures that appear in written language may not be common in oral language because the purposes of written language are often different from those of oral language.

    a. The writer has to use elaborate means to provide for the reading audience images about people, places, and events, since the writer and the reader do not share a common time and place:

        When the bushes and trees were seeking to outdo each other in the color and extravagance of their Easter outfits . . .[2]

        The barn was very large. It was very old. It smelled of hay and it smelled of manure. It smelled of the perspiration of the tired horses and the wonderful sweet breath of patient cows.[3]

    b. An author may choose to write very formal language that many readers seldom use either in listening or in speaking:

        The motionless, who struggle with no such unnecessary inherited encumbrances, find it labor enough to subdue and cultivate a few cubic feet of flesh.[4]

    c. Archaic language or language variation due to regional, ethnic, racial, or age differences can confront the reader who may never have heard either the old form of the language or the particular dialect represented.

    d. Written language can present new and abstract ideas. Philosophical, theological, or legal points of view can often be expressed in language that is very different from the reader's oral language. The reader often confronts new concepts but has no opportunity to ask questions or have a face-to-face discussion in order to clarify those concepts or make them simpler to understand.

3. *Limited reading experiences.* Although limited reading experiences may be caused by or related to the problems we have just listed, this factor deserves separate focus because it is so prevalent. Students limited to reading one or two types of materials throughout their reading instruction, such as the same basal reader or programmed material, to the exclusion of a wide variety of reading materials, are doomed to having difficulty in predicting certain grammatical structures. The constant use of reading materials that are unduly controlled for vocabulary, patterns of spelling-sound relationships, or types of sentence structures can interfere with reading development. Reading such materials exclusively reinforces the tendency to predict only the structures with which the reader has had experience. When readers encounter structures that do not fit the patterns to which they have become accustomed, they are often confused and find it difficult to make an easy transition from highly controlled materials to more natural language. The ability to predict varied grammatical structures as well as the ability to handle complex and unpredictable structures will be enhanced by reading a wide variety of material that is close to natural language that students use, is close to written language children have heard, includes a variety of sentence structures, is interesting, and is within the concept development of the readers.

---

[2]Marie Killilea, *Karen* (New York: Dell Publishing Co., Inc., 1952), p. 70.

[3]E. B. White, *Charlotte's Web* (New York: Dell Publishing Co., Inc., 1952), p. 19.

[4]Henry David Thoreau, *Walden* (New York: Holt, Rinehart and Winston, Inc., 1948), p. 3.

NOTE Although it is important for writers and publishers—especially those producing materials for developing readers—to be concerned with what makes their work hard to read, we would not want rigid standards imposed on authors—standards that would thwart creativity, produce strange and unnatural language, and cause reading to be boring and uninteresting. Instead of controlling language, we help readers to anticipate and appreciate the unique and the original in written language; we must teach them not to lose confidence about reading when they encounter complex grammatical structures. We must help students realize that all good readers produce predictions that do not work out, and that it is acceptable to reread or rethink when a prediction has been disconfirmed.

Given the infinite variety of written materials and individual structures or sentences that might be problematic for readers, it is impossible to suggest lessons for all the structures of sentences that might be problematic for readers. However, strategy lessons for a few constructions that cause some students difficulty have been formulated. These lessons should serve as models for developing strategy lessons for other complex grammatical structures with which your students seem to have difficulty. The lessons we present deal with two different types of sentence complexities:

1. Sentences with hard-to-predict phrases and clauses
2. Sentences with a variety of hard-to-predict grammatical structures

Strategy lessons for other hard-to-predict grammatical structures are provided in "Pronouns," "Relational Words and Phrases," and "Negatives" in chapter 4; "Indicators of Direct Speech" in this chapter; and "Does This Make Sense?" in chapter 7.

HARD-TO-PREDICT PHRASES AND CLAUSES: STRATEGY-LESSON PLAN

Specific Rationale

Stories read by students of all ages often include phrases and clauses that are hard to predict because the main noun or verb phrase is complicated through the use of additional noun phrases or prepositional phrases. Consider these examples:

From a fourth-grade text
All the men and women and children of the tribe went to the cranberry swamp near the Winnebago Islands. They would spend their days picking the ripe cranberries.[5]

From a third-grade text
One picture showed a large black crow with a long piece of string in his bill. He was standing on a rock in the rose garden.[6]

From a picture-storybook
First son was called See Trouble. He had the gift of seeing trouble a long way off. Second son was Road Builder.[7]

Students who tend to read word by word often lose the interrelationship of various phrases within a sentence and, when reading a passage like that in the first example, are usually more concerned with sounding out words like *tribe*, *cranberry*, or *Winnebago* rather than with understanding that a group of people who share a relationship have gone someplace.

Some students do not make an easy adjustment from the subject-verb-object sentences of much of the instructional material for beginning reading, to the more complex structures found in materials of greater literary quality. They tend to predict the end at a point too early in the

[5]Ruth M. Tabrah, "Billy Whitemoon," in *Along Friendly Roads*, ed. Emmett A. Betts and Carolyn M. Welch, Betts Basic Readers, 3rd ed. (New York: American Book Company, 1963), pp. 153–157.

[6]Ruth G. Plowhead, "Kitten Jones," in *Beyond Treasure Valley*, ed. Emmett A. Betts and Carolyn M. Welch, Betts Basic Readers, 3rd ed. (New York: American Book Company, 1963), pp. 60–66.

[7]Gerald McDermott, *Anansi the Spider* (New York: Holt, Rinehart and Winston, 1972).

sentence and are often left with a dangling phrase or clause, which may not be attached to a complete sentence. The reader who has not had much experience in developing proficient strategies to handle a series of phrases or clauses can easily confuse meaning by rearranging or transforming phrases, as the following readings of the examples demonstrate:

> All the men and women and children of the tribe went. To the cranberry swamp near Winnebago Islands they would spend days picking the ripe cranberries.

> One picture showed a large black crow with a long piece of string. In his bill he was standing on a rock in the rose garden.

> First son was called. See Trouble had the gift of seeing. Trouble. A long way off second son was road. Builder . . .

Proficient readers can also transform or rearrange sentences. However, they either produce sentences that are acceptable or reread and correct their prediction if they are not acceptable:

> All the men and women and children of the tribe went to the cranberry swamp. Near the Winnebago Islands they would spend days picking the ripe cranberries.

A second type of hard-to-predict sentence includes a series of noun phrases that are all objects of the verb:

> *From a fifth-grade text*
> In his tool box he found another battery, a ruler, a coil of copper wire, a small bulb and tape.[8]

> *From a sixth-grade text*
> There were glaring spotlights and floodlights, and cables rigged up everywhere.[9]

> *From an eighth-grade text*
> They snarled down on Peggy with teeth bared, ears flat, the hair on their backs raised and their feet spread for a sudden spring.[10]

Sentences of this type can cause problems even for proficient readers. In oral language we use a particular type of intonation as a cue to the listener that a list of items is coming. In writing, such as we find in social-studies or science materials, colons, numbers, or an actual listing of items in a column format serve this function. In nonfiction, however, there are few cues provided early enough to indicate that the author is going to list a group of items. The reader, therefore, often predicts other possible structures. The more proficient readers, as they continue to read, tend to recognize a listing by the series of noun phrases, including the commas, and the meaning of what they are reading. They then reread or rethink if their initial prediction proves to be an inappropriate phrase structure. The less proficient reader needs to be helped to approach this type of structure in the same way.

A third type of hard-to-predict structure gives information that cannot be fully understood until the reader has read further into the story. This structure often consists of a dependent clause preceding an independent clause:

> But when the heavy snow was gone from Winnebago lands, Billy was very happy.[11]

> After the cut in his allowance, Freddie's experiments narrowed to those outlined in his book.[12]

---

[8]Lillian Moore, "Freedie Miller, Scientist," in *Adventures Here and There*, ed. Emmett A. Betts and Carolyn M. Welch, 3d ed., Betts Basic Readers (New York: American Book Company, 1965), pp. 61–68.

[9]William D. Hayes, "My Brother Is a Genius," in *Adventures Then and Now*, ed. Emmett A. Betts and Carolyn M. Welch, 3d ed. Betts Basic Readers (New York: American Book Company, 1963), pp. 246–56.

[10]James C. Stovall, "Sheep Dog," in *Widening Views*, ed. William D. Sheldon and Robert A. McCracken, Sheldon Basic Reading Series, 8th ed. (Boston: Allyn and Bacon, Inc., 1965), pp. 80–99.

[11]Tabrah, "Billy Whitemoon."

[12]Moore, "Freddie Miller, Scientist."

Off he went, making a road.[13]

Sentences or groups of sentences of this third type require readers to predict what might occur and at the same time hold the processed information in memory for a short period of time until they can process the needed information that follows. Only as they begin to understand how all the information fits together can they integrate the whole idea into the developing story. Such sentences become difficult to process if readers are not concerned with predicting possible structures, holding on to ideas as they read, and if they do not continuously integrate what they are reading into what they understand about the written material.

This strategy lesson is intended to help students become aware that meaning is conveyed through the interrelationship of phrases and clauses. It emphasizes the need to concentrate on the construction of meaning through reading. When readers are concerned with building or integrating events and plots, they can often anticipate the kinds of information presented, even though they cannot quite understand their relationship to the story. As they gain additional information, they can use these early elements to process the whole idea.

The lesson provides experiences with different types of hard-to-predict grammatical structures. Through reading a wide variety of unpredictable sentences, students will become better able to anticipate potentially confusing constructions. It is therefore unnecessary to present lesson plans for every possible type of unpredictable structure. If a student consistently miscues on the same kind of structures there might be some justification in writing a specific lesson focussing on the unpredictable structure.

NOTE   Any additional pupil material that you write for this strategy lesson should include only a few unpredictable phrases and clauses. If there are too many complex structures in one piece of reading material, or if the structures are in too close proximity in the material, the students may easily get bogged down and become discouraged.

EVALUATION

The strategy lesson for Hard-to-Predict Phrases and Clauses will benefit

1. Students who avoid reading *long* stories or books about things they are interested in, or find it difficult to finish such books. These students may say that they prefer "little" books or tend to count pages before they start reading to make sure they do not have an overwhelming amount to read.
2. Students who do a great deal of regressing or rereading during oral reading, yet their attempts at correction do not produce acceptable sentences. Such students tend to reread a word or two but not whole phrases or clauses.
3. Students who rearrange sentence structure by omitting appropriate intonation or inserting inappropriate intonation, which produces unacceptable sentences, yet do not make any attempt at self-correction.
4. Students who seem to become confused about the relationship of significant and insignificant information in the material they read; or students who may treat information as discrete items, making no attempt to discern relationships.
5. Students who almost never make miscues involving any rearranging or transforming of phrases or clauses, but usually make simple word-substitution miscues as they read. Miscue analysis of such students' reading should indicate that most word substitutions are the same part of speech as the text word, yet the syntactic and semantic acceptability score should be less than 60 percent.

Reading-Strategy Instruction

INITIATING

MATERIALS   Simple Sentences for Rewriting (A), (B), and (C)

---

[13]McDermott, "Anansi the Spider."

Simple Sentences for Rewriting (A)

Sharon had been burned.
Now Sharon was careful.
She would not let her little sister use the stove.

The weather was getting warm.
John invited his friends to his house.
John had ice cream of all flavors.
John had topping of all kinds.
Everyone made his or her own ice-cream sundae.

The girl was singing.
She sang softly.
She had a high voice.
She sang a sad song.

The man was walking to the bus stop.
The man took long steps.
The man carried a briefcase.

Simple Sentences for Rewriting (B)

Jonathan looked in the window.
He saw his mother.
She sat at her desk.
She was typing.
Jonathan saw the bookshelves.
He saw all the books.
The books belong to his mother.
He saw the rug.
The rug was orange.
He saw the couch.
The couch was brown.
The couch was old.
There were books on the couch.
The books belonged to his brother.
Jonathan smiled.
He had been away all summer.
He was home.

There were three boys in the family.
There were three girls in the family.
There was a mother and father in the family.
There was a grandfather in the family.
They lived in a big house.
The house was white.
The house had green trim.
The house was on a shady street.

Simple Sentences for Rewriting (C)

The clown sat on a chair.
The clown had big shoes.
The shoes were black.
The shoes were floppy.
The clown had green hair.
The hair was curly.
The clown was named Happy.
The clown was frowning.
The clown had a large mouth.
The clown had a big nose.
The nose was round.
There was a fly on the nose.
The clown's eyes were crossed.

A boy was sitting on the grass.
It was spring.
The grass was green.
There were flowers nearby.
Some flowers were tulips.
The tulips were red.
The boy picked a tulip.
A bee was inside the tulip.
The bee flew at the boy.
The boy was scared.
The boy screamed.

Distribute copies of Simple Sentences for Rewriting (A) or make a transparency of the sentences to use on the overhead projector. Together with the students, rewrite each of the simple sentences into two fuller sentences. Explain that the goal is to try to combine as many of the ideas from the simple sentences into as few acceptable sentences as possible. The sentences provided explore all the various kinds of complex sentences discussed in the Specific Rationale. (For those who find this lesson helpful, you might want to explore sentence combining references. See Bibliography.)

INTERACTING

Impose only one restriction on your students: They are to write fewer sentences than the number originally supplied. It is not necessary that they use every sentence from the original text.

During the discussion and rewriting of the simple sentences in (A), accept any rearrangement of words, and interrelationship of phrases. Allow the students to work individually or in small groups to produce a variety of sentences for the examples in (B) and (C). Discuss the variations they produce.

QUESTIONS FOR DISCUSSION

1. *Do the sentences sound acceptable to you?*
2. *Is it possible to take the same ideas and combine them in a variety of ways?*
   Help students realize that structuring sentences in different ways is what authors do. Authors choose a particular structure although they always have other options. Readers need to understand what an author means even if the sentence he or she has written is somewhat different from what they might expect or from what they might write themselves.
3. *Do the various arrangements of the sentences cause some shifts in meaning?*
   Use the students' examples to explore how variations in sentence organization affect the meaning relationships that are built. Syntactic shifts are related to shifts in meaning focus and emphasis. For example, the sentence *The man with the briefcase took long steps as he walked to the bus stop* allows for the suggestion that the man can be distinguished from others on the street by the briefcase that he carries. But the variation *The man walked to the bus stop taking long steps and carrying his briefcase* focuses our attention on the man and his destination.

APPLYING

The most important aspect of learning to handle a variety of grammatical structures and applying this knowledge to a variety of reading experiences is simply that it enables students to read a wide variety of materials. Permit, encourage, and plan for periods of sustained silent reading. Encourage the students to read for a minimum amount of time daily. With young children, or those who have had little success in reading, you might start with as little as ten minutes each day. The students should be permitted to select their own reading material and to read silently and independently. Increase the minimum amount of time regularly until young children are reading for thirty minutes daily, and middle-grade and older readers are reading silently and independently for at least forty-five minutes daily.

Students of all ages, but especially young readers, should be read to as frequently as possible. The importance of this activity lies not only in the appreciation and enjoyment of literature that it can nurture in the listeners, but also in the exposure to a wide range of linguistic structures and styles uncommon to oral language that it offers students. Teachers can read to small or large groups of students, and students of all ages can read to each other. A variation of this activity is tape-recording a student's or teacher's oral reading of a book for others to listen to and read along with at another time.

You and your students may want to devise a *record-keeping system*. Discuss with them what aspects of their reading they would like to record. Decide together the purposes and criteria for recording. The purposes might include: (1) to be able to see our progress, (2) to remember books or articles we liked best so we can share them with others, (3) to remember those we liked least so we won't be bothered with them again, (4) to recall authors that we like so that we might read more of what they wrote, (5) to remember ideas, knowledge, and language that were interesting that we might want to share with others or preserve for other purposes.

Record-keeping should be kept simple and should be based on the students' purposes. The aspects that are to be recorded should be changed as students have experiences with recording and as they expand their interests. One first-grade class decided to keep their individual records on cards shaped like book marks. Each student wrote his or her name on the card, as well as the name of the book and its author; then drew in a happy or sad face depending on the individual response to the book:

Child's Name ___Betty M.___

Book Name ___Anansi the Spider___

Author ___McDermott___

A group of fourth graders kept a record of every book or article that they completed. These students used file cards, entering on each one the name of a book or article read and a reason why they thought their friends would also want to read that selection. The books or magazines, which were eventually shared with the whole class, were placed in a class file so that individuals might follow up on selections that interested them:

Name of Book or Article

Harriet the Spy

– –

Why would your friends want to read it?

If they like stories about girls that get into trouble.

A group of sixth graders kept their individual records in a file folder; these students used a chart format:

Student's Name Jaime G.

Title	Author	Type of Material	Fiction or Nonfiction
Journey Outside	Mary Q. Steele	paperback	fiction
Today's Weather	none	newspaper	don't know yet
Peanuts	Charles Schultz	paperback comics	fiction

In some cases students have recorded aspects of reading material related to particular strategies on which they were working. Categories such as "sentences that caused me trouble and what they mean" or "words I met for the first time and learned to understand" were among those created. Other possible categories include "hard-to-predict sentences" or "new words and phrases" but no matter how they are labeled, the categories should focus on the readers' concern for constructing meaning.

Students often like to share reading experiences with others (1) when they are involved in deciding how sharing should be done, (2) when there is a good deal of variety in sharing, (3) when they are excited about their reading, and (4) when opportunities to share do *not* become required, uninteresting chores.

Do not use the same kind of *reporting system* over and over again. Provide a variety of ways for students to share their reading with others. For example, sharing may be done through drama, oral reporting, or art, as well as through writing. Newspaper articles may be presented as TV or radio news broadcasts. Students reading the same books or stories might discuss their shared reading among themselves or plan a panel presentation. Decide with the students their purposes for sharing and the criteria for what and how to share. It is important that students not only choose the kinds of reading they want to share but have control over their own presentations.

EXPANDING

Since the focus for strategy lessons on Hard-to-Predict Grammatical Structures can best be facilitated and expanded through reading a great deal of a wide variety of materials there are no special activities for the Expanding phase. Instead the teacher is urged to refer to the Bibliography, which lists references of book lists as well as titles for students which contain various types of complex grammatical structures.

To ensure that students have a wide variety of reading experiences, it is essential to have a wide variety of easily accessible reading materials. (See the Grid of Reading Materials in chapter 3, p. 38.) If students have access to the school library throughout the day, a duplicate library in the classroom may not be necessary. However, if a student can only go to the school library at scheduled times, the classroom library should include at least three titles for each student.

IDENTIFYING HARD-TO-PREDICT STRUCTURES: STRATEGY-LESSON PLAN

Specific Rationale

Even in the primary grades, it is obvious that students have varied backgrounds in terms of the kinds of language structures they have come across in their reading. What may be predictable for one reader who loves to read science fiction and the encyclopedia, or another reader who can handle a *TV Guide* with ease and is read to every night by mother or father, may be unpredictable for a third reader who is unaware that he or she can read anything but instructional reading materials. It is therefore helpful to have students examine their personal hard-to-predict grammatical structures by using the technique of Reader-Selected Miscues described in chapter 2.[14] This procedure gives the teacher and students an opportunity to pinpoint structures that individual students or small groups of students find hard to predict. It is an informal evaluation that can be applied to any silent reading experience.

EVALUATION

The strategy lesson for Identifying Hard-to-Predict Structures can be used with any group of students.

Reading-Strategy Instruction

INITIATING

MATERIALS A book or any other material that individual students have never read before or are currently reading
Approximately ten bookmarks or strips of paper

READER-SELECTED MISCUE PROCEDURE

1. The students read silently without interruption, for a period of ten minutes (for the more proficient readers you may increase this time to fifteen minutes).
2. Students read a text that they have not read before. Or they can work with materials that they are currently reading, in which case they should begin their reading at the point where they last left off.
3. At any point that students are aware they are having a problem with their reading, they insert a bookmark and then continue reading.
4. At the end of the specified reading period the students go back to each marked place in their reading material. On a page headed *Reading Miscues* they write out the complete

---

[14]See pages 26–27. See also Dorothy J. Harper Watson, "A Psycholinguistic Description of the Oral Reading Miscues Generated by Selected Readers Prior to and Following Exposure to a Saturated Book Program" (Ph.D. dissertation, Wayne State University, 1973).

structure in which the problem occurred, underlining the segment they believe caused the problem, and next to the structure they note the number of the page on which it appears, as well as the title of the book. (You or the students may eventually need to refer to the book if more of the context is needed to understand why the sentences were hard to predict.)

5. Collect all the structures with the underlined miscues.
6. Categorize the miscues according to similarity of problems. As your students develop an understanding of this process, you may involve them in the categorizing.
7. Select one category of structures including the underlined miscues, and duplicate the examples, indicating the name of student, the title of the reading material, and page number.
8. These examples will be used for the Interacting phase of the lesson, and students should bring a copy of the reading material to the group.

INTERACTING

Allow the group members to suggest individually why they believe the structure caused difficulty. Start the discussion of each sentence with the student who selected that sentence as a problem, and then encourage interaction and elicit additional ideas from the rest of the group.

QUESTIONS FOR DISCUSSION

1. *Why do you think this* [indicate the sentence to be discussed] *was a problem?*
2. *What did you do or what strategies did you use to try to work yourself out of the difficulty?*
3. *If you were not able to work it out, do you think you know what the sentence is supposed to mean?*
4. *How did* [or could] *you figure out the meaning? What strategies did you use* [or could you use] *to figure it out?*

    See if the student is able to come up with a partial meaning for the material and relate it to previous statements in the context of the material. Encourage students to refer back to the reading material whenever appropriate.
5. *Can you restate or rewrite the sentence in your own words so that it makes more sense to you?*

    Continue these questioning techniques with six or seven different examples as long as students continue to be interested. In closing, try to get the students to be consciously aware that getting meaning was their major consideration. If they are able to restate or rethink the ideas in the sentence in their own language, then they are in turn able to gain meaning even if they had difficulty dealing with the sentence.

APPLYING

The best way for students to apply the ideas they have learned through this lesson is to read a variety of materials. Have the students read for a period of one or two weeks and then try the Reader-Selected Miscue procedure once again. As students begin to handle more complex reading materials, more complex structures will show up in their selection of miscues.

EXPANDING

The greater opportunities students have for broader reading and writing experiences, the more interaction and practice they will have with hard-to-predict grammatical structures. For this reason no additional suggestions are offered in the Expanding phase.

Chapter 6

Predicting Graphophonic Cues

UNCOMMON SPELLING PATTERNS

General Rationale

The reading strategies of selecting and predicting common graphic cues are easily learned by young readers. Common cues are the ones readers have become accustomed to through their reading experiences: the spacing between words, the various ways the same letter appears in print (A, *a*,), the various punctuation marks.

As mentioned in an earlier discussion of the graphophonic system (see chapter 1), research has suggested that young readers naturally build a logical relationship between the graphic patterns they encounter in print, and the sound system of their language. This relationship is reflected in their own invented spellings. Readers are aware of which spelling patterns are more likely than others to appear in written language; specifically they are able to predict the most common consonant and vowel patterns in English.

Since students are usually able to handle these kinds of predictions, the strategy lessons in this section will focus on two kinds of uncommon spelling patterns—less predictable because they occur less frequently in written materials for young readers:

1. *Eye dialect.* The use of nonstandard English spelling to indicate a character is speaking English in a different or unusual manner or in a specific dialect of English.
2. *Foreign language words or phrases.* The use of non-English words, phrases, or sentences for any of a variety of reasons.

It is important that students become aware that the same strategies they are successfully using to predict common graphic cues can be applied to the predicting of uncommon spelling patterns. To predict what they believe an author is saying, proficient readers select minimal graphic cues based on their past experience with written language. Readers tend to pay most attention to initial consonants, although the endings of words and certain other distinctive features are also taken into consideration. Effective readers do not utilize all the information in the graphic field because to do so would hinder efficiency. Rather, they have the ability to select and predict using only the information they need to make the meaningful prediction. As an example of this strategy, consider the following to see how easily you can construct meaningful sentences:

John w _____ ked as _____ truck dr _____ .
He was a str _____ g m _____ .

The more background about language and/or the subject matter that one brings to a piece of written material, the fewer the cues one needs to select. Also, fewer graphic cues are needed as context is built through reading a story or article; that is, as a reader begins to understand the motivation and writing style of the author, he or she will depend less on graphic cues. Of course, the structure of language, and the meaning, are supportive systems that readers use to help them in their predictions.

When readers encounter uncommon spelling patterns—as occur in words, phrases, or names from foreign languages or dialects of English—they will often predict common spelling patterns or known words. These readers are likely to predict *seven* for *Sven*, a name based in a foreign language, the first time that word appears in a story because there are very few words in English that start with an *sv* pattern. Often a foreign-language word or phrase, such as *pièce de résistance*, will be treated as English, and therefore misunderstood, by readers who have little or no experience reading uncommon spelling patterns. When an author tries to represent a speaker's dialect with an unusual spelling, such as *fer* for *for*, or *wuz* for *was*, readers may become confused and not make appropriate predictions.

Proficient readers who have experience in reading language that includes uncommon spelling patterns will usually recognize such words, phrases, or sentences and will be able to predict them as they read. In order to comprehend these uncommon spelling patterns, proficient readers usually do the following:

1. They recognize the language cues that help predict that foreign language or eye dialect may appear in written material.
2. They predict the words or phrases that are different from common spelling patterns.
3. They decide whether these words or phrases are significant.
4. If they decide the words or phrases are significant to the story, and if appropriate cues are available, they then try to understand them.

EYE DIALECT: STRATEGY-LESSON PLAN

Specific Rationale

When authors want to indicate differences in the socioeconomic class, regional dialects, or national origin of the characters in their stories, they often use speech as a means of representing those differences. They usually change the spelling of particular words so that the reader can quickly recognize that some of the characters speak differently from the author or other characters in the story. Since spelling remains the same in English regardless of dialect, authors may employ unconventional spellings to represent a particular way a person speaks. We call this use of nonstandard spelling *eye dialect*. With rare exceptions, eye dialect is confined to dialogue.[1] Examples of eye dialect include

1. The representation of informal or nonstandard speech as in
   He was gonna go home.
   They are runnin' fas'.
2. The representation of people who speak English as a second language, as in
   Zat iz a sveet leedle shild.

The strategies used by proficient readers to read eye dialect involve predicting the uncommon spelling pattern, relating it to its oral equivalent, and translating the conversation to themselves. Some readers, however, are confused by these spelling patterns. They do not predict that such language can appear in written material so they try to sound out the eye dialect to produce legitimate language. Sometimes readers are surprised when they discover that words and phrases that their teachers correct in their own writing are being used in legitimate written material.

---

[1] See Special Note on page 131.

Through these strategy lessons, readers should

1. Broaden their reading experience to include eye dialect
2. Predict the kinds of materials in which eye dialect is likely to occur
3. Predict eye dialect through its uncommon spelling patterns as well as the use of apostrophes, quotation marks, italics, or other printer's conventions
4. Confirm the spelling patterns by relating them to oral-language equivalents
5. Focus on comprehending the passage in which the eye dialect occurs

SPECIAL NOTE   Authors sometimes use eye dialect in ways that tend to indicate low educational status of speakers. This use of eye dialect has helped perpetuate the myth that certain speakers are careless and sloppy. Students will find such examples of eye dialect in their reading. They need to be helped to understand that some authors do use eye dialect in this manner, which shows that even writers can have misconceptions about language.

Students, with the help of informed teachers, must understand that everyone says what sounds like *gonna* and *hafta* in some oral-language contexts and that many people say *kin* for *can* and *git* for *get*. People who talk this way are as likely to be educated as uneducated. How people pronounce words and phrases depends as much on where they grew up and learned to talk as on their educational background. Most people say *swimming* and *dancing* as if they were spelled *swimmin'* and *dancin'*, especially if those words appear in the middle of a sentence. Using your normal speech pattern, try saying the phrases *west side of town*, *ham and eggs*, and *I'm going to go to the store* in a sentence. What happens to the sounds represented by *sts* in the word *westside*, by the letter *d* in *and*, and by the words *going to*? In most cases you will find that these words are pronounced as if they were spelled *wesside*, *an'* or *'n*, and *gonna*. Students should be helped to develop a true picture of how people talk and the relationship between oral and written language so they can be critical of uses of eye dialect that tend to stereotype a group. Through discussion with the students and examples from literature, you should help them become sensitive to the positive use of dialect—which is to express the sensitivity and humanity of people, as opposed to building negative stereotypes.

EVALUATION

The strategy lesson for Eye Dialect will benefit

1. Students who indicate they do not like to read certain books, comics, or magazines because they have too many "funny" words.
2. Students who stop at a word or phrase expressed in eye dialect and sound it out differently each time, often producing nonwords rather than approaching some oral-language equivalent.
3. Students who always ask you or other students to read or interpret eye dialect for them.
4. Students who make fun of the way other people talk or seem insensitive to, or intolerant of, language differences.

Reading-Strategy Instruction

INITIATING

MATERIALS   "*She'll Be Comin' Roun' the Mountain*," or any folk song familiar to the children that has eye dialect reflected in print

Any cartoon that uses eye dialect: *Snuffy Smith, The Ryatts, John Thorp, Gordo, Pogo*

Distribute copies of the song, or make a transparency to be used on an overhead projector. Have the students sing along with you, or, if you prefer, ask one of them to lead the group in singing the song. If you are working with the transparency, sweep along the line of print with a pointer (your finger or pencil point will do) as the students sing the song.

The words in parentheses on the song sheet are usually spoken at the end of the first, second, and last lines of each verse and are accompanied with motions (described below). At the end of each verse only you can repeat all of the spoken words with accompanying motions which occur up to that point of the song and get an accumulating effect by the end of the song.

Chorus

1. She'll be com - in' roun' the moun - tain when she comes. (Toot, toot)

She'll be com - in' roun' the moun -tain when she comes. (Toot, toot)

She'll be com - in' roun' the moun - tain, She'll be com - in' roun' the moun - tain,

She'll be com - in' roun' the moun - tain when she comes. (Toot, toot)

2. She'll be drivin' six white horses when she comes.
   (Whoa, Bill; Toot, toot)

3. An' we'll all go out and meet her when she comes.
   (Hi, Babe; Whoa, Bill; Toot, Toot)

4. An' we'll kill the ol' red rooster when she comes.
   (Ek, Ek; Hi, Babe; Whoa, Bill; Toot, toot)

5. We'll all have chik'n an' dumplin's when she comes.
   (Yum, yum; Ek, ek; Hi, Babe; Whoa, Bill; Toot, toot)

6. She'll havta sleep with gramma when she comes.
   (Snore, snore; Yum, yum; Ek, ek; Hi, Babe; Whoa, Bill; Toot, toot)

Source: *Harcourt Sandburg Songbag* (Adapted and arranged by Yetta Goodman and Kelly Smith.)

1 toot, toot!	Move as though you were pulling a train whistle.
2 whoa, Bill!	Move as though you were pulling back the reins as you ride.
3 Hi, Babe!	Wave.
4 ek, ek!	Draw a hand across your neck to indicate the chicken is being killed.
5 yum, yum!	Rub the stomach.
6 snore, snore!	Close eyes and lay head on hand.

After singing, ask the students to read the song to themselves quickly. Tell them that you will be distributing a cartoon (or placing it on the projector) when they finish reading the song, and you will want to know in what ways the writing in the song and that in the cartoon are the same.

Distribute the cartoon or place it on the projector. Ask the students to read it silently.

INTERACTING

QUESTIONS FOR DISCUSSION

1. *What is happening in the cartoon? In your own words, what is each of the characters in the cartoon saying?*

   Permit discussion and accept any answer that the students are able to justify. Respond to all answers—whether you think they are right or wrong—with: *What makes you think so? How has the author shown you that?*

2. *What is the author trying to tell you about the characters in the cartoon or the people in the song?*

   After the students discuss general characteristics, help them focus on the fact that the language is written in an unusual manner. This is another means the author can use to provide the reader with cues about the characters.

3. *In what ways are the print of the song and that of the cartoon similar?*

   Accept all answers that can be justified. Respond positively to all answers dealing with meaning, but also help the students focus on the use of apostrophes, italics, and unusual spellings—that is, the relationship between written language and oral language. (You may want to tell your students that one term used to indicate unusual spelling that represents oral language is *eye dialect*.)

4. *In what kinds of material do you think you will find language printed in this way? In what kinds of material do you think you would be unlikely to find language printed in this way?*

   Write on the board all the examples suggested by the students. Leave examples on the board for a few weeks, or put them on a chart and leave the chart up for a while. The students can add to or change this list as they continue to learn more about eye dialect. If there are disagreements among the students, encourage them to solve the controversy by doing related research. (See suggestions in the Applying and Expanding sections.)

5. *When you notice eye dialect[2] in your reading, what strategies can you use?*

   Help your students focus on the necessity of gaining a general understanding of what the characters are saying rather than focusing on the author's spelling. If they think about what is happening in the story and relate it to their oral language, they may then be able to grasp what the author is saying through the characters. (See suggestions in the Applying and Expanding sections.)

APPLYING

MATERIALS   "Hambone," adapted and arranged by Yetta Goodman

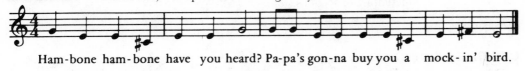

Ham-bone ham-bone have you heard? Pa-pa's gon-na buy you a   mock-in' bird.

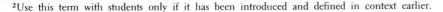

[2] Use this term with students only if it has been introduced and defined in context earlier.

VERSES FOR HAMBONE

If that mockin' bird don't sing.
Papa's gonna buy you a diamon' ring.

If that diamon' ring don't shine,
Papa's gonna buy you a bottle of wine.

If that bottle of wine get broke,
Papa's gonna buy you a billy goat.

If that billy goat run away,
Papa's gonna buy you a chevrolet.

If that chevrolet don't run,
Papa's gonna buy you a b.b. gun.

If that b.b. gun won't shoot
Papa's gonna buy you a baseball suit.

If that baseball suit don't fit,
Papa's gonna say "Aw, shoot! I quit!"

Build a collection of reading materials that will give students the opportunity to read eye dialect. Involve your students in helping you accumulate such a collection. The Bibliography lists materials in which eye dialect appears.

Students should read the materials provided and any others that you have collected or that they find independently. Help students apply what they have learned about eye dialect when it appears in their reading by having them talk about what they think the language means and what the author was trying to convey about the characters. If students ask, "What does this say?" encourage them to discover the meaning themselves from the context.

Students might organize a chart or notebook, similar to the one below, to record examples of eye dialect. Help them develop criteria for the kinds of eye dialect they want to categorize. Encourage students to work in groups of two or three, rather than alone, as group work often creates opportunities for stimulating discussion.

Where We Found It	What the Author Wrote	Why the Author Wrote It	What It Means to Us
Cartoon	[Example could be cut out and pasted here to avoid having to copy it]	Purpose related to characterization	
Newspaper: sports section	[Could be dialogue found in a reporter's account of a football game]	To provide factual reporting	

Every few weeks the examples collected in this activity should be shared and discussed to see if the students have discovered new purposes for use of eye dialect or new places where it is found. Provide local and up-to-date newspapers in which students can look for interviews in sports, feature, or entertainment sections.

EXPANDING

CREATIVE WRITING   Encourage open-ended creative writing that uses eye dialect for a purpose, where it is appropriate. These stories could also be used as additional reading material for other students in the group who need help with eye dialect.

LANGUAGE DISCUSSION   Have students listen to different types of people on television or radio—actors and actresses, announcers, disc jockeys, people in commercials. Suggest that they try to write down any language differences by using unusual spelling patterns. Discuss how different people use language in different ways. The use of tape-recorded examples collected by the students would provide opportunities for repeated listening, discussions, and more accurate decisions.

Explore the notion that even though people do pronounce the same words in different ways, written language does not reflect those differences. In other words, American English spelling is standard across dialect differences. Because there is no standard way to spell for eye-dialect purposes, it is possible to find a variety of ways to spell the same words when authors choose to use eye dialect.

ART ACTIVITY   Suggest that students draw cartoons with appropriate uses of dialogue. They may refer to the chart they are keeping on eye dialect and authors' purposes for its uses.

MUSIC ACTIVITIES   Provide students with the verses of songs that they know well. Avoid the use of eye dialect when you prepare the material. Have students listen carefully as they sing. Then have small groups of students work on rewriting the song in eye dialect that more closely represents their actual singing. They may compare their uncommon spelling patterns with those of other students to note any differences.

Students might (1) examine collections of folk songs that they bring from home or find in the library, to discover how many use eye dialect in written verses of songs; (2) compare the same songs found in different books to see if they do or do not use eye dialect; and (3) compare the different uncommon spelling patterns used in versions of the same song. They might look for "She'll Be Comin' Roun' the Mountain" and "Hambone" and compare the versions they find with the version originally presented to the class, noting how each handles uncommon spellings as well as various phrases and verses.

READ ALOUD   Collect materials that contain eye dialect (the Bibliography lists several sources) and read pertinent passages. Broadening the kinds of literature students hear will better enable them to predict similar kinds of language as they read. You should only read aloud dialects you are familiar with and can reproduce without giving the impression that you are making fun of the characters represented by the eye dialect. There are recordings of poets, authors, and actors reading different literary selections in various dialects. You may want to begin a collection of such material.

FOREIGN-LANGUAGE WORDS AND PHRASES: STRATEGY-LESSON PLAN

Specific Rationale

Authors use foreign-language words or phrases to[3]

1. Provide cues to the background of a character, to develop the setting, or to establish a mood:
   Maria said, "*Vámanos*, we really must hurry."
2. Convey meaning and subtleties of meaning for which, in the authors' opinion, there are no adequate equivalent terms in the dominant language of the text:
   It is *oeuvre* of life, not death.
3. Provide emphasis or status to the setting or to the characters in the story:
   He saved the *pièce de résistance* for last.

---

[3]There are many different languages spoken in the United States. Unfortunately, it is often common to refer to languages other than English as "foreign languages." As used here, "foreign language could refer to Spanish, French, or other language phrases embedded in English; however, it could also refer to English phrases embedded in Spanish, French, or other language texts. In other words, foreign language words or phrases are those written language units which occur in a language different from the dominant language of the text the reader is using.

There are times when italics or some other print variation is used as a cue to help the reader predict a foreign-language unit. However, the foreign language is often graphically similar to the dominant language of the text. In these cases the reader must use the syntactic and semantic language cues to predict the foreign-language word or phrase and then build meaning for the unit through the use of context.

Proficient readers handle such units in a variety of ways, depending on their knowledge of the languages being represented. Those who know the foreign language (or languages), or have had experience with the particular word(s) or phrase(s), will treat the unit as if it were part of the dominant language they are reading. Or, those proficient readers who are familiar with the spelling patterns used to represent the other languages may be able to identify the language of the word(s) or phrase(s). This may help them build some of the context needed to comprehend even if they have never seen the particular word(s) or phrase(s) being used.

Proficient readers who have little or no knowledge of the foreign language(s) can comprehend the foreign-language units only if the author has provided enough contextual language cues to help the reader construct meaning. If the phrase is significant to the story, the author will usually provide the necessary context cues for the reader to comprehend it at some level of meaning. Then proficient readers using these cues can make predictions relating to the setting of the story. If the foreign-language unit is insignificant, readers will probably ignore it and in any case will not lose much meaning.

If the author has erroneously assumed that the experiential background of the readers includes knowledge of the particular foreign-language unit, even proficient readers may indeed lose meaning. Readers need to be aware that such limitations in written material do exist. In such cases concepts or knowledge may have to be postponed for future experiences. Readers should not become insecure when they are not completely sure of everything that is happening. They must be willing to continue reading, confident that they have the appropriate strategies to build meaning as unknowns are discovered in the future.

Nonproficient readers, on the other hand, often tend to treat foreign-language words and phrases as if they were English, if that is the dominant language of the text. They may try to sound them out using English rules or continue to look at the word believing that if they look long enough they will recognize it. They are likely to be overly concerned with surface pronunciation and unaware that exact pronunciation is not only unnecessary but also not often helpful in constructing meaning. Sometimes even proficient readers revert to sounding-out strategies when they meet foreign-language units in their reading, allowing this to interfere with their usual ability to use syntax and semantics. Other readers may simply refuse to read material that has foreign language sprinkled throughout. Many adults who consider themselves good readers have limited their own reading experiences because they have not learned proficient strategies for handling foreign-language words and phrases in their readings.

This strategy lesson should help readers to

1. Broaden their reading experience to include material with foreign-language words and phrases
2. Use context surrounding foreign-language units to try to understand what the author or a character is saying
3. Understand that reading contains unknowns that may not be understood at the moment of the reading experience, but the reading should be continued despite these occasional lapses in comprehension

EVALUATION

The strategy lesson for Foreign-Language Words and Phrases will benefit

1. Students who indicate they do not like to read certain books because they contain too much foreign language.
2. Readers who frequently stop at a foreign word or phrase to sound it out, or who try to produce words that relate to the sound system of the dominant language, for a foreign-language unit.
3. Readers who usually ask for help from others to read foreign words or phrases.
4. Students who make fun of people who speak a language foreign to them.

Reading-Strategy Instruction

INITIATING

MATERIALS "Open House," by Yetta Goodman

Open House

The boys and girls in Ms. Peters's fifth-grade class had been busy preparing many things for Open House. This was an important day for everyone. Ms. Peters wanted the parents to see all the hard work the children had been doing and how much their work had improved during the year.

The boys and girls were excited too. They wanted to show their parents what a beautiful room they had. And they wanted their parents to meet their favorite teacher, Ms. Peters. Ms. Peters had a way of getting them to learn and at the same time she made learning fun.

The parents were also excited. Many of them had never met Ms. Peters. Many of the parents spoke Spanish. But other parents spoke Italian, French, and German. When the parents spoke English, it sounded different from the teacher's English. They wondered if they would like the school and the teacher. Still, they wanted to see the work their children had done and they wanted to see the teacher their children talked about and liked so much.

It was seven o'clock, and Ms. Peters was at the door of the room waiting for the parents and students to arrive.

Theresa was the first to arrive with her mother.

"Buenos noches," Ms. Peters said to Mrs. Orcaza. "Welcome to our classroom."

Ms. Peters then turned to Theresa and said, "Theresa, that's a very pretty dress."

Mrs. Orcaza smiled when Ms. Peters said to her, "Bonita, muy bonita," pointing to Theresa's dress.

"Sí," said Mrs. Orcaza proudly. "She made the dress herself."

Ms. Peters saw the other parents coming. She turned to Theresa and said, "Show your mother your work, and I'll be with you as soon as I greet the other parents."

YETTA GOODMAN

INTERACTING

Have the students read "Open House" silently and independently.

QUESTIONS FOR DISCUSSION

1. *In what ways does the story seem unusual or unfamiliar to you, or different from other stories you have read?*

   Accept any answers that the students can justify, but continue to encourage discussion until someone indicates that there are unusual or foreign words or phrases in the story.[4] If the students do not point this out, you may do so when the discussion begins to lag. Either you or the students may write the unusual words or phrases they noticed on the board. Do *not* ask for oral pronunciation of the units.

2. *What makes the words listed on the board unusual? What clues are there that help you know that these are not English words?*

   Students may notice unusual spellings, as in *buenas* or *muy*, or the use of accent marks. (When you are working with other materials in which non-English words appear, answers to these questions may also include the use of (1) question marks in unusual places, (2) italics, boldface, or underlining, (3) superscripts like tildes, apostrophes, or accent marks, (4) different alphabetic letters such as those used in Greek and Arabic, or (5) nonalphabetic symbols or other unusual symbols.)

3. *How can you find out what these unusual words or phrases mean?*

   Ask students to remember what they did to understand the foreign-language units in "Open House." Help them to realize that by predicting and relating to ongoing events while reading the material, they can best discover meaning. Have students reread "Open House" quickly and examine the English-language context that provides clues to the meaning of the foreign-language units, and encourage discussion of the meaning of those units. Ask any students who know Spanish to explain to the others how the context of the story provides clues to the translation. At the same time, explore the idea that knowing the general meaning in English (for the English speaker) is more important than knowing the exact word-for-word translation or pronunciation.

4. *What can you do if there is no way that you can understand the foreign-language units from the context?*

   Agree with students that they could ask you or look in a dictionary. But continue to explore what they would do if an expert or a dictionary were not available. Emphasize that it is acceptable to continue reading without recognizing or being able to pronounce the unusual words or phrases. If the word or phrase is significant, they will discover its meaning as they continue reading, since the author will *probably* provide additional information. If the author does not do so, the students may then have to postpone understanding until they read the word or phrase in some other context. Remember that your main goal is to produce independent readers who are concerned with comprehension and aware that in certain situations there are limitations to what can be understood from reading.

5. *Does anyone know which languages are represented by the words or phrases listed on the board?*

   Have students refer to the story and explore the aspects of the context that provide clues. Do *not* give them the correct answer. Those students who are interested should be encouraged to do further research (see Expanding section).

6. *In what kinds of materials or stories are you likely to find foreign-language units? Have you read any stories or other materials that contain such language units?*

   This discussion should help students explore types of materials in which to predict foreign-language words and phrases. You might want to discuss the use of foreign

---

[4]Help students become aware that the United States is a multilingual society. They need to understand that although a language may be foreign to them, it may be native to the United States.

languages in menus and recipes, and you might begin to collect such material to make use of during relevant lessons.

7. *Why does an author use foreign language in his writing?*

As the students begin to respond, you might suggest the development of a cumulative list which can be kept as a chart for the whole class or in separate notebooks for each reader to be added to by the students as they have more experience with such language in their reading. There are the beginnings of such a list in the Specific Rationale (see page 135); however, permit the students to discover the purposes of foreign-language units—both those we list and any others the students find—through their own reading experiences.

8. *When is it important to know how to pronounce foreign-language units and phrases?*

Explore with students the idea that it is not necessary to know the pronunciation when they are reading silently for understanding. Only when the language is to be used orally does it become important to find out how the native speaker pronounces the word or phrase. They should explore the notion that some native speakers might be offended, feeling that others are making fun of their language, if words are mispronounced. Students should also know that in some cases the only accurate source for the way a language is pronounced is the speaker of that language. Even pronunciation guides may prove fallible in giving appropriate pronunciations. Point out, also, that speakers of the same language vary in their pronunciation. When an important foreign name or place is in the news a great deal, have the students listen to radio and TV commentators to discover variability in pronunciations even among professionals. *Viet Nam* and *Alexander Solzhenitsyn* are recent historical examples.

APPLYING

MATERIALS   "A Letter from Brazil," by Barry Sherman
"The Map," by Yetta Goodman

A Letter from Brazil

March 28, 1980

Dear Jim,

I am sorry that I did not write to you last month. You're my only pen pal from the USA, and I should write to you at least once every two weeks. Now that you are back home, I don't get a chance to speak English anymore. I don't think that you get to speak Portuguese anymore either. If you don't write to me and I don't write to you, you will forget the Portuguese you learned when you were here in Brazil, and I will forget English. We can't let that happen.

You asked in your last letter if there have been any changes in our little town since you left. You should know that things change slowly in a little town on the seashore in Brazil. You can be pretty sure that everything here is *como sempre.* If you came back tomorrow, you would recognize everything. Sr. Santos still sits outside his grocery store all afternoon, smoking thin *bahiano* cigars. The flowers in all the little gardens still smell sweetly. The sea rolls in toward the shore, making big waves on our white sand beaches. And the *palmeiras*—the beautiful coconut palm trees—wave in the ocean breezes. Yes, everything is the same.

But a few new things happen all the time, *amigo.* We had a terrible time two weeks ago. We were all very frightened. It was terrible—*terrível mesmo!* I will tell you about it.

It started two weeks ago, when my father and uncle went fishing early in the morning, as they do every morning. Do you remember our fishing boats, our *jangadas?* Most of the men of our town are fishermen. Each day they sail out to sea on *jangadas. A jangada* is like a big raft. It is made of big logs of balsa wood, a wood that is so light that it floats on water easily. The logs are tied together, and each *jangada* has one sail. Usually, our fishermen start out together in the morning and return at sunset. When you see all the white sails coming into the harbor, it is very *bonito*—a beautiful sight.

Two weeks ago, on Monday, the fishermen sailed out as always. I watched until they disappeared from sight. Oh, how I wished I could be with them. All during school vacation, I sailed on the *jangada* with my father and uncle. But now I had to go to school. *Que pena!* It is a real pity.

That night I walked down to the beach to watch the fishermen come home. One by one the boats pulled up to shore. But my father's *jangada* did not come back. Old Tomas put his arm around my shoulder and said, "Come, Carlos. We will walk to your house together. I want to talk to your mother."

We didn't say a word to each other, but inside I was very, very scared. Maybe you remember the old saying among the fishermen, that sooner or later the Goddess of the Sea, *Yemanjá,* takes a *jangada* down to the bottom of the ocean. Every day the fishermen go out to sea, but every once in a while someone doesn't return. This time I was afraid that *Yemanjá* had taken my father and uncle.

When we got to my house, old Tomás said to my mother, "I came here tonight to tell you that we had a storm at sea today. It was one of those quick storms that come from nowhere and disappear as quickly as they come. Your *jangada* was separated from us when the mast broke. The last time we saw it, the boat was drifting farther out to sea. We could not move fast enough to catch the *jangada.* Your husband is lost at sea. I am afraid that *Yemanjá* has claimed another victim."

My aunt and two brothers and sisters began to cry when they heard about the storm at sea. I wanted to cry, too, but I am the oldest boy, and I must learn to act like a man. But I tell you, *amigo,* it is hard not to cry when you learn that your father is lost at sea.

But my mother did not cry. I could see that she was holding her feelings inside herself, but she did not cry. Instead, she said, "Tomás, we thank you for coming to us, even though your news is sad. It is very possible that the cruel sea has taken my husband. We are in God's hands, and what must be, must be. But I feel in my heart that my husband is not dead yet. So we will wait."

My mother and I sat on the beach all night, waiting. We were both very sad. We waited and waited. Ten days passed. It was impossible that they were still alive, but my mother would not give up hope. She said that she knew they were still alive. Every morning, before dawn, she would leave our house and walk down to the beach. It was still dark outside, but I would wake up and follow her. I saw my mother sit down on the sand and I heard her cry. I knew she was hoping against hope.

Then, yesterday, we saw a big *helicóptero* flying toward us from the sea. It came closer and closer until it reached the beach. Then it began to come down for a landing. None of us had ever seen a *helicóptero* before, even from far away. All of a sudden, here was one close up. I even forgot my sadness for a minute. On the side of the *helicóptero* were words that said it belonged to the Brazilian Air Force—the *Força Aeréa do Brasil.* After a few minutes a door opened in the side and out jumped my father and my uncle! Can you imagine! They had been drifting at sea for more than ten days until they were picked up by a ship heading for Africa. The ship radioed the *Força Aeréa* and they sent a *helicóptero* to get my father and uncle. We were so happy to see them. And my mother, who didn't cry when we all thought they were lost at sea, suddenly started to cry when she saw my father. She didn't stop crying for a long time.

That night, the whole town got together for a big *festa* in honor of my father and uncle. We had all kinds of good food to eat. You would have loved it. The next day, everything was back to normal. I went back to school. My father and uncle began to build a new *jangada.*

I'd better say *adeus* now because I want to mail this letter today. I hope you remember to write soon. Your friend, Carlos

BARRY SHERMAN

The Map

Beth and Mary were waiting at the bus stop for the school bus. Other kids were waiting, too.

"I hope the bus gets here soon," Mary said. "I don't want to be late for school. Mr. Roberts was reading a good story yesterday. He said he would finish it at the beginning of school today if all the buses got there on time."

As they stood there, they saw a family walking toward them, all dressed up. They looked like they were going somewhere special on a holiday. There was a father, a mother, and two small children.

The man came up to them and said, "Guten Tag."

The two girls looked at each other. They did not understand what the man had said, but Beth answered speaking very clearly.

"Can we help you?"

The man said, "Ve vant go to town. Vich bus ve take?"

Mary said, "This is a school bus stop not a city bus stop."

The man said, shaking his head, "Ich versteh nicht. . . . I speak not very vell English. Ve vant a bus to go to town."

Beth turned to Mary. "I don't think he understands you. You'd better try again," she said.

Beth turned to the man and said, "This bus does not go downtown. I will show you how to go. Give me some paper and a pencil, Mary."

Mary took paper and pencil from her school bag. Beth began to draw on the paper, talking and pointing at the same time.

"We are here on Royale Street."

"Royale Street," the man said nodding.

Beth nodded, too, and continued to talk, draw, and point.

"You go one block north in that direction to 15th Street."

She pointed and the man nodded his head.

"At the corner you cross the street and walk two blocks past Superior Road to Johnson Road."

She looked at the man's face. He was watching her drawing carefully and seemed to understand.

"Then cross over Johnson and take the No. 44 bus there. It will say Central Station on the front."

She gave the man the map. Her bus was coming.

When the man saw the bus he said, "Oh, *school* bus." He smiled and said something to his family which Beth and Mary did not understand. They all smiled, too.

As Beth and Mary got on the bus, the man said, "Tank you, very much, girls. Tank you." He waved at the girls and so did all his family.

The girls waved back. They both felt very good.

YETTA M. GOODMAN

When the students have had some opportunity to select and read materials, all of which include foreign-language words and phrases, help them explore, through discussion, the following ideas:

1. It is not necessary to be able to pronounce foreign-language units in order to understand them. It is not even necessary to recognize the languages to make an educated guess about the meanings of specific words or phrases.
2. It is the language context familiar to the reader that provides cues to the foreign-language units.
3. It is often necessary to read the whole story or poem before the meaning of a particular foreign-language unit can be grasped.

Many of the questions used in the Interacting phase of this lesson can be used again to establish these principles.

Have the students keep a list of any foreign-language words or phrases they encounter as they read. Have them write any of the known language cues they found in the story that helped them understand the meaning, mood, and/or purpose of the foreign-language unit. A class or individual record, such as the following, may be kept:

Sentence with Unusual or Foreign-Language Words or Phrases	Which Language?	Where Found?	Meaning	Cues to the Language and Meaning

EXPANDING

CREATIVE WRITING Have the students expand the story "Open House," (presented in the Initiating phase) with a description of Ms. Peters greeting other visiting parents who speak a language other than English. Students might have to interview people who speak such languages, or do some library research to find appropriate greetings. They might act out the story after they have collected a number of episodes.

Suggest that students act out the story *The Map* (see Applying above), and then discuss the problems of people traveling in foreign countries. They might write a handbook called, for example, "How to Help Non-English Speakers," "Non-Spanish" speakers or "Non-French" Speakers, or others, depending on the community.

Have students create stories in which they include non-English words or phrases that they know. Stories may be shared with others and kept for a collection of such materials to be used with later classes.

LANGUAGE DISCUSSION If any students want to experiment with pronouncing the foreign words or phrases they encounter in poems or in any other materials, suggest that they interview people who speak particular languages to obtain a more accurate pronunciation. Even if you know the language yourself, encourage this kind of independent research. Students will find that all speakers of French, Navajo, German, and other languages do not pronounce their language the same way—as is true of English speakers.

Students may categorize the various foreign-language units they discover as they read to see if there are similar spelling patterns that help them predict which language is being represented.

SOCIAL STUDIES There are many names not common to English spelling patterns used in social-studies materials. Students should be helped to build concepts related to place names and characterizations for the names of people, rather than worry about the pronunciation of the names. (See the strategy-lesson plans for "Nouns as Names for People," and "Nouns as Place Names," in chapter 5.)

SCIENCE Scientific names of plants and animals are usually derived from Latin and Greek. When students read materials that have scientific terms, help them use reading strategies similar to those they use with foreign-language words or phrases so they do not become overwhelmed by the reading task. Usually the rest of the language context will be available to provide clues to what is being described. Often common names are also provided. Many scientific terms are concepts for which students must build meaning. Students could also begin to discover that some scientific terms have bound morphemic endings, such as *ology* or *ium*, which can provide clues to the meanings of the word. (See the strategy-lesson plans "Developing Meaning through Context," in chapter 7.)

GRAPHIC VARIATIONS

General Rationale

We shall examine two ways in which authors and publishers make use of graphic variations:

1. *Variations in print.* Readers with limited reading experience may be unfamiliar with the variety of print they will encounter in written material and may be unaware of the purposes of such variations. In either case, they may not know how to handle print variations appropriately.
2. *Variations in the organization of print.* The format or organization of written material is indeed various. Differences in format may be due to conventions of publishers and printers, space limitations, and purposes that the organization will serve. Unique formats may also be conceived by authors to emphasize the nature of the material or highlight its meaning.

The strategies necessary to read graphic variations are usually easily learned and cause few problems for most readers. However, there are students who are puzzled by graphic variations. Some find it easier, because of their experience, to read one format as compared with another, while others may not have much opportunity to read any materials that vary in print. There is no way to anticipate which students will have difficulty with any one of the many possible variations. Therefore, instead of providing reading materials for such strategies, we shall make suggestions that can be adapted for a particular student and a particular graphic variation.

PRINT VARIATIONS: STRATEGY-LESSON PLAN

Specific Rationale

There are many written conventions that give the reader cues to greater understanding of the writer's purposes. Such conventions include varying the type face, as in *italics* or **BOLDFACE**, placing words and phrases in "quotation marks" or ALL CAPITAL LETTERS; or underlining them.

Authors use these conventions

1. To indicate emphasis:
   Her father said, "Don't you ever, *ever* let me catch you smoking."
   But nothing, **absolutely nothing** would stop her from running away.
2. To show a change in the mood or tone of a story or of a character:
   The storm got worse and WORSE.
   His voice got softer and his whole body began to *tremble*.
3. To indicate titles of publications or institutions:
   She read *Les Misérables* three times.
   He went to visit the *Empire State Building*
   Her father works for the *Tucson Public Schools*
4. To indicate an overused or unusual statement:
   She was "no better than she ought to be."
   He was "as strong as an ox."
5. To indicate that a word or a phrase is being referred to as a unit in itself:
   "Is" is a two-letter word.
   Write three sentences with the word "beautiful."

6. To identify eye-dialect or foreign-language words or phrases (see the two preceding strategy lessons):

" *'Enry pahk the cah,"* commanded the passenger.

The attractive young man said very politely, *"S'il vous plaît."*

Students should become aware that authors generally have a purpose for using print variation. Readers' awareness of that purpose will usually enhance their understanding of the written material.

EVALUATION

The strategy lesson for Print Variations will benefit

1. Students who pause, frown, or in some other way appear to be bothered when they encounter print variations.
2. Students who do not use appropriate intonation when they read aloud language written in varied print, or otherwise indicate they have not understood what they have read.

Reading-Strategy Instruction

INITIATING

The strategy lesson should be related to a critical moment in the learning/teaching situation. As you are working with a student who is reading orally, or in reviewing a tape of a student's oral reading, you may hear evidence of a particular problem with graphic variations. Make a note of the problem and later, during an individual conference, have that student reread the section that caused difficulty.

INTERACTING

QUESTIONS FOR DISCUSSION

1. *What do you think the author wants you to know when a word or phrase is printed in that way?* [Use the exact term of "in that way." Say, "in all capital letters," "with underlining."]
2. *How does the change in print help you to understand what the author is trying to say?*

INDEPENDENT OR SMALL-GROUP ACTIVITY Encourage students to look for print variations in everything they read: newspaper and content-area texts, as well as other reading. Ask them to keep a record of all the print variations they find over a period of two weeks or so. They are to list the print variations, including a significant segment of the language context; and next to each they should indicate (a) the author's meaning and (b) the author's purpose:

Print Variation	Author's Meaning	Author's Purpose

At the end of the designated time period, help the students categorize the various reasons for which authors use print variations. Although the categories will no doubt be similar to those listed in the Specific Rationale, do not provide any of those categories for the students; they should emerge from discussion. It is important to permit students to use their own organization and labels. Students' examples might be collected, put on Ditto masters, and duplicated. Then the students can work as a group sorting or categorizing the combined examples in order to discover new or different reasons authors use print variations.

APPLYING

Encourage the students to record only those print variations that they do not understand or that they believe are different from others they have found. In a small-group discussion or in an individual conference with the teacher, the students can explore the uniqueness of, or the problems caused by, the print variations, what the print variations mean, and why a particular author is using them.

EXPANDING

CREATIVE WRITING   Encourage students to use print variations in their own creative writing and to give reasons for their use. Discuss with them what happens when print variations are overused in a story or article.

Have the students explore the use of print variations in poetry or rhyme to enhance meaning. For example, they may write a poem about the world or an orange and arrange it in the shape of a circle.

Have other students read the creative writing and poetry to give them more experience with print variations.

Students can look for cartoons that use print variations (*Pixies*, for example), and make up their own.

ART ACTIVITIES   Suggest that students draw words or phrases in such a way that the meaning of the unit is conveyed graphically. The word *cracked* may be written to look as if it is actually cracked, and *tall* may be written vertically to represent height. Students may also draw a word or name in cursive writing, then copy its mirror image and fill it in with crayons or a watercolor wash. This exercise can convey the idea that written language has aesthetic quality and may be examined as an art form. Samples of Chinese and Arabic script may also be used to illustrate this concept.

FORMAT VARIATIONS: STRATEGY-LESSON PLAN

Specific Rationale

Written material can be presented in a wide variety of formats. The format to which students are most exposed during reading instruction—that of uninterrupted print running across the page from left to right margins, and down the page from top to bottom margins—may not be the most common format. This may account for the difficulty some students have in adapting their reading strategies to other formats.

Although the same basic reading process—predicting, confirming, and integrating—is used with all formats, the strategies comprising that process are used in different ways, depending on the material being read. Only when students have varied reading experiences can they learn to adapt their reading strategies to various formats.

Variations of format may be due to publishers' conventions or the physical limitations imposed by the organization of written material. Or they may serve to enhance the meaning of material or to make it easier to read. Sometimes a particular format is required because of the subject matter itself. Recipes, math problems, and science experiments are set up in certain formats because they are best understood when presented in those organizational patterns.

Formats may vary in some of the following ways:

1. Double columns on one page
2. Magazine or newspaper format
3. Print that wraps around maps, pictures, or graphs
4. Captions describing art or photographs
5. Lists

Formats may vary because of the nature of the material to be read, or its purpose:

1. Poems
2. Recipes

3. Directions
4. Ingredients on containers
5. Television guides
6. Telephone listings
7. Indices or tables of contents
8. Headlines
9. Signs
10. Dictionaries
11. Menus
12. Shopping lists
13. Art, photography, or picture books
14. Cartoons or comics
15. Tickets for theaters, games, transportation
16. Advertisements
17. Guarantees

These examples emphasize the need for a reading program that includes a great variety of reading materials.

EVALUATION

Since problems with format variations are usually very individual, it is advisable to keep records of the problems each student has with particular kinds of formats, and plan accordingly. For example, make note if a student *frequently* loses his place while reading double columns, newspaper columns, or wraparound formats; then plan a strategy lesson for that particular format. Or plan a strategy lesson on reading headlines if a student has difficulty with them. Problems with headlines are often due to a lack of redundant language cues.

Encourage students to share with you any problems they encounter in reading new material. You may ask as a regular part of individual conferences: *Was there anything about your reading that caused you difficulty?* Help your students broaden their reading experiences by providing opportunities to read types of materials to which they have not been exposed. Remember that even very young readers encounter print variation on cereal boxes and gum wrappers, in TV captions, advertising, games, and toys, among others. The use of materials listed in the Specific Rationale or those included in the Grid of Reading Materials in chapter 3 (page 38) will expand your students' contacts with a variety of print formats.

Reading-Strategy Instruction

INITIATING

The most important aspect of these strategy lessons is to encourage students to read broadly so that they have many opportunities to adapt their reading strategies to different materials. The teacher will need to (1) plan with students experiences that will provide the necessary purposes and motivations that will make them want to read broadly; (2) make available materials printed in the various formats needed by the students; (3) be aware of the types of material the students read most and those they read least; and (4) help students understand that a particular format, or way of organizing materials, is often intended to serve a specific purpose.

INTERACTING

QUESTIONS FOR DISCUSSION [You must know something about the reading habits of the student to ask the first four questions.]

1. *In what way is* [one type of material the student usually reads] *like* [another type of material the student reads]?

    Students may tell how comics are like the sports page, or how science fiction is like an encyclopedia. Then they may compare some more similar formats such as recipes and directions for building something.

2. *How are these formats different, and why are they different?*

Students can explore the reasons for format differences.

3. *What must you do differently when you read each type of material?*

Explore with students that often different reading strategies are used in different ways for different materials. For example, some materials may be read faster than others, depending on the reader's purpose. In reading newspaper articles, one need only read the first paragraph to get an overview of a story and then decide whether to read the rest of the article. In the case of recipes, pattern instructions, and other directions, it is sometimes important first to read everything through once to know what the final outcome will be and what ingredients or materials are required; the reader then rereads and implements the directions step by step.

4. *When a picture or graph accompanies the reading, at what point is it best to read the caption related to it? Why is it important to do so? What special strategies are needed for this task?*

Since not much research has yet been done to discover the different ways in which reading strategies are used for various formats, you and your students may explore what each reader does and then discuss which strategies have proved to be more or less effective and why.

5. *What kinds of problems do you have when you read material* [of a particular format that caused difficulty or that is seldom read]?

Help students understand that the difficulty lies in their unfamiliarity with that kind of reading material, not in their reading ability.

6. *As a reader of* [a particular type of material] *what do you need to know? Why do you need to know it? How will you find out most easily?*

7. *If you were the author of* [a particular type of material], *what would be your reason for arranging the material in a particular manner? What problems could this arrangement cause the reader?*

Help the student separate the role of reader from the role of writer.

APPLYING

With your students, decide what strategies can be used most successfully with a particular format without interfering with the search for meaning. Suggest, or help the students select, materials that will provide opportunities to try these strategies.

EXPANDING

ARITHMETIC   For the primary classroom, set up a corner store stocked with empty cans, boxes, jars, and the like. Encourage the children to use the print on these items as they simulate the ordering, shopping, and purchasing of household products. This gives them an opportunity to interact with print in various formats. In addition, units on cooking can be developed to encourage the reading of the various formats in recipe books. A gasoline station may be set up to provide other experiences with numbers and reading.

READING   With the students, collect samples of different kinds of reading materials. You may want to develop a kit of such materials. Discuss with students each kind of written material in terms of the following questions:

1. *For whom did the author intend the material?*
2. *What purpose did the author have in writing it?*
3. *Why would a reader read it?*
4. *In what different ways would different readers read the same material? Why?*
5. *What should be read; and what does not need to be read? Why, how, and when?*
6. *Why is the written material organized the way it is?*

All students benefit from reading a wide variety of materials. You may wish to share with your students parts of the Grid of Reading Materials (see chapter 3, page 38). For each kind of material they read, they may record the specific problems they have with the materials, indicating why the particular materials presented a problem, why the author chose the particular format, and in what ways reading strategies are used differently for different materials.

Chapter 7

Confirming Semantic Cues

RETHINK/REREAD

General Rationale

Because of the speed with which newspapers must be printed, it is not uncommon to encounter typesetting errors in them. Depending on the language systems these errors involve,

> The jury and the spectators sat in <u>stuned</u> silence as the <u>sorbid</u> story of the butchering unfolded and this man who had perpetrated one of the most hideous crimes ever committed in the state of Indiana bared his soul.   From *The Evening World*, Bloomfield, IN, Tuesday, September 11, 1979.

> A new "report card" on the state of education in America is out, and it <u>say</u> the country is letting down a whole group of kids whom now you will mostly find doing things like . . .   From *The Herald-Telephone*, Bloomington, IN, Thursday, August 30, 1979.

> Fugitives Rudy and Helena witness the 1941 massacre of Jews at Babi Yar; Josef and Moses are <u>become</u> a part of the Warsaw Ghetto resistance; and Inga smuggles letters to Karl at Buchenwald.   From *The Herald-Telephone*, Bloomington, IN, Tuesday, September 11, 1979.

we find them more or less disruptive to our processing. Graphic-level alterations are often ignored or even unidentified. We simply process what we know was intended to be there, with little or no disruption to our train of thought. More disruptive are those instances when whole structures are altered. We find our minds and our eyes skidding to a halt and the thought registering, *That doesn't make sense*. But even with this interruption to our reading we generally reread a portion to confirm the problem and to pick up the thread of meaning and then proceed with what we assume was intended.

Physically disrupted texts are not the only instance in which we can find ourselves reprocessing. Because reading depends upon the reader's use of predicting and interpreting strategies it is only natural that that reader will arrive at points in text where the information being processed does not appear to fit with the portions already read.

Good mystery writers depend upon this phenomenon. They present the reader, who is acting as the guest detective, with all the relevant clues and interim hypotheses, just as they are arrived at by the protagonist. Even with this shared information, the reader can be unsure of the resolution right up to the ending of the story. Any set of circumstances can have more than one logical interpretation. The fictional detective and the reader cannot be expected to share the same set of background knowledge.

Informational pieces on controversial topics—say, the proposed construction of a nuclear-power plant—also help us explore the reader's use of the confirming strategies. It is possible for the author to carefully expose the major advantages and disadvantages, for the reader to agree with this exposition, and then for the two of them to arrive at opposing conclusions because of their individual weighting of the various factors. When this happens, the reader tends to reconsider the issue in an attempt to identify the pivotal decision-making points; in this way the reader is able to reassess the author's sense of the situation.

Read the cartoon in Fig. 7-1. Did you find yourself going back to one of the earlier frames to examine more closely the faces of the three knights once you had learned their names?

The ultimate responsibility of a reader is to continually ask the question, *Does this make sense?* As each new chunk of data is generated—either by the text itself or by the reader's experience, which the text acts to stimulate—the reader attempts to assimilate and accommodate this information and then to integrate it with the conceptual whole that has already been processed. The function of the reading process is the search for meaning, not the resolution of it. There will always be a certain percentage of miscalculations generated by any reader.

As long as the reader feels that the search for meaning is proceeding with some degree of success, then the reading process proceeds through the application of predicting and confirming strategies. Only when the question *Does this make sense?* generates a no response must the reader decide upon the application of one of four available courses of action.

Fig. 7–1 *"The Wizard of Id"* by permission of Johnny Hart and Field Enterprises, Inc.

Specific Rationale

When a reader is faced with a no-sense situation, the processing options include

1. *Reread.* Seek additional cues from the graphic information. These may be semantic, syntactic, or graphophonic cues, depending on what caused the material not to make sense.
2. *Rethink.* Determine if reevaluating the already processed context allows for any alternate interpretations and predictions.
3. *Self-correct.* Do this if the first two options provide clues that suggest correction will be beneficial.
4. *Continue to read.* Determine if additional context will clarify the confusion.
5. *Stop reading.* If the content is important enough, either find some more predictable reading material or a nonreading experience.

The determination of which of these courses of action should be implemented must be based upon consideration of four interrelated factors from the reader's schema:

1. The value the reader places on the content
2. The language resources the reader can bring to bear
3. The experiential knowledge the reader can bring to bear
4. The semantic support the author has provided

Rereading is the most frequent confirming strategy used by readers when they begin to have difficulty integrating meaning. It is a strategy toward which writers in the field of reading instruction have always shown an ambivalent attitude. In some instances, when teachers feel that the student has not given due attention to the print, they will tell the student to go back or to look more closely at what is there. They are operating on the premise that missed or misread words are the basis of the student's problem and that more careful attention to the text is the appropriate resolution. They are further assuming that "if it had been done right the first time," there would be no need to reread. This view is clearly articulated in some testing settings where regressions are counted as additional reading errors.

Certainly, reprocessing is a strategy common to all expressions of language. Conversational comments like "Would you repeat that?" "What did you say?" and "Did I hear you say that . . . ?" are all alternate ways of saying, "Wait a moment, your thinking took a twist that I hadn't been anticipating and now I must adjust my own thoughts." Perhaps the ambivalent feelings concerning the reprocessing of text have been generated because that reprocessing has so often been related to word-level analysis. The reader is counseled to reexamine the text when the student fails to produce the expected lexical item. This attempt to refocus the student's attention most often leads to an impromptu miniphonics lesson or to the teacher's "giving" the reader the word, which diverts attention from meaning. Our research concludes that repeated processing attempts at one point in text are very unproductive because they are so bereft of language cueing. (See General Rationale for "Initial, Medial, and Final Graphic Cues" in chapter 9.)

Rereading becomes much more productive when its application is related to larger-than-word units. One teenager, in an interview about his reading, provided some perspective on this issue:

Question: When you are reading and you come to *something* you don't know, what do you do?
Answer: Read back over it.
Question: What is the "it" that you read back over?
Answer: The sentence that I didn't understand.
Question: Do you ever do anything else?
Answer: Then, if I don't really understand that, I usually go back farther.

This reader is attending to semantic units and is aware that they must be sought within larger syntactic units.

These examples of attempts at *self-correcting* further demonstrate this point:

You can see ⓒevery feather on that bird. *[handwritten: father, bi-]*

One picture showed a large black crowⓒ with a long piece of string in his bill. *[handwritten: peck]*

Rethinking is the same mental process as rereading. In both instances the reader reinvestigates the cues that have been accumulated from the already processed text as well as those experiential cues that have been selected. The task is to project alternative interpretations for these data by reweighting and realigning the interrelationships. There is always more than one logical prediction for any setting or process. If the reader can generate an alternate that "makes sense" of the sum of available cues, the reading may proceed. All of this processing can be accomplished with the reader's eyes closed.

There are times when the reader will be aware that rereading or rethinking will not or has not generated any additional perspectives. It may be the case that the reading has only progressed into the first hundred or so words of text. At this point the context is just beginning to take on texture. The available semantic cues are sparse, and the reader is drawing the initial assumptions in relation to his or her appropriate experiential knowledge or schema. In this case there is little to be gained by reprocessing. (The reader is well aware of the limitations on his or her understanding.) However, in moving ahead the reader hopes that the text will supply additional cues and that the relationships with experiential knowledge will be strengthened.

Instances in which the reader is dealing with conceptualizations far removed from experience are often best handled by *continued reading*. When a reader (or a learner in any setting) is dealing with new information, two things must be expected:

1. The possible relationships that exist with personal knowledge will only be discovered over time.
2. Some cues to the conceptualization may be recognized as such long before they are fitted into the construct or schema that the reader is generating. One aspect of treating reading as a developmental process is to value the partially constructed concepts that are the products of initial encounters.

A nine-year-old from an urban setting who encounters coyotes in a story set in sheepherding country may conclude that because *coyotes are able to climb over high rocky places* they seem very like wild goats. After reading the same story, an adult may conclude that coyotes are like wolves because *they attack in pairs*. Both concepts are incomplete but indicate not only the knowledge the readers had before their reading about goats or wolves but what information they were using to develop concepts about coyotes.

Finally, the reader must learn that it is a legitimate strategy to *stop* when the communication function of reading breaks down. There are points at which the limits of the reader's resources and the limits of the textual support combine to make reading nonproductive. Adults avail themselves of this strategy when they pay a lawyer to read and interpret a contract for them; a doctor, a lab report; or a teacher, a curriculum.

Initially readers should be supported in the development of this strategy during the reading of their personally selected reading materials. Students need to learn how to read to themselves silently a sample passage from the material that they have chosen for pleasure reading and then to explain to themselves what they are thinking and understanding in relation to it. If they are formulating ideas and if their interest is maintained, then, without regard for the number of miscues made or the differences between the author's intended meaning and their own, they should be encouraged to read the selection. If, however, the communication function of reading has broken down, the appropriate response is to stop reading and disregard this material. Students need to be helped to make such decisions themselves. Self-monitoring the degree of understanding is a major goal of reading instruction.

EVALUATION

The strategy lesson for Rethink/Reread will benefit

1. Students who read for extrinsic reasons—because someone else has set the task and raised the questions. They have no personal investment in the process.

2. Students who seem more concerned with "correct" answers to preset questions, than with understanding.
3. Students who are able to give smooth oral readings of material, which they are then unable to discuss.
4. Students who hesitate to pause or regress, placing a value on flawless oral performance above that of meaning-gaining.
5. Students who make regular use of rereading and rethinking strategies but who feel guilty about doing so. Previous instruction may have taught them that value is placed on a continuous left-to-right treatment of print. They believe it is a form of cheating, which they practice because it usually goes unobserved in silent-reading settings. But they harbor the belief that really proficient readers do not need to fall back on it.

Reading-Strategy Instruction

MATERIALS   "Jim's Adventure," by Dorothy Watson

Jim's Adventure

page 1

There were three ways of getting from the Robinson farm to Sam's cabin. Sam was the Robinsons' nearest neighbor and it was two miles to his place if you took the path that went safely along the edge of the forest. Jim's father always made him take this path to Sam's if he were going alone. The other two ways to Sam's were by river.

page 2

The quickest route was by turning off the main stream about half a mile from the landing, shooting twenty feet of narrow rapids, then proceeding on the river's branch until you landed almost at Sam's back door. This route was very dangerous, and Jim's father had forbidden him ever to take it.

The third way to Sam's was also by river and was quite safe, especially with two people handling the canoe. This river route simply involved staying to the right bank of the river all the way from the landing to Sam's waterfront dock.

page 3

Jim's heart was pounding as he guided the canoe into the icy water. As he paddled along the dark right bank of the river, his arms began to ache but he did not slow his pace. At the first sound of the rapids, Jim slowly began to edge the canoe toward the left bank. His muscles strained and he felt his heart jump as he aimed the canoe into the rapids.

DOROTHY WATSON

INITIATING

Prepare "Jim's Adventure" as a three-page booklet. The text should be so divided among the pages that the reader must turn back to the first two pages in order to reprocess desired material.

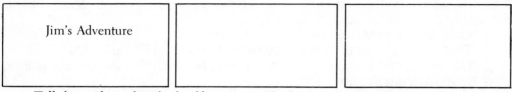

Tell the students that the booklet contains the beginning of an adventure story and that you would like them to read it through silently to determine what might cause the adventure.

Observe the silent reading, noting the individuals who do reread portions of the text from either of the first two pages.

INTERACTING

QUESTIONS FOR DISCUSSION

[Name student], *I noticed that you turned back to the first page of the story. What happened to make you do that?* Encourage the student, and then the others who reprocessed, to indicate just what information was being sought and what prompted the search. Did any of you want to reread certain parts but decided not to? Why? Encourage them to share their reasoning.

The significant points that need to be developed through this discussion include

1. You cannot always judge ahead of time the relative significance of information.
2. Not remembering does not always mean that you were careless. It can mean that you initially thought something else would be more important.
3. Rereading or rethinking can sometimes help you make sense of what you read. You can help yourself.

APPLYING

MATERIALS "A Day at the Zoo," by Charlotte Hazelwood

A Day at the Zoo

The day was bright and sunny—a good day to be at the zoo. Many animal sounds and shouts of laughter filled the air.

"Look at that funny fellow!" said Ambrose.

"Throw him a peanut, quick, before he turns away!" cried Judy.

"Oh, he caught it and is going to throw it back! Clever fellow. Sometimes they seem fairly bright, don't they?"

"He's scratching his head. They always scratch their heads. Maybe they think it makes them look wise, but they're probably looking for fleas."

"It's feeding time! First one down is a rotten monkey!" Ambrose shouted as he swung himself deftly down from the top of the cage to the floor.

"Oh, Ambrose, wait for me," cried Judy. "Visitors' day at the zoo gives me such an appetite."

CHARLOTTE HAZELWOOD

Introduce the group to "A Day at the Zoo" by telling them that this is another story that may make them want to rethink or reread. Ask them to read the story silently and to place a mark on the page at the point where their ideas about the story are suddenly changed.

In the discussion that follows the reading, identify the section of text that does not make sense with the processing and predictions that have gone before: "It's feeding time! First one down is a rotten monkey!" Consider the fact that this author purposefully set out to play a trick on the reader by providing clues that could be misleading for a while but that would make a new kind of sense when the final clue was provided.

The Clues	The Reader Predicts
1. " . . . animal sounds and shouts filled the air . . ."	*It's people talking about monkeys.*
2. The fact that Ambrose and Judy are talking.	
3. "Throw him a peanut . . ."	
4. "He's scratching his head!"	
5. "Maybe they think it makes them look smart, but they're probably looking for fleas."	*This doesn't ring quite true.*
6. "It's feeding time! First one down is a rotten monkey!"	*Wait a moment! It's monkeys talking about people.*

You may also want to discuss the notion that the reprocessing necessitated by this text can easily be handled by rethinking, whereas rereading is more probably called for in "Jim's Adventure."

EXPANDING

ART   Have students make game boards that include steps to retrace or take other circuitous routes. Help students see the relationship between such games and the various reprocessing that occurs in reading.

DEVELOPING MEANING THROUGH CONTEXT

General Rationale

A citizen examining the daily newspaper reads a feature article concerning some papyrus scrolls that biblical scholars are translating, learns that the Gnostics were members of a religious sect existing about the time of Christ, and wonders how this newly acquired information may be related to what she already knows about agnostics.

A person looking for entertainment may decide to read a novel because the author finds unpredictable, unusual, and yet logical ways of developing the plot or of providing provocative information. The robber in one novel is an engineering genius and outwits an electronic, computer-supervised burglar-proofing system. In another story the foreign spy, posing as a native New Yorker, is eventually exposed because he casually tells a cocktail-party companion that he waited "in line" for two hours to obtain tickets to a championship fight. Men who are trapped in a mine cave-in are rescued at the eleventh hour by the daring use of explosives. The reader, incidental to the pleasure-seeking purpose, learns from these stories that interrupting the electrical source of a computer can cause it to dysfunction; New Yorkers stand "on line" while midwesterners stand "in line"; the "fire boss" is the man in a mining crew who places and explodes the dynamite charges.

A person pursuing a hobby, meeting a professional commitment, or following a scholarly investigation will have more explicit needs that generate reading. The search might be for a chemical that can be used to aid the polishing of semiprecious stones, the list of manufactured products that contain elements of the peanut plant, the necessary components for the speaker on a stereo set, or the cultural and political factors that led to a revolt in the Ukraine.

The prospect of the unknown is one of the most enticing lures of reading and one of its major functions. As a result, written language constantly presents the reader with unfamiliar words, phrases, and concepts. However, there are degrees to which a reader may be unfamiliar with something that is encountered.

1. The reader knows the item in oral language but may not immediately recognize the written form:

She had a bad case of *pneumonia*.

When will our *victuals* be ready?

He is the *spit and image* of his father.

In these cases there is not a close graphophonic relationship between what the language user says—

$$/n\upsilon m\mathfrak{I}ny\mathfrak{d}/, \; /v\mathfrak{I}t\mathfrak{d}lz/, \; /sp\mathfrak{i}tn\mathfrak{i}m\mathfrak{d}\hat{\mathfrak{f}}/ \; —$$

and the way the items are represented in print.

2. The reader has an adequate synonym but does not recognize its meaning relationship to the text item:

He is a *laconic* person.

This is a *propitious* occasion.

A *davenport* was the only thing in the room.

In the same circumstances the reader would have referred to a *terse* person, a *fortunate and significant* occasion, and a *sofa*.

3. The reader is familiar with the use of the item in contexts other than the author's:

There was a *pregnant* pause when the speaker concluded.

Debra is a *sabra*.

The reader recognizes the first item as usually describing a woman who is going to give birth, but is not familiar with the concept of filled with meaning, which it holds here. *Cactus* is the reader's understanding of the second item; that this term is used to describe a native Israeli is unknown.

4. The reader is totally unfamiliar with the word or phrase and its related concept:

His model of how language works will be a *heuristic* tool for linguistics.

Her *mien* was fair.

What happens when the reader meets the unknown? If the author provides little evidence that the word, phrase, or concept is significant, it will probably be ignored and forgotten. If the word, phrase, or concept is significant, the author will usually need to make reference to it more than once, provide synonymous information, and use enough redundant information cues to provide the reader with opportunities to construct meaning for the concept.

There are times, of course, when the author does not provide sufficient information about a significant concept. This can happen because of poor writing on the part of the author or because the author presupposes necessary background and experience to deal with the information which the reader does not have. In either case, the reader will have difficulty comprehending the material.

Usually, however, the proficient reader can develop meaning for the unfamiliar through reading. The strategy used involves

1. Deciding that the concept is significant
2. Predicting a meaning based on the author's cues and the reader's own background information
3. Confirming or disconfirming such predictions based on additional context and gained through continued reading
4. Constructing a meaning that fits the text

There are two limitations on the reader. Firstly, many of the words and phrases with which the reader must deal are ones that exist mainly in writing, or are ones that have not been perceived by that reader in listening. This means that the reader can be unsure about their pronunciation even after having developed a workable concept for them. *Dowager, misled, parameter, compromise,* and *boatswain* are all examples of words that proficient readers can have difficulty pronouncing.

Secondly, the development of an expanded and complex concept proceeds only through a series of experiences and across time. A young child may understand that he has a brother and know the meaning of brother within the context of the family—for example, that his mother is his brother's mother. It will take a year or two longer for him to realize that he is his brother's brother. And many years and experiences might pass before he will understand *all men are brothers* as a concept that includes all women, too.

As mentioned earlier, one young reader from a large urban area, in reading a story about a series of coyote attacks on a grazing sheep herd, decided that coyotes must be a lot like wild goats. The story indicated that the coyotes were about the size of a large dog; were good fighters; could climb, and live in rocky places; and were wild. These were all things that this reader had perceived about the mountain goats housed at the city zoo and that were compatible with the needs of the story.

No reader can go beyond present information or past personal experiences. Within the context of a single reading experience the reader can simply make use of the available text cues to formulate a concept that is compatible with the story meaning and that reader's personal knowledge.

Specific Rationale

The students will be asked to write stories that contain blank, unfamiliar, or nonword slots so that they must

1. Predict what they believe should go in the text slot
2. Adjust and confirm their predictions based on additional context

The use of blank, unfamiliar, or nonsense slots allows the reader to minimize the use of graphic cues, leaving available to the readers the syntactic and semantic cueing systems. The slots must be filled with text that fits the structure of the sentence and that makes sense within the story. The objective of the lesson is to convince readers that the best way to handle unknowns within context is to concentrate on the structure and the meaning of the text as a whole.

Readers will discover that predictions can be refined and limited only as the reading continues and additional text information becomes available for confirming to occur. They will focus on making a speedy and useful prediction and then moving on. The constant refining of predictions will necessitate not rereading but rethinking. The process is one of making closer and closer semantic approximations to the text. Story meaning will not be lost by the less useful early predictions. The logic of the whole will simply be readjusted as the predictions are confirmed or disconfirmed and, therefore, refined.

The following example describes what this strategy looks like when applied to natural text during an uninterrupted reading setting. The reader, an adult with a history of reading problems, was in the very early phases of developing effective reading strategies. He was reading a story called "Bill Evers and the Tigers[1]" in which the word *baseball* occurs seven times.

The first six times that *baseball* occurred the reader read it as *basketball*. This was a most effective prediction as it reflected a close graphic relationship to the text item and maintained the grammatical function. An examination of the semantic cues in selected sentences in the text indicates that there was no information present up to this point to disconfirm the reader's initial decision.

The boys on the Tiger baseball team were excited.
Bill Evers, the baseball star, was in town.
They wanted him to write his name on a baseball.

---

[1]"Bill Evers and the Tigers," in *Readings for Taping: Reading Miscue Inventory,* ed. Yetta Goodman and Carolyn Burke (New York: The Macmillan Company, 1972).

Ben felt funny about calling a baseball star.
I'm on the Tigers baseball team.
He wanted to show the boys how to play better baseball.

However, following the sixth occurrence of *baseball*, this sentence occurred.

Then, just when Bill Evers was showing Ben the right way to hold his bat, a newspaperman came.

When the reader arrived at the word *bat*, he paused for an extended time, turned back to examine previous text, and only grudgingly produced *bat*. Five sentences further on in the text he read without miscue:

Bill Evers wrote his name on the baseball.

There were, in this whole story, only two cues to the game that was being played: the word *baseball* itself and the reference to a bat.

It is important to remember that experienced readers also meet the unfamiliar or unrecognized when they read. Sometimes the only difference between them and the less proficient reader is that their semantic problems may go undetected.

A group of university graduate students read an article that began as follows:

Recently, I spoke with a man twice my age who expressed great faith in the future of American youth: "There's nothing wrong with them that ten years, a family, mortgage and car payments won't be able to cure." He, of course, envisions millions of young troublemakers shaving their beards, dropping their hems, marching across the generation gap and acculturating in a sea of baby food, weed killer and convertible debentures.[2]

Among other questions posed following the reading, they were each asked to define *convertible debentures*. While none of these people had produced an oral miscue on this segment of text, their responses included

"I don't know."
"Payments on a car."
"Some kind of debt."
"False teeth."

Obviously, this term had proved to be unfamiliar to them, even though they were perfectly capable of applying the appropriate graphophonic rules to produce an expected pronunciation for it. Most of them, like the reader in the previous example, had also made use of individual knowledge and semantic context to develop a meaning prediction. The "false teeth" predictors had related debentures to dentures; those who arrived at debt had drawn a relationship between it and debentures; while those who produced "car payments" had combined the debt/debenture relationship with one concerning car/convertible. Because convertible debentures represents only one of a number of related examples upon which the author relies to convey his meaning in that paragraph, he supplies no additional cues to their meaning and his message may be gained even if the individual reader does not already have, or cannot develop, a fully effective meaning for them.

We can never presume to know beforehand which specific terms, knowledge, or concepts a reader will find unfamiliar or unrecognizable in some degree. We can only expect that reader to make use of available semantic context to develop progressively more effective semantic predictions.

EVALUATION

The strategy lesson for Developing Meaning through Context will benefit

1. Readers who focus on the graphophonic or syntactic systems at the expense of the semantic system; when they encounter unknown words, these students may sound out words but fail to understand their meanings.

---

[2]Roger Rapoport, "Why We Need a Generation Gap," *Look*, April 1973.

2. Readers who limit themselves to minimal use of language context within phrases or sentences but who are not making use of these strategies within the total text.
3. Readers who effectively read material within their own experiential background but who become upset when faced with reading material that contains new concepts or ideas.
4. Readers who have the background or experience to deal with new concepts in nonverbal or oral settings but who are not able to understand new concepts through reading.

Reading-Strategy Instruction

INITIATING

MATERIALS   For recognizing familiar concepts: "Something Is Missing," by Carolyn Burke and "The Blog," by Barry Sherman
For developing new concepts: "Petoskeys," by Yetta Goodman

The Blog

As Jack approached the blog, he shivered in anticipation. Sitting down on the edge of the blog, he took off his shoes and socks, and rolled up his pants legs. Then he gingerly put first one foot in the blog, then the other. Brrr: It was cold! Standing up, Jack waded to the center of the blog. His feet squished the mud on the bottom of the blog, and ripples splashed his trousers. Oh, but it was cold!

"There's nothing better on a hot day than the old wading blog," Jack thought.

BARRY SHERMAN

Something Is Missing

I was really mad. All of the _____ was missing.

It had been in the box on my desk. But not one piece of _____ was in the box now.

Who could have taken it? I had baked that _____ myself.

It was whole wheat. I had wanted to have a slice of _____ with butter and jelly for a snack.

CAROLYN BURKE

Petoskeys

THE BOY WAS LOOKING FOR PETOSKEYS.
HE WAS WALKING SLOWLY TO MAKE SURE HE WOULDN'T MISS THEM.
EACH TIME HE LOOKED, HE FOUND A NUMBER OF THEM.
PETOSKEYS ARE NOT EASY TO FIND BECAUSE THEY ARE ALMOST THE SAME COLOR AS THE SAND.
THE BOY ENJOYED LOOKING FOR THE PETOSKEYS ON THE BEACH. HIS MOTHER USED THEM IN HER WORK.
SHE WAS AN ARTIST AND MADE JEWELRY WITH THEM.
WHEN PETOSKEYS ARE POLISHED THEY TURN DEEP SHADES OF BROWN AND GRAY.
A PATTERN OF SIX-SIDED FIGURES SHOWS UP ON THEM.
PETOSKEYS ARE FOUND ONLY ON THE SHORES OF THE GREAT LAKES.

YETTA GOODMAN

The qualities that are important in the materials for this strategy lesson are the same whether they are prepared using a blank slot, as in "Something Is Missing"; a nonword slot, as in "The Blog"; or an unfamiliar-term slot, as in "Petoskeys." The cues relating to the slotted term must be scattered throughout the text, with the more general of the cues coming before those that are more specific and limiting.

This strategy lesson is most effective as an oral group experience so that individuals will become aware of the range of predictions possible and of the productive use of prediction strategies by others. The text can be produced on an overhead transparency and should be arranged so that you can expose one segment at a time.

Tell the students that they will be reading a story that has blank slots in the place of missing words or phrases, nonword slots containing nonsense items; or unfamiliar-term slots containing words or phrases (select the appropriate one), all of which they will probably not recognize. The purpose of their reading will be to discover the word, phrase, or meaning for each slot.

INTERACTING

Expose the first segment and ask the group to read silently. In situations where students may have difficulty, you may wish to read it to them aloud.

Point to the slot and ask, *What do you think this* [*blank, blog,* or *petoskey*] *means?* Write down all the suggestions on the board as the students supply them. Encourage the students to share all their predictions. Discourage students from laughing at or dismissing the unusual answers of others. Tell them that often creative thinkers come up with answers that other people may think are not plausible.

Expose the second segment and have the students read. Review the list. Cross out any earlier suggestions that *ALL* the students disconfirm. Ask for new predictions and add these to the list.

Expose and read each subsequent text segment. Cross out the items that are disconfirmed, and add new predictions to the list on the board. On a selective basis, have the students share the thinking that lead to their disconfirming and their new predictions, but do not allow this procedure to evolve into extended discussions, which slow down the pace of the lesson. Point out that individual experiences and backgrounds lead to unique predictions.

When the whole text has been read, consider all remaining prediction(s) that have been confirmed. It is entirely possible to arrive at the end of a text and be left with more than one useful prediction ("Petoskeys": rocks, shells, fossils; "Something Is Missing": bread, whole wheat cake). Demonstrate, by noting all the disconfirmed predictions on the board, that the students did make use of the progression of text cues to narrow and refine their predictions.

Allow the students time to read silently through the complete text making use of their final predictions. Help them realize that even if they are not sure of the exact meaning, they do have enough information to understand this particular story.

APPLYING

Students may work in teams of two. Each team will need two copies of a slotted story, pencils, and two sheets of paper. Independently of each other, the two students will apply the procedures established in the Interacting phase of this lesson. They will

1. Read silently each story segment
2. Generate a list of predictions to fit the meaning slot
3. Cross out and add to their prediction list as they read successive segments

When they have completed the story, they will share their prediction lists with each other, noting

1. How similar or dissimilar their predictions are
2. The text cues and personal knowledge that each one is aware of having used in the decision making

EXPANDING

ORAL LANGUAGE Two to four students may want to play the game "I Spy." One of the group chooses an object within the view of the total group, selects one identifying trait, and informs the group, "I spy something [(name a trait)]." The group members take turns asking one question each until someone identifies the object. That person selects the next object to be guessed. An optional rule may limit the guesses by time or by number.

WRITING Individual students can try their hand at writing slotted stories. They will need to

1. Select an object they feel is familiar to most of their classmates (a squirrel, an ivy plant)
2. Develop a list of traits ("a good climber," "enjoys the sun," "hardy")
3. Number the traits from most general to most specific
4. Incorporate the traits in a text

The student-author may then want to have the slotted story used in a group interaction session or by a team of two. In either case, observation of the reader predictions can be used by the author in considering any necessary rewrites.

Chapter 8

Confirming Syntactic Cues

PUNCTUATION

General Rationale

Writing is used when time and/or distance separate the producers of language from their audience.

The family recipes are set down to be passed on from generation to generation.

The diary is written so that in years to come the writer can reexamine experiences and evaluate his or her life.

The play is penned so that the playwright may focus the consciences of his or her viewers/readers on a social issue.

When the production of language is removed from the situation to which it refers, the possibilities of receiver difficulty increase:

Is the flour to be sifted before it is combined with the other dry ingredients?

Were my immediate reactions to the mishap ones of resignation as they are now, or were they ones of panic and depression?

Does the playwright side with the revolutionaries?

Because the author is usually unavailable to the reader to help in the resolution of such questions, writing has some conventions that have developed to offer redundant cueing to the reader in the process of reconstructing the message. These conventions, both structural and semantic, are directed at limiting ambiguity.

Semantic conventions include such devices as paraphrasing, the use of examples, and even direct repetition. The author may make a statement:

He was a tyrant.

Then the author defines just what it is intended to imply:

She was allowed no personal spending money. She was discouraged from developing friendships or from any activity which took her out of the house.

167

The author's statement may be explicated by example:

> Once, when the local YWCA was canvassing door to door for dollar contributions to the summer-camp program, she had to ask them to return when her husband was at home.

Newspapers, contending with space restrictions and responsible for factual reporting, have devised and popularized a whole complex of such conventions: the *wh-* questions (who, where, why, what, when); the sandwich paragraph (say it, explain it, say it again); the caption under the photograph, which is either directly repeated or closely paraphrased within the story.

Structural conventions include a standardized spelling system, spacing between words and paragraphs, justified margins, capitalization, and punctuation. Written language can and has functioned without their benefit. Early alphabetic systems made use of an undisrupted flow of capital letters and only gradually was this flow interrupted by spaces. It was not until the Middle Ages that scribes experimented with a mixture of lower- and upper-case letters. Printers, imposing their own preferred spellings on submitted manuscripts, generated a conventional spelling system.

> KANYOUREEDTHIS
> KAN YOU REED THIS
> Kan you reed this?
> Can you read this?

The employment of conventions is not a prerequisite of language usage. It is a support that is offered to the reader. Increased speed, decreased effort, focus on the message, and restriction of ambiguity, all of which benefit the reader, are paid for by the added efforts their use demands of the author.

Specific Rationale

"You just ran through a stop sign!" "Read it with feeling." "Pay attention to the punctuation marks." These and similar instructional statements have come innumerable times from teachers made uncomfortable by some student's oral-reading rendition. There is, within these directions, the presupposition that the reader is simply not attending to a key feature of print: that if the punctuation is sighted, the voice then takes on the necessary inflection, or the pause is inserted.

There are problems with such an assumption. Punctuation, like all conventions, is not a basic cueing system of language; it is intended only as redundant information. Not only can the language user function without it, but that language user must already be making syntactic and semantic decisions for punctuation marks to provide usable information.

The reader must be committed to second-guessing the author: to constructing the message as it is assumed the author chose to construct it. Read the following story segment and complete the final sentence:

> Ben was only five years old
> and he had already been missing
> for more than three hours. Where

Whether you chose to generate a question such as "[Where] would he be likely to wander?" or you decided on a statement such as "[Where] the ground was shaded from the sun, it was already quite chilly," your basic decision concerning the intonation pattern for that sentence was made as you processed the word *Where*. Only as you would continue along the fourth line of text were you able to confirm or disconfirm your original prediction, with the concluding period or question mark acting as the last of the confirmation points.

Instances in which punctuation marks are said to be inserted or shifted by the reader are a further documentation of the generative role that readers take:

> It was a very exciting occasion. People were spread all over the house. The kids ran madly
> through the back yard.[1] While the men congregated in the living room,[2] the women were examining the newly decorated den.

---

[1] Period omitted.

[2] Period substituted for the comma.

For these changes to be taking place, the reader has to be functioning as a decision maker, not passively waiting for the punctuation to announce the end of a structure. An apparent disregard of punctuation is a symptom of a problem that the reader has already experienced. It is not the problem itself.

Punctuation marks always provide cues that are redundant of information otherwise available within the language, and they operate mainly to confirm or disconfirm decisions already made.

EVALUATION

The strategy lesson for Punctuation will benefit

1. Readers who limit themselves to minimal use of language context in phrases or sentences but who are not making use of these strategies within the total text. They produce miscues that result in sentences that are only partially acceptable grammatically and semantically.
2. Readers who consistently produce many intonation-related miscues.

Reading-Strategy Instruction

INITIATING

MATERIALS The material selected or developed for this strategy lesson needs to be relatively brief, direct in its message, and not overly complex in structure. Single-concept informational pieces—an explanation of how last names evolved, a description of the seasonal cycles of a tulip bulb, or a report on a day in the life of a veterinarian—work well, as will folktales and traditional tales that make use of a simple plot, clearly delineated events, and repetitive phrasing.

Preparation of the material involves producing a version typed entirely in capital letters and without punctuation. All other written conventions are maintained without change.

The reader is presented with the material and directed (a) to read it orally into a tape recorder so that it makes sense and (b) to be prepared to discuss what has been read.

Once the reading begins, it must proceed without interruption. There are some effects that this punctuation-free text can be expected to have upon the reader:

1. Reading speed will be slowed.
2. It will become necessary for the reader to rethink and reread at points where predictions do not work out.
3. If the author is a consistent writer, the reader will become more effective at predicting as the text progresses.

INTERACTING

When the reader has concluded, the teacher may return to hear the student's discussion of what was read. Or the student may be asked to provide that information on the recording. The student then plays back the recording, following the tape while reading the printed version of the story.

As the students listen to their own readings, they should be helped, through questioning, to

1. Become more aware of the active role played by the reader while reading
2. Develop intuitive knowledge of those structural points where the reader is faced with alternate available predictions
3. Recognize punctuation as a confirmation of reader-made decisions
4. Value correction as a confirmation strategy

APPLYING

Students work in teams of two. Each member must produce a piece of writing (either informational or fictional) with their team member as the intended audience. They then exchange writings and tape-record their reading of each other's material. The student-author is to provide no aid to the reader.

Following the reading, each author may use the taped reading to reexamine the work and then edit on the basis of observed reader difficulty. This will provide the authors with firsthand evidence of the support system that their use of conventions can offer the reader. It should also make them better predictors of other authors' use of written conventions.

EXPANDING

LANGUAGE Have students collect punctuation conventions that are unusual to them. These can be kept in an individual or class notebook. A chart such as the following may be developed, and added to, for each punctuation as additional examples are found.

Punctuation (In complete phrase or sentence)	Where Found	What It Means	What It's Called
Harry repeated the magic words to himself—and disappeared.	Book-Dragon Takes a Wife	separates one part from the other	dash
h _____	magazines	a dirty word and something is left out	dashes

REPEATED SUBSTITUTIONS

General Rationale

Sometimes a reader will develop a persistent relationship between selected sets of words or phrases. Upon encountering one of these items, the reader is apt to produce the associated item rather than the expected response. Teachers probably view this occurrence as one of the most prevalent and persistent encountered in their classrooms and the mark of a reader experiencing problems. Such repeated substitutions produce miscue sequences like the following:

She was a small yellow *the* canary, hanging very still in the air. Her wings were folded quietly *cardinal* at her sides. She could stay that way because nothing has any weight in space. Before I recovered from the surprise of seeing a *the cardinal* canary in our space station, she did a kind of backward loop. No earthbound *cardinal* canary could have done it.

The most traditional explanation given for the occurrence of repeated substitutions is that the reader is not attending to the graphic display. It is assumed that if only the reader would or could examine the print more carefully, the substitution would not occur. The instructional procedures that are generated out of this theoretical assumption are designed to focus the reader's attention upon key graphic differences between items:

Doll and *ball* are to be identified by attending to the fact that the stick comes before the circle in forming a manuscript *b* as opposed to the sequence of circle/stick for *d*.

Was is to be distinguished from *saw* by attending to the initial letter of each word and associating this letter with the appropriate sound.

Miss and *Mrs.* are to be handled by noting their medial letter variations (*i* as opposed to *r*, and the doubling of the *s*).

Sometimes readers who exhibit these confusions are labeled as having some perceptual disease.

Repeated substitutions tend to be looked upon as perceptual problems best handled by intensifying the reader's attention to letter shape and sequence. However, our view of reading, based on some accompanying linguistic phenomena, causes us to question this interpretation. For example:

1. Results from miscue analysis have shown that associated words or phrases are not *consistently* substituted by any reader in different text settings. There will be instances when such words or phrases are produced as expected, and still others when they are involved in miscues quite different from their usual associated response.

2. No reader demonstrates a persistent and consistent problem with any specific letters other than the specific associated pairs. The reader who seems unable to discriminate between *doll* and *ball* will not have the problem spill over to *all* other words beginning with *d* or *b*.

3. There are still other repeated substitutions that bear little graphic relationship to each other, such as the substitution of *wolf* for *coyote*.

If we place the significance for such occurrences wholly on the reader's perception of the graphic display, we will be forced to conclude that the readers who get involved in these associations suffer from metaphoric shorts in their graphic circuitry: that there are times when currents flow unobstructed from graphic perception to output and others in which the flow is either prohibited or distorted.

If, however, we view the miscues in relationship to the syntactic and the semantic systems as well as the graphophonic system, a variation in the quality of individual repeated substitutions is discernible.

The Grid of Repeated Substitutions categorizes selected reader miscues according to (a) the language systems involved within them and (b) the effectiveness of those miscues within the text. (An explanation of the latter follows.)

GRID OF REPEATED SUBSTITUTIONS

	High Quality	Low Quality
Syntactic	a:the proper name:proper name no:oh:go	typical:typeical:tropical saw:was said:and when:then
Semantic	baseball:basketball canary:cardinal coyote:wolf she:he Mrs.:Miss	happy:birthday come:here
Graphophonic		at:it down:brown on:no

NOTE   The quality of any particular repeated substitution depends on the surrounding context and the application of self-correcting strategies.

A general inspection of the grid will establish that these repeated-substitute pairs do have a strong tendency to have high graphic similarity. Examination will indicate that for any individual reader these miscues tend to have a closer graphic relationship than will the rest of that reader's miscues (an argument to add to the three already given in countering the notion that such miscues are simply perceptual; see page 171).

Miscue research demonstrates that the largest percentage of repeated-substitution miscues serve grammatically as function words (noun determiners, clause and phrase markers, among others) and that the reader, in making the repeated substitutions, almost always maintains grammatical function.

This information introduces the involvement of the syntactic language system into the generation of repeated substitutions. Function words serve a basically structural role within the context of language. They announce the syntactic pattern that the phrase, sentence, paragraph, or text is taking. Determiners announce the presence of a noun phrase, and clause and phrase markers establish the relationships between objects and actions. Although all these words carry some semantic information in the text, this is much less prominent than the syntactic information that they provide.

To establish a feeling for the syntactic role these words play, read the following paragraph supplying appropriate function words for the blanks:

> While we are quite often oblivious _____ our environment, nature can periodically intrude upon our consciousness _____ a most startling manner. Yesterday I was working at my desk _____ I gradually became aware of thunder _____ rain. However, I continued to work, letting the weather serve only _____ background to my efforts. Gradually, almost imperceptibly, the noise increased. Just as gradually, and without conscious decision, I was drawn away from my work _____ the window where I became _____ spellbound witness to a magnificently violent hailstorm.

The task should have been a relatively easy one. You might have found yourself with the word already formulated in your mind before arriving at the blank; or perhaps you handled the blank and the whole chunk of sentence following it as a single unit. Even though the blank intruded on your attention more than a filled slot would have done, you still probably focused your interest on context-laden items like *oblivious, environment, thunder, weather, witness, hailstorm*. It is doubtful that anyone reading this passage would bother to try out available alternatives—that is, "[*to* /*of* /*concerning*] our environment"; "[*and* /*when*] I gradually became aware"; "[*a* /*the*] spellbound witness"; rather, the reader simply proceeds using the first effective slot filler considered. Not much changes in this process when the blanks are filled with function words. The reader's attention is focused on the meaning units while the function words unobtrusively organize the setting.

Since it is natural for the reader's attention to be drawn away from the function word, it becomes predictable that a greater percentage of miscues will occur at these pivotal points in text than at others.

High-quality syntactic. Let us examine three examples of repeated substitutions that have high syntactic quality. These miscues can often be generated by efficient readers.

The *a:the* substitution is the most common repeated substitution, generated even by highly efficient readers of all ages. We learn from the numerous contexts in which these two words are substituted that they frequently operate as semantic synonyms:

> It was Dick's last day in Harbor City. He was going home on the **a** train.
>
> We waited in silence while he held Claribel against his ear, trying to hear **the** a heartbeat.
>
> You just happen to do your studying in the **a** room where your baby brother is sleeping, that's all.
>
> At the station Mr. Barnaby rushed us into **a** the studio and pushed **the** a crib for Andrew under one of the big cameras.

Although there are shifts of meaning in the following examples, they either fit unobtrusively into the story or cause such minor changes in meaning that the reader tends to self-correct silently or ignore the shift in favor of more significant information:

May we take pictures and send them to *a* the contest?

They took pictures of *a* the father in the garden.

I guess *the* a fellow has to work off steam once in a while.

In the following examples the miscue disrupts the syntactic acceptability of the sentence. While the syntactic cues are available to predict the presence of a noun phrase, prior to the occurrence of the determiner there are no semantic cues available to predict between *the* or *a*.

One day Penny rushed up *the* front steps . . .

They went to the floor where *the* handbags were.

Philosophical: showing calmness and courage in *the* face of ill fortune.

There are but rare instances when semantic cues precede the occurrence of *the* or *a*.

Dick looked in *all the* windows.

The examples we have discussed indicate that although the grammatical slot for the determiner function is quite predictable syntactically, it is not nearly so predictable semantically and will therefore always be involved in the miscues of even the most efficient of readers.

When a reader encounters an unfamiliar or unrecognized name within a text, the most significant function of that name is to consistently signal the actions, words, and thoughts of a specific character. Sometimes the only additional information available comes from the presence of *she* or *he* to mark the gender of the character.

In these settings one of the most effective strategies that readers adopt is to choose and consistently apply an alternative name—whether it represents a real name that shares graphic similarities with the text item, or an attempt at a phonemic reproduction. (See the strategy lesson "Nouns as Names for People," in chapter 5.)

Judy Juby is my oldest friend. He lives in Los Cordovas where the schoolhouse is.

I first saw *Clardo* Clarabel when I was working in my office.

We had just never had any pets until *Steven Awsom* Sven Olsen decided he wanted one.

Repeated *no:oh* substitutions would, on first appearance, seem to support the graphic-perception argument and to violate the role of syntactic features, which we have been building, since these two words do not fill the same grammatical function slot. However, a closer look at the text of some preprimers will supply a syntactic relationship of a slightly different nature:

No, no, no.   Oh, oh, oh.
No, Dick, no.   Oh, Dick, oh.
"No, Polly!" she said.   "Oh, Polly!" she said.
"No," said the man.   "Oh," said the man.

Clearly, in these syntactic units the verb and the negative can interchangeably fill the same surface structure position. With the very generalized story lines, heavily dependent on pictures, the meaning of the text will frequently be unchanged.

This combination of weak semantic structure and stilted syntax makes it possible for yet another word to form a triumvirate of repeated substitutions in this instance:

No, no, no.   Oh, oh, oh.   Go, go, go.
No, Dick, no.   Oh, Dick, oh.   Go, Dick, go.
"No, Polly!" she said. "Oh, Polly!" she said. "Go, Polly!" she said.
"No," said the man.   "Oh," said the man.   "Go," said the man.

There are language instances, then, when few semantic constraints are available to interact with compatible syntactic features and graphic similarity to minimize the probability of repeated-substitution miscues for efficient readers. These are miscues that seldom occur in material representing more natural language.

Low-quality syntactic. Let us now explore some settings in which a less effective use of the syntactic system is involved in the generation of repeated substitutions. Essentially these substitutions break down into two groups:

1. Those in which the syntactic slot is maintained without regard for semantic cues
2. Those in which the immediate syntactic cues supporting the miscue are not confirmed by the larger structure

In the first instance the reader is much like the person who is humming a tune but has forgotten the lyric. What is produced sounds like language but does not make sense. In a story centered around the relative intelligence of a baby brother, the word *typical* occurs thirteen times. Story contexts such as the following clearly build the meaning of *average* or *everyday*:

. . . a pretty good brother . . . As little brothers go.

He'd do just as good as anyone else his age.

A baby like everyone else's baby.

All babies cry . . . He wouldn't be typical if he didn't cry sometimes.

Many young readers encountering *typical* do not recognize it, in many cases choosing instead to say either *typeical* or *tropical* for each text occurrence. Although these two responses demonstrate a consideration of both graphophonic and syntactic cues, they do not reflect semantic considerations.

The repeated substitutions below, which illustrate the second category of low-quality syntactic substitutions, fit this pattern of the reader's use of syntactic structuring without regard for meaning. The available graphophonic, syntactic, and semantic cues prior to or closely surrounding the miscue are consistent with the prediction. However, when additional syntax and meaning indicate the need for disconfirming the earlier prediction and self-correcting, the readers do not choose this strategy:

At last Dick *saw* (was) a large policeman.   He rushed up to him and said, "Please will you help me?"

"I see a monkey," said / *and* Ted.

But when Ted came to the fair / *then* a little boy ran up to him.

For the less efficient readers, most repeated-substitution miscues fall in this low-quality syntactic category. These readers have available semantic cues that signal the ineffectiveness of the repeated substitution; however, they reject these cues in favor of syntactic and graphophonic cues.

High-quality semantic. There is, however, a category of repeated substitutions in which the reader does make use of the semantic system. In these instances there tends to be a certain amount of "play" in the semantic cues: some ambiguity of meaning that allows meaningful alternative responses.

As presented in the previous chapter, *Bill Evers and the Tigers* is a story about boys on a baseball team who meet a professional player who gives them playing tips. The word *baseball* appears seven times, and there are a number of references to the game:

"team"
"watched his games on TV"
"could play ball"
"a baseball star"
"to write his name on a baseball"
"go on with the game"

Yet except for the key word *baseball*, all the contextual cues, except the second to the last one, are general enough to refer also to football or basketball.

It is something more than coincidence, then, when three very different readers (an eight-year-old in California, an eleven-year-old bilingual in Arizona, and a twenty-three-year-old in Indiana) all read *basketball* in place of *baseball* the first six times the word appears. These readers stopped to assess their choices when, eight lines from the end of the story, they encountered the sentence "Then, just when Bill Evers was showing Ben the right way to hold his bat, a newspaperman came." Upon arriving at the word *bat*, they all paused in their reading, turned back through the text to hunt for the word *baseball*, and then went on to read *baseball* in its final text appearance two lines before the end of the story.

In another story about a pet bird on a space station, a dozen or more readers, ranging in ages from seven and a half to fourteen produced *cardinal* for *canary* each of the six times that word appeared. Their only semantic cue that *cardinal* might not be appropriate was one early reference to the bird's yellow color.

In reading "Sheep Dog," the story about a sheep dog's efforts to save a flock from the attacks of coyotes, a group of somewhat older youngsters chose to read *wolf* for *coyote*. Within the context of this story there were no semantic cues disruptive to the reader's use of *wolf*.

Very similar semantic circumstances can exist for *she:he* and *Mrs.:Miss*. Animals are the major characters in any number of stories written for young children. Their gender, in many cases, is irrelevant to the story. With neutral names such as Kitten Jones, Pepper, or Yellow Bird, the only reason for assigning gender is the need to use either the masculine or feminine pronoun for purposes of word repetition:

Kitten had been playing in the rose vines.

he
Now she walked over to the camera.

Pepper [a dog] saw Jimmy ride to a house and stop.

she
He saw Jack stop, too.

Such miscues are less likely to occur if the pronoun refers to a male or female person who has already been introduced with appropriate cues about gender.

A text will usually have pronoun cues available to the reader in determining *Mr.:Mrs.* / *Miss* substitutions, but *Mrs.:Miss* alternatives are frequently semantically ambiguous especially when no reference or significance is placed on the character's family relationships:

Miss
One morning old Mrs. Duck said, "What a good day for a walk!"

Mrs.
We want to surprise Miss Parks [the teacher].

She will come in soon.

In semantically ambiguous settings many young readers fall back on their own personal experiences, thus calling an animal *he* or *she* depending upon their own or friends' pets, or tending initially to address a female teacher by *Miss* or *Mrs.* depending on the marriage status of their last female teacher.

There is, then, a grouping of repeated substitutions in which the text supplies semantic support for the reader's choice. There actually are instances—as with the *coyote:wolf* substitution—when the reader's consideration for the semantic system overrides graphophonic concerns.

Low-quality semantic. Yet a second variety of semantic repeated substitutions is generated by experiences prior to the immediate reading. Our language is filled with lexical items that change their meaning and grammatical function on the basis of changed context:

The *bear* went over the mountain.

Bear with me for one more minute.

I *saw* what you did.

We will cut the wood with a *saw*.

Old Mrs. *Duck* went for a walk.

Duck when someone throws something at you.

Young language users accept these multiple structure uses as a natural function of the process. However, in a few rare instances a reader can develop a strong specific meaning relationship that is allowed to override considerations of both syntax and the meaning. *Happy Birthday* is a phrase that some young readers find so semantically powerful that they are apt to produce such miscues as the following:

He is called Happy ~~Joe~~. *Birthday*

On his *happy* birthday Franklin woke up early.

The appeal of *Happy Birthday* probably grows out of children's natural interest in growing up and in the social pleasures attached to this holiday.

A second semantic repeated substitution, however, is closely tied to instructional procedures that stress word-level-vocabulary development and that make use of repetition. For the sake of vocabulary practice, particular items are repeated a number of times across the stories in a reading series. While the instructional intent is to make such items (*here* and *come* in the following example) *sight* words for the reader, the actual result can be to build a strong semantic relationship between them. The reader will then be found producing the following kinds of phrase-level repeated substitutions:

Come ~~Here~~ is my blue airplane.

Here ~~Come~~ and look in here.

Here ~~Come~~ with me.

"*Here* ~~Come~~ out here," said Jimmy.

These miscues also become inconsequential as readers work with material of greater literary quality.

Low-quality graphophonic. The miscues clustered in the final box of the grid seem to have little linguistic relationship to the text other than a graphic one:

Look *it* at my toy train.

See it go.

Look *it* at my little train go.

Here I go *brown* down.

Come, Sue.

Come *brown brown brown* down, down, down.

Jeff said, "Come *no* on, Mother."

Daddy said, "*On* No. It is not the picnic."

"*On* No," said Daddy.

These miscues represent a very small portion of the repeated substitutions made, and are produced almost exclusively by young readers and generally in material like the above which is linguistically impoverished. Older readers who are having significant problems with reading rarely make miscues of this type, as examination of their repeated miscues indicates. Over time, all readers, effective and ineffective, seem to become more sensitive to the constraints of language cues. This sensitivity allows them to make higher quality reading predictions initially or to disconfirm and self-correct.

We evaluate repeated substitutions by the same criteria we use to evaluate all miscues: Does the structure in which the miscue occurs sound like language? Does it make sense? When such questions are asked, it becomes clear that some repeated substitutions are of high quality. These kinds of miscues should cause no concern and should not be corrected by teachers; nor should they become the focus of reading instruction. The great majority of repeated substitutions are influenced by syntactic and semantic cues. However, when semantic cues are ignored, syntactic constraints coupled with close graphic relationships generate the greatest percentage of low-quality repeated substitutions. Repeated substitutions are rarely generated out of an isolated application of graphic cues.

Following are some additional repeated substitutions that readers have made. Consider each example in light of the possible involvement of the semantic, syntactic, and graphophonic systems and use this information to place it appropriately on the Grid of Repeated Substitutions:

I want to go back to the *farm* fair. This is the last day of *farm* fair week.

Mary said, "I think Mrs. *Brooks* Brush will be glad to live there too." Everyone laughed. Mrs. *Brooks* Brush was Mary's cat.

The children met *Grunts* Gus as soon as they got off the train. "That's *Grunts* Gus," smiled Aunt Betty. Gus was a tall, sad-looking man with a mouth that turned down at each corner.

There was a swing in a big tree too. "I like the *switch* swing," said George.

"I *wash* wish I could go, Father." Ted's father said, "I *wash* wish we could all go."

Run Run Run Run Run Ride, Pepper. Ride, Sue. Ride! Ride! Ride!

I am *my* new in this house, and oh, I am *my* not happy!"

"This boy would like a flowered handbag *from* for his mother," said Aunt Betty. Then he thought, "I have looked at the toys *from* for a long time."

He saw the spring flowers. He saw *was* the green trees. Then he saw *was* the man.

REPEATED SUBSTITUTIONS: STRATEGY-LESSON PLAN

Specific Rationale

Repeated substitutions that disrupt meaning vary in terms of their linguistic quality. The relationship that readers form between pairs of items has to do with the varying involvement of cues from the three language systems. Individual repeated substitutions will be more or less disruptive to the meaning of the text.

Just as these miscues vary in quality, there are also a variety of circumstances that encourage the formulation of graphophonic and syntactic substitutions. They may result from a combination of instruction, text, and reader strategies.

Conditions generating low-quality repeated substitutions. When instruction focuses on the word as the key language unit, the cues provided by the syntactic and semantic systems are devalued by the reader. With attention focused on the word, graphic contrasts become the main source of information. The reader associates *look* with the two *o*'s, *my* with the *y*, and *there* with the initial *th*. This system *seems* to function adequately until additional vocabulary items, such as *book*, *may*, or *three*, which contrast minimally, are introduced.

It is clear that readers perceive the graphic similarity between the two items—otherwise they would not have a tendency to substitute one for the other. However, what is less clear is that they are not lacking in their ability to recognize fine perceptual differences between *b* and *l*, between *my* and *m-y*, and between *ere* and *ree*. If this were actually the case, their problem would spread like wildfire to other graphically related items. They would be awash in a sea of undiscriminated words. Their problems would not be limited to a relatively few pairs.

Problems with minimal contrasts are not related just to children or to reading. All of us are susceptible to such confusions. A medium-priced car will closely follow the body lines of a luxury model, and many of us will find the two difficult or impossible to distinguish as they pass us on the road. How many of us can distinguish, on the basis of a sight examination alone, between a stick of butter and one of margarine, or between a Paris original and its copy? Our solution, in these settings, is not to intensify our visual scrutiny of outward appearances but to vary the focus that our examination of the objects in question takes. When you raise the hoods on the two cars, will one have a more powerful engine? Will the butter taste sweeter or richer than the margarine? Will the material feel finer and the seams be more finished on the Paris original?

In such nonlanguage settings we do not expect a single cueing source to carry the total weight of the information processing. We seek information from alternative sources in order to make our distinctions. It is not that there are not fine distinctions available within a single system—the recessing of a rear window, the texture and melting point of the butter, a depth of tone in the color of the cloth. But limiting ourselves to these minimal contrasts is uneconomical and increases the chances of error when more rapidly applied and obviously significant cues are available from other sources.

Likewise, when readers narrow their information processing to graphic cues, they increase their encounters with minimal contrasts and enhance their opportunities to make disruptive predictions. The more systems that are considered in the decision-making process, the fewer will be the possible minimal-contrast pairs available and the more varied the information cues available.

| | Minimal Contrasts | | |
Items	Graphic	Syntactic	Semantic
book:look	yes	no	no
my:may	yes	no	no
there:three	yes	no	no

Insisting on making one system carry the total burden of the process can actually strain the use of that system. The reader who has a repeated substitution between *book* and *look* is not in need of instruction that provides more practice with the sounds related to *b* or *l* nor is the reader failing to attend to initial consonants. Instead, the reader is simply placing too much stress on the graphic system. This overuse makes the graphophonic system which has the least discriminating cues the focal point of the decision-making process.

Some readers do take a slightly more expanded view of reading and attend to short sequences of words. They, like the producers of graphophonic repeated substitutions, focus on the word as the significant language-processing unit. However, they consider the word in relationship to the immediate, preceding, and following text. It is as if they had a keyhold view of the sentence, seeing section by section as they shift their visual focus through the opening.

This slightly increased focus provides for the inclusion of some limited grammatical cues as these readers predict so that their repeated substitutions tend to have a minimal contrast syntactically as well as graphically. But their view is seldom broad enough to pick up syntactic alternatives; therefore, their substitutions produce many partially acceptable structures. Of course, their perspective is much too narrow to admit semantic relationships.

| | Minimal Contrasts | | |
Items	Graphic	Syntactic	Semantic
for the school: from the school	yes	yes	no
when guests came: then guests come	yes	yes	no
but then who would: but then who could	yes	yes	no

As noted earlier, the reader's failure to take syntactic and semantic information into account can also be encouraged by the reading material. The reader will be forced back to relying on graphic cues and snatches of syntactic structure if the material has hard-to-predict or unnatural structures or deals with information irrelevant to or beyond the knowledge and understanding of the reader.

Selecting or writing strategy lessons. The student must be encouraged to attend to meaning and to place high value on the semantic cues that the text offers. To do so the amount of text that the reader considers must be increased. The control of three factors will help this expansion to occur naturally. First, the text should have strong experiential relationships for readers. It should be within their background of experience, and it should be important to them. (There are many things for which we have experience but no real interest.) Second, the items involved in the repeated substitution should be placed in unambiguous syntactic and semantic structures. The text structure should not encourage possible substitution.

Third, the items from the repeated-substitution pair should not be introduced in close proximity to each other within the text. In some instances only one of the pair might appear in any single text. The reader's attention should be drawn away from any minimal distinctions (such as high graphic similarity) between the two and should be focused, instead, on the distinctive semantic and syntactic features of each.

EVALUATION

The strategy lesson for Repeated Substitutions will benefit students who repeatedly substitute one item or phrase for another across multiple text settings, with little regard for semantic acceptability.

SPECIAL NOTE   Repeated substitutions of high quality should not become the focus for instruction. If they are generated because of ambiguous semantic structure and/or are not maintained across various text selections, they simply represent an example of the minimal, nondisruptive changes that all readers will make. Such repeated substitutions are not indicators of any reader problem.

Nor should an attempt be made to develop lessons for all of the low-quality repeated-substitution pairs that any reader may have. It must be remembered that the focus is not on specific vocabulary items but on the limited use of semantic and syntactic cueing systems, which places undue stress upon the graphic system. As experiences with selected repeated-substitution pairs encourage an increased focus on meaning, the occurrence of all repeated substitutions will begin to diminish.

Reading-Strategy Instruction

INITIATING

MATERIALS   "I Had a Party," by Valerie Gelfat (*bought*)
"Camping," by Dorothy Watson (*bought/brought*)
"The Trip around Cape Horn," by Barry Sherman (*through*)
"The Argument," by Debra Goodman (*through/thought*)

I Had a Party!

I had a party!
I went to the store,
I bought lots of candy,
and cookies galore.

I bought fancy napkins,
I bought paper cups,
I bought Alka-Seltzer,
For those with hiccups.

I bought a big cake
And pink lemonade,
I got out my money,
and the grocer was paid!

I bought all these goodies,
and took them on home,
"Happy Birthday to me."
(That's the end of this poem.)

VALERIE GELFAT

Camping

Rusty was at camp. He would be there for three weeks. He loved going to camp. He had carefully planned the things that he would bring. He brought with him all the things he knew would help make camp fun. He brought his old sleeping bag. It was really warm and cozy for those cold nights when all the kids would backpack into the mountains for three or four days. He brought his beautiful guitar. His mother used to play it. Rusty had been really popular at camp last year because he could play so well. He would always play at the evening camp fires. But the thing he brought to camp which he knew would help him have the best time of all was his scuba-diving equipment.

Rusty had carefully looked over the list the camp had sent him to see that he had everything he would need. He only had to go to the store to buy one thing. He had left the batteries in his flashlight last year, and the acid ran out and rusted the flashlight. So he went to the store and bought the best flashlight they had. He also bought enough batteries at the store to last all summer.

Now Rusty was at camp and would have many adventures with the sleeping bag, the guitar, the scuba-diving equipment, and the flashlight that he had brought with him.

DOROTHY WATSON

The Trip around Cape Horn

It is hard to understand what it was like to take a trip on the great wooden sailing ships of the past. Today, ships have powerful engines that can move them through even the roughest seas. A long time ago, ships were made of wood and had only the wind blowing against canvas sails to push them through the water.

In those days, one of the hardest trips to make was the trip around the southern tip of South America from the Atlantic Ocean to the Pacific Ocean. This trip around Cape Horn was called "Rounding the Cape," and it was very dangerous. Many ships were lost at sea and on the rocks. And many people died. But the ships had to get through. Today, ships don't have to go anywhere near Cape Horn to get from the Atlantic to the Pacific or from the Pacific to the Atlantic. Today, ships sail peacefully through the Panama Canal. But in the days of the sailing ships, it was another story.

First, a ship would try to cross from the Atlantic to the Pacific around the Cape itself. At the place where the cool waters of the Atlantic Ocean meet the ice-cold waters of the Antarctic Ocean, there would be cold weather and fog and very high waves. If the people on the ships looked to the north they would see the low hills of Tierra del Fuego, the southern tip of South America. If they looked to the south, they would see open ocean. Beyond the open ocean to the south was Antarctica, covered with snow and ice all year 'round.

As the ships would try to sail west toward the Pacific Ocean, they would meet terrible storms. These storms would push the ocean waves higher and higher, until they were as tall as the masts of the ships. Imagine looking up at a wave taller than the highest mast of the ship! When such waves hit a ship, they would roll it back and forth in a terrible way. There would be wind and rain and snow and sleet. Sometimes, the weather would be so bad that ships would have to turn back.

Ships that turned back because of weather could try another route, the dangerous trip through the waters and rocks of the narrow Strait of Magellan. The sailors who passed through the strait would see the wrecks of ships that had crashed on the rocks. And if a ship made it through to the very end of the Strait of Magellan, it had to pass the point where the waters of the Atlantic Ocean meet the waters of the Pacific Ocean. Can you imagine the kinds of waves that a ship would have to pass through? At the end of the Strait of Magellan, the giant waves of the Pacific rolling in toward the east meet the choppy waters of the Atlantic moving toward the west. A wooden sailing ship caught in this kind of water would be in for a rough time. It was so rough that captains would order their sailors to tie themselves to the ship. All openings on the ship would be closed. Then, the ship would head into the waves. Many ships never made it.

But if a ship was lucky enough to pass that dangerous spot, and reach the Pacific Ocean without sinking, the waves would get smaller until the ocean was peaceful again. Then, as the ship sailed northward, the sun would shine, the water would be blue and peaceful again, and everyone could relax. You can be sure that everyone who lived through a "passage around the Horn" had a story to tell when he reached San Francisco or Hawaii.

BARRY SHERMAN

The Argument

Richard and Sean were through with their bath. They both stood wrapped up in towels feeling very clean. They were leaning over the edge of the bathtub, watching the water flowing down the drain.

"I wonder where the water goes," Richard said.

"If I was the size of a small mouse," said Sean, "I would put on a mask and an oxygen tank and jump down the drain. Then I could take a ride through the pipes and find out where that water is going."

The two boys walked into the kitchen. And Richard got the cookies, while Sean poured the milk.

"Well," Richard said, "if I was a mosquito, I'd fly right into your body, through your nose, and I'd bite you on the inside of your head!"

"Oh, yeah?" Sean said. "Well, if I was a germ, I'd hide in your milk, and you'd drink me and I'd go swimming through all your blood vessels and poison you on the way!"

"You would, would you?" Richard demanded, looking at his milk fearfully. "Well, if I was a—if I was a—" Richard thought and thought, but he couldn't think of anything smaller than a germ. "You just wait!" he shouted as he ran out of the kitchen and into the living room.

"Momma," he asked, "what's smaller than a germ?"

"Hmmm," Momma said, "everything on earth is made of tiny, tiny things called molecules. If the molecules are very close together, the thing is hard like a rock. If the molecules are farther apart, the thing is liquid like milk. And if the molecules are very far apart, the thing is a gas like the air. Molecules are so small you can't even see them when you look with a microscope."

Richard wrinkled up his nose and thought about what his mother had said. Then he asked, "What do molecules do?"

"What do they do?" his mother said. "Well, they move around. Sometimes they bump into each other and float off in another direction."

Richard laughed and ran back to the kitchen. "If I was a molecule," he shouted, "I'd float right through your body and bump into everything, and you couldn't even see me!"

"If you were a molecule," Sean said seriously, "I don't think I'd feel you."

Richard yawned just as their father came in and said it was time for bed. He picked up both boys at the same time and carried them into their bedroom. He tossed Richard into the top bunk and dropped Sean into the bottom bunk. And he turned off the light as he left.

"If I was a beam of light," said Sean in a very sleepy voice, "I'd peep through the keyhole and watch you sleeping."

Richard didn't say anything, because he was fast asleep.

DEBRA GOODMAN

The specific sets of repeated substitutions that individual students develop are dependent on their unique encounters with print. For this reason relevant strategy lessons will often be conducted with individual students.

Preparation of materials constitutes the most important aspect of this strategy lesson. Select, from among the sets of repeated pairs that the particular student generates, those which you can comfortably manipulate in writing text or for which you have appropriate materials. Remember that the specific examples with which you deal are not important. What is important is that you will have available several appropriate selections. Once this strategy is initiated, it must be maintained over an extended period of time. Low-quality repeated substitutions are a symptom of a reader's preoccupation with word-level graphic cues. Such miscues can be expected to fade only gradually.

The first piece of each set of materials to present to the reader should include only one of the item pairs: for example, *bought* in "I Had a Party!" and *through* in "The Trip around Cape Horn." In both of these stories the initial occurrence of the key item is preceded by strong semantic support. A reader could predict appropriately on the basis of context if this were a selected-slotting procedure.

> I went to the store.
> I _____ lots of candy . . .

> Today, ships have powerful engines that can move them _____ even the roughest seas.

Also, the particular lexical meaning initially established for the item is maintained throughout the material.

The second piece to present to the reader includes both of the repeated substitutions, but a careful distance is maintained between them. For example, in "Camping" (*bought*/*brought*) *brought* is introduced first, with both semantic (*bring*) and syntactic (*with him*) constraints:

> Rusty was at camp. He would be there for three weeks. He loved going to camp. He had carefully planned *the things that he would bring*. He _____ *with him*. . . .

Bought is then introduced in the second paragraph, again preceded by appropriate semantic cues:

> He only had to *go to the store to buy* one thing. . . .
> So he *went to the store* and _____ . . .

Now, examine "The Argument" and identify the syntactic and semantic constraints that are intended to aid in the prediction of *thought* and *through*.

The selections are representations of the text structuring that will support readers' increased use of semantic cueing and larger syntactic patterns. You will need to have multiple selections available at each of these stages.

INTERACTING

Repeated-substitution lessons reflect one clear instance where the teacher's purposes should vary from the learners'. Neither the teacher nor the materials should call attention to the specific items around which the lesson is built. The whole purpose of these experiences is to demonstrate to students that items are better handled when readers' attention is focused elsewhere. An instructional focus for the initial *bought*/*brought* lesson is outlined below.

1. *What are some reasons you can think of for having a party?*
   Accumulate a list on the chalkboard.
2. *What different kinds of things might you like to do at each of these parties?*
   Add to your chalkboard list. Examples include:

HALLOWEEN	BIRTHDAY	VALENTINE'S DAY
Wear costumes	Have cake and ice cream	Exchange cards
Have a costume parade	Give presents	Have punch and cookies
Have a haunted house	Play games	Play games
Read scary stories		

3. Have each student select one of the listed parties to think about. Have them make out a shopping list of things that they would need to buy for the party.
4. Then provide the students with copies of "I Had a Party!" and explain that it tells what someone else had to buy for a party. They should read the poem silently, and then you will discuss their party and the things that they plan to do there. Following the discussion, the poem may be read aloud once (by an individual or group) to culminate the session.

APPLYING

In each instance a selection to be read must be chosen on the basis of how successfully the student(s) handled the repeated substitutions embedded in the previous selection. In making this judgment the teacher should not be distracted by other, unrelated miscues that are generated.

When an appropriate text has been selected, the teacher simply needs to provide enough time for the student to read through the selected material orally. Since all the interaction will be between the reader and the text, the teacher may listen to the reading without comment or have the student tape-record the reading. The value in the lesson lies in the effect that the text has upon the student's use of strategies.

The effects of repeated-substitution strategy lessons will only be felt gradually and over an extended period of time. No immediate discernible lessening of repeated substitutions can be expected when the student reads materials not specifically structured to support the use of semantic predicting. The teacher will simply want to observe the continued occurrence of repeated substitutions in such cases in order to determine the support that will still be needed in materials written for additional repeated-substitution strategy lessons; and other selected repeated substitutions that would lend themselves to strategy lessons.

EXPANDING

WRITING   Have students write stories using their own repeated substitutions when you observe through their reading that they are gaining control over these substitutions.

Chapter 9

Confirming Graphophonic Cues

INITIAL, MEDIAL, AND FINAL GRAPHIC CUES

General Rationale

When readers scan a page of text, they must make use of both their eyes and their minds. Their eyes view the print, but their minds tell them which of the written symbols to pay attention to (to perceive). Not all of the available graphic cues are ever used by any one reader.

Written material incorporates a number of graphic cues developed as conventions by literate language users: capitals, punctuation marks, spelling patterns, spaces between words. These graphic items do not necessarily correspond directly to oral-language units. For example, the hyphenation of a word at the end of a line of text can occur only in print:

The cattle gradually moved across the plain toward the river as they grazed.

The ways in which individual readers perceive graphic symbols change as a result of instructional and developmental experiences as well as context. Preschoolers make one of their first reading distinctions when they note the difference between a picture and a page of print. Of the latter they are apt to begin to inquire, "What does it say?" At some later point comes the recognition of words as meaningful written units only indirectly related to speech pauses.

Oral: He hada hartime.

Written: He had a hard time.

As with all other graphic cues, attention to and use of spelling patterns develop gradually. Words can generally be conceived of as having three parts: initial, medial, and final. In short words these three segments are pretty much of equal length. But as words get longer, the segments do not grow proportionately. The middle segment does most of the expanding. The initial and final segments of words are relatively short and stable in size regardless of word length. Readers' selected use of spelling-pattern cues can be examined in relation to these three word segments.

Readers use both predicting and confirming strategies in response to graphic cues. The initial word segment and configuration (word length and shape) are used for predicting. Of these, the initial word segment (with emphasis placed on the initial letter) is developmentally

185

the first spelling-pattern cue attended to by beginning readers, and the one most frequently used by proficient readers. When used in the syntactic and semantic context of the text portion already read, it offers the most economical cueing—the reader has the best chance of making an accurate or semantically acceptable guess when it is based on the fewest graphic cues.

The medial segment usually contains the significant portion of a word's vowels. Vowels are much less economical predictors in English than are consonants. A vowel or vowel nucleus (that is, *ai, ou, ie, eo, oa*) can represent any of several sound sequences, and any sound sequence can be represented by alternate spelling patterns:

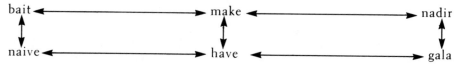

The medial word segment only becomes a significant graphic cue as a reader makes use of confirming strategies. When a prediction turns out not to sound like language or not to make sense with the subsequent language of the text, the reader can reconsider (review or rethink) the available graphic cues and readjust them in an attempt to produce an alternate choice that will fit syntactically and semantically with the rest of the text.

The two examples below typify the confirming role of medial word segments:

He ⟨*hoped*⟩ hopped down from the truck.

Penny ⟨*rooshed*⟩ rushed up the front steps and into the house.

It was on the basis of the rest of the sentence context—*down from the truck* and *up the front steps*—that the first predictions were disconfirmed and adjustments made to the medial portions of the miscued words.

A further example can demonstrate the relative insignificance of vowels as predicting cues. Languages such as Hebrew and Arabic do not bother to represent most of their vowel sounds in print. The consonants are presented, and the reader uses context to "read in" the necessary vowels. Some secretaries use a process called speed-writing, which operates on the same principle:

Brng hm sm hmbrgr nd rlls.

The only ambiguity you are likely to encounter with this sentence will involve whether *hm* represents *him* or *home*. This would be immediately resolved if the sentence were placed in further context and you then knew that Mrs. Balarian had stuck a note in her husband's lunch to remind him of an errand.

Through lots of reading experiences most readers become effective users of spelling patterns (as well as other graphic cues). While they may show varied proficiency in dealing with different spelling patterns and different word segments, they have established the relationship between spelling patterns and sound patterns, use graphic cues both for predicting and confirming, and have developed an inductive procedure for recognizing new spelling/sound patterns.

A major problem experienced by some students actually involves an overemphasis on graphophonic rules—attention to sound/letter strategies to the exclusion of available syntactic and semantic cues. Such an emphasis can result in the following kind of reading miscue:

The boys walked around the ⟨*cureve*⟩ curve in the road.

This reader actually read *curve* initially, then went back and abandoned the expected response in favor of the nonword *cureve* (pronounced as a single-syllable word, of which the first portion sounds like *cure*). When asked to explain why he had made the change, the reader said that because the word ended in *e*, it had to have a long *u* sound. Not only has this reader treated sound/letter relationships as involving a one-to-one correspondence (a single sound for a single letter or letter sequence) but he has let application of such relationships override all available semantic cues. He would rather apply a spelling-pattern rule than produce something meaningful.

There are two important considerations in evaluating a reader's use of graphophonic cues. First, many testing instruments will score as ineffective or minimal users of graphophonic cues those readers who successfully use or even overuse such cues. Second, a reader's application of graphophonic strategies will usually differ depending on whether they are applied to words in isolation (as in a word list) or to words in context.

Most tests now in use credit the student only for "correct" responses. In many instances such a response is dependent on the student's prior knowledge of the item. Graphophonic cues, when applied in isolation from syntactic and semantic cues, can really only guarantee a close approximation or possible alternate pronunciations for a truly unknown item. For example:

Circle the correct pronunciation for *krait*. [1]

/krait/ [1]   /kriyt/   /krat/

All three choices are possible alternates for the spelling pattern as it can be found in *trait*, *faille*, and *plaid*. The sound/letter relationship that occurs most frequently is represented by *ai* (as in *trait*), and this is the one most often selected. However, it happens not to represent the conventional pronunciation of *krait*. Many of the "wrong" answers selected by students in phonics tests represent alternate available sound/letter relationships for a particular spelling pattern. This indicates the students' awareness of sound/letter relationships.

Testing and instructional settings frequently require students to demonstrate their use of the graphophonic system in isolation from the other two language systems: They must respond to words out of context (as the *krait* example forced you to respond in isolation). Readers differ in their handling of words depending upon whether they are in an isolated list or in context, as the example demonstrates:

Key Word	In a List	In Context
there	[thore]	there were many windows . . .
pieces	prizes	Then some of the pictures were painted.
sail	smile	. . . boats sail on its waters.
blue	blue	. . . with a little door.

The first column lists the key words; the second column, what the reader produced when looking at that word in a list; and the third column, what the same reader produced when the word occurred in the context of a story.

There is no direct relationship between the reader's responses in these two settings. Reading a word in the list does not guarantee that the reader will retain it in context (as in the case of *blue*). Nor will a reader's miscue necessarily remain constant between list and text (as with *pieces*). In the setting of the list readers have only two choices: They can recognize an item or they can attempt to use spelling-pattern relationships to sound out the item. With only the graphophonic system available to provide the cues, a great many miscues produced will involve either nonwords or look-alike words:

red
Ted
[caward]
carried

some
same
[droove]
drove

all
call
[stirning]
string

Some determined attempts at sounding out an item will generate a broken-record effect, seldom producing the expected item. (Each of the miscues are numbered in the order produced, with 1 representing the reader's first attempt, 2 representing the second attempt, and so on.)

4. s –
3. [sin + why]
2. [sinwhile]
1. sin –
sinewy

4. [soothing]
3. sow
2. [smoothing]
1. smooth
soothing

3. [diferations]
2. dif –
1. difers
definitions

---

[1]Square brackets—[ ]—indicate a nonword; the spelling represents the way it sounds.

If sounding out fails to produce a recognizable item and the reader is uncomfortable with nonwords, the choice will be simply to omit the item.

There are some readers who tend to treat reading in context as a word-recognition task. They fail to take advantage of the syntactic and semantic cues that context provides and apply only the graphophonic system—spelling-pattern relationships—to unrecognized or unfamiliar items:

The
Then they will know the circus is coming.

noise
What a long nose he has.

3. [*as + harmed*]
2. *as* –
1. [*a harm*]

I began to feel a little foolish and ashamed.

Billy was very afraid. He shook with (fear).[2]

Self-taught readers and effective readers never display this pattern of a limiting dependency upon the graphophonic system. Overuse of spelling-pattern relationships results from instructional procedures and materials that treat word recognition as the key to reading and therefore isolate and stress the use of the graphophonic system. Although many students are exposed to instruction that so distorts the reading process, only some succumb. Peter Board has termed those susceptible students "instructional dependent personalities," indicating that they allow outside authority to override their intuitive language strategies.[3]

SPECIAL NOTE   In a few cases it is possible that a student is not making effective use of the graphophonic system. Miscues involving a similar spelling pattern as it appears in a number of items throughout the text:

grow	led
grape	heard
grab	word

or repetitive miscues on particular word pairs:

when/then	what/that

could be cause for concern. To place this possible difficulty in perspective, search the text from which the miscues have come and list all the words which contain the problem spelling pattern but on which the reader did not miscue. In other words, did the reader accurately produce *green*, *ground*, *grade*, *great*, and *grandmother* in the same texts where he or she miscued on *grow*, *grape*, and *grab*? Are *who*, *whole*, and *white* no problem, even though *when* and *then*, *that* and *what*, are substituted repeatedly?

Almost one hundred percent of the time this analysis will indicate that the reader's difficulty with a spelling pattern is not total—that the same spelling pattern occurs in items that the reader has accurately produced. The research data from hundreds of readers of all ages have yet to yield one reader who shows a total lack of any one spelling pattern throughout a whole story. Allowing readers to informally induce the relationships for any weakly developed patterns as they meet them in context is the most effective instructional strategy. Direct instruction runs the risk of encouraging an overuse of graphophonic cues and, at best, may only speed up a discovery that the student would have made independently.

Instructional procedures for students who make repetitive miscues on particular word pairs are further handled in the strategy lessons for Repeated Substitutions.

Specific Rationale

Because graphic cues provide only an approximation of the conventional pronunciation of any item, and because a portion of graphic-cueing strategies become economical for use only as

---

[2]Circle indicates omission.
[3]Peter Board, "A Descriptive Analysis of the Oral Reading Behavior of a Selected Group of Disabled Readers," (Master's thesis, University of Toronto, 1974).

confirming strategies (not as predicting strategies), the most frequent reader problems related to their use involve overdependence.

The three strategy lessons that follow are directed only toward those students who allow concern for graphic similarity to override their intuitive sense of language structure and their construction of meaning.

The lessons are concerned with freeing the reader from past instruction. Students are very hesitant to abandon instructional procedures even when they are not producing desired results. After all, these procedures were introduced by a person who already successfully practices the desired process. Students' usual assumption—underlying any overt hostility or disinterest—is that the problem lies within themselves. They tend to believe that they either are not applying the process as directed or are lacking in some necessary ingredient.

The first lesson, "Spelling Patterns through Language Experience," is intended to draw the student's attention to meaning as the prime focus of a reading setting. A language experience technique is used so that the relationship between purpose and reading can be highlighted. Six steps are suggested for developing and using the material, but it is the final one—rereading the experience story at a later date—that takes on central significance.

If the first five steps have been meaningfully developed, the student's entire attention has been placed on the meaning relationship between what was experienced and what was recorded of the experience. In returning to that record at a later date, the student is more likely to seek support for unrecognized or unrecalled items from memory than from application of graphic strategies and in so doing will be led to discover the usefulness and availability of context.

The second and third lessons, "Meaning without Graphophonic Cues" and "Synonym Substitutions," are intended to extend the concept demonstrated in the first and to indicate that a problem in graphic handling of some items within an unfamiliar text does not necessarily draw the reading process to a halt or insure a loss of meaning.

Two variations of selected slotting are used. In the first, selected, highly predictable words are deleted from a text that is well within the reader's capabilities. The reader is asked to supply any available semantically acceptable terms for the slots. Successful handling of this experience should support the discovery that we read meaning, not words, and that the meaning carried for any one sentence slot is developed and supported by the surrounding structure.

In the second variation the student is presented with a text in which selected words have been underlined rather than deleted. The student is asked to read the text, supplying an alternate semantically acceptable item in place of the underlined item. To do so, the reader is forced to go beyond (but not really to ignore) the graphic cueing to confirm the meaning.

EVALUATION

The strategy lesson for Initial, Medial, and Final Spelling Cues will benefit

1. Students who produce a significant number of nonwords and/or omissions of unknown words.
2. Students who abandon expected or semantically acceptable responses in favor of non-words or semantically unacceptable words that they view as being graphically closer to specific items.
3. Students who make multiple attempts on an unknown item at one point in the text.
4. Students who do not demonstrate a qualitative difference between application of graphophonic strategies for words in a list and words in context.
5. Students whose miscue-analysis profile indicates semantic and syntactic acceptability of less than 50 percent with a combined graphic similarity score of more than 70 percent for miscues showing some similarity and those showing high similarity.

SPELLING PATTERNS THROUGH LANGUAGE EXPERIENCE

Reading-Strategy Instruction

INITIATING

As a reading approach, language experience incorporates the learner's experience, thought, and language in the production of a narrative. The teacher, in the role of scribe, translates the learner's oral language into written expression and so makes use of the learner's competencies to extend language development. Application of language experience involves a six-step process.

Step 1: Provide or focus in on an experience. This strategy lesson must be generated out of an attention-arresting, highly meaningful experience. The students maintain their focus on the experience and not on any reading instruction because they are going to be encouraged to handle all print on the basis of meaning and intent.

Because the strength of the focus on meaning is so critical it is best if the first several engagements of this strategy are generated out of teacher-planned experiences immediately participated in.

While the experience can be one shared by the total class, the reading-strategy instruction should be limited to the specific group of students meeting the evaluation criteria. In this way they will not be passive observers of the facility with which other, more effective readers use meaning and context. At the same time, a group setting will encourage them to support each other and to share insights.

The effectiveness of the experience will be measured by the intensity of the intellectual and/or emotional attention it draws, not by its exoticness or uniqueness. Finding a dead bird, making cupcakes for a class treat, taking a tour of the school boiler room, examining a drop of water through a microscope, are all relatively common and accessible occurrences that generate true intellectual curiosity.

INTERACTING

Step 2: Establish a reason for recording the experience. While it is true that the teacher's purpose in recording the learner's narrative is to create a vehicle for learning to read, the learner needs to see a less abstract purpose for the turning of speech into print: for example, giving directions to another group, planning an event, communicating with someone distant from the event, sharing with others, providing a personal diary. We need to help our students value writing for its function of preserving and extending events.

Step 3: Organize and evaluate the experience through discussion. Discussing the experience with the learners is the most critical part of the language experience. When learners are invited to explore all aspects of an experience, they are exposed to the viewpoints of their classmates and are provided with the time to reflect upon the experience.

The discussion should be a comprehensive one in which the children organize and reconsider the topic through the familiar expression of speech. It is important in the initial stage to allow the children to make uninterrupted statements and to mentally and verbally roam the experience at will, highlighting aspects that generate their interest.

As the discussion progresses, the teacher can be prepared to ask selected questions designed to bring out significant points that have not been considered, suggest unexplored alternatives, and provide organization. The general discussion period provides the teacher with the opportunity to develop, through questioning, any overriding concepts within the experience.

As the topic is explored, the students select the ideas that are important to them, discard the frivolous, and eliminate the repetitive. In this way the discussion is elevated from a loosely related series of descriptive phrases to an all-of-a-piece narrative. When the teacher feels that the discussion has distilled the ingredients of the experience into a clarified narrative, the dictating/recording sequence is initiated.

Step 4: Dictate/record the experience. At this point the teacher changes role, acting now as scribe rather than discussion leader. To insure that the language of the student is preserved, the scribe needs to follow certain conventions, recording on the chalkboard or paper as the student dictates:

1. Standard English spelling conventions should be observed. It is the nature of language that graphic changes lag behind changes in the sound system. English has a standard spelling pattern regardless of oral dialect. Be sure to use standard spelling for root words and inflectional endings such as *-s* and *-ed* (whether or not they are heard).
2. Use standard punctuation forms.
3. Use the student's vocabulary.

4. Use the student's grammar. If the student says, "Me and Jane learned Jim his spelling words," this should be recorded as dictated.

Step 5: Reread and edit the story. The fully generated story should be read through without interruption before the close of the session. This reading allows the students to edit any material they find awkward, inappropriate, or inaccurate within the context of the whole. It allows the teacher to catch any inadvertent alterations that may have been made in recording the learners' language.

But most important to the learning process, this reading acts to complete the cycle from uninterrupted whole (step 1), through consideration to and analysis of the components (steps 2 through 4), back to uninterrupted whole (step 5).

APPLYING

Step 6: Select future readings. A balance needs to be struck between materials that are to be read again, and so will be preserved, and one-shot materials whose main value lies in focusing and clarifying the students' perceptions of an experience. The decision concerning permanency should be based on the communication needs of the setting. Seeing a percentage of the produced materials wiped off the board or placed in the wastebasket frees the students to take more risks, to share their developing thinking on a topic, to value written language for organizing their ideas.

One-shot language-experience materials can be generated for such purposes as

1. Planning a class party: What activities should we have? What refreshments should there be?
2. Reviewing the day's activities: What did we accomplish? Did anything unusual or exciting happen? Are there any messages for home?
3. Predicting the author's position prior to reading a text or trade book: What topics might be covered concerning the development of a railroad system in America? I wonder what kind of wild things we will encounter in a book called *Where the Wild Things Are?*
4. Delineating the positions taken by class members on some topic of current concern: Who will win the presidential campaign? Should the school have a dress code?

Language-experience materials selected for preservation should have communication needs that extend beyond the present moment:

1. Topics of interest to persons not present: articles for a class newspaper; letters to parents or community members
2. Good literature for the class library: fiction or nonfiction written by individuals or groups; stories written for the entertainment of children in other classes; the script for a class play
3. Informational material for the class library: how-to material on growing plants, raising guppies, making a scooter; research reports on people, events, time periods; reports on hobbies; such as "All I Know About Rock Collecting/Stamps/Baseball"
4. Bulletin-board displays: a timeline of famous people or events to accompany a social-studies unit; the developing record of a seed growth experiment
5. Material samples for self-evaluation: personal work folders that are used for periodic evaluation of developmental progress

Language-experience materials should be reused only when they have application to some new or extended need; they should never be viewed solely as a form of reading practice.

Early in this approach, the reader should be encouraged to be a scribe for his or her own experiences or those of others. The teacher should take over the scribe function whenever the reader-writer tires but still has more to record. When the reader acts as the scribe, he or she should be encouraged to use invented spelling (see chapter 2).

MEANING WITHOUT GRAPHOPHONIC CUES

Reading-Strategy Instruction

INITIATING

This second lesson is intended to draw readers' conscious attention to the fact that it is possible to apply, in more general reading settings, those meaning strategies that they used to handle unrecalled text items within the language-experience stories developed in the preceding lesson.

Because the readers for whom these lessons are intended overdepend on graphic cues, they will be supplied with a text that prohibits the use of this strategy. In this way they will be relieved of any responsibility or compulsion to use it.

A series of one- or two-page materials containing selected deletions should be prepared. These materials should be of two types: familiar stories and highly predictable texts. Each text should be examined for those meanings that are most predictable, based on reader experience and contextual development. Each of these items should then be deleted from the text and replaced by a five-space line.

Examples of familiar stories:

MARY HAD A LITTLE LAMB

    Mary had a little _____. Its fleece was white as _____. Everywhere that Mary went the _____ was sure to go.

THE THREE LITTLE PIGS

    Once upon a time there were three little pigs. One day the three little pigs left home. Each little pig wanted to build a _____. The first little pig made a house of _____ . The second little pig made a house of _____ . The third little pig made a house of _____ .

Use any materials—nursery rhymes, folktales, songs, storybooks—that the children have read or have had read to them and that they have a special fondness for.

An example of a highly predictable text:

TREE ANIMALS

    Trees are really fun to watch because many different kinds of animals make their homes in them.

    Some of these animals can fly and have feathers. They use sticks, and twigs, and leaves to make a nest. These animals are _____ .

    Another animal likes to live in holes in the trees. This animal eats nuts. It is a _____ .

    Some animals are very small. They like to live on the leaves. They eat the leaves for food. Sometimes the birds eat these animals for food. These animals are _____ .

The bases for predictability of material are

✓ Familiar concepts, relationships, and story line
✓ Straightforward sentence structure
✓ Familiar lexical items

Prepare the materials either on an overhead transparency or on duplicate sheets. Explain to the students that (a) they will be reading about things they are familiar with and (b) when they come to a blank, they are simply to fill in an appropriate item.

Move rapidly through the materials, alternating familiar and highly predictable selections. Alternate between group oral reading (this should not be choral reading: do not attempt to keep everyone together or read with dramatic intonation) and oral reading by individual students. Make no corrections, and supply no aid (remind the students, if necessary, that they can guess or skip the unknown). Following each selection, accept any brief remarks concerning concepts or content. Encourage the students to save any comments on strategy or any problems for later discussion.

INTERACTING

QUESTIONS FOR DISCUSSION

1. *How did you know what to put in the blanks?*
   Reexamine the individual pieces of material. Let the students discover that the material can be sorted on the basis of stories that they have read before and information that is familiar to them. They need to come to the realization that they have made use of already-known material in reading this text.
2. *Were there many blanks that generated alternate answers?*
   The structure of this material will tend to produce convergent responses. Examine slots that produced alternates. How many alternates are synonyms? How many are semantically acceptable even though meaning varies? Examine the text for the cues the readers used in arriving at their choices, as illustrated below:

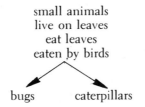

small animals
live on leaves
eat leaves
eaten by birds

bugs   caterpillars

APPLYING

Have available, for student selection, a collection of one- or two-page readings which are highly predictable semantically and in which selected items have been deleted and replaced by five-space blanks. Students can work in pairs, or individually with a tape recorder.

Reader-listener team. The reader reads the text aloud to the listener, pausing at the blanks while the listener fills in any appropriate item. The team should make an effort to proceed as quickly as possible. If the listener fails to produce a slot filler, the reader should continue with the text. The team should not interrupt the process to discuss the relative merits of their choices. All discussion should be saved until the end of the selection has been reached. No list of expected or acceptable responses should be provided. The team must determine what they find acceptable.

Reader—tape recorder team. The reader reads the text aloud to the recorder. Encourage the reader to proceed as quickly as possible, filling in the blanks as they are encountered and choosing to skip a slot rather than pause. On completion of a selection the reader plays back the tape to evaluate choices and/or attempt other available alternates. The student can discuss these choices with the teacher during an individual conference.

SYNONYM SUBSTITUTIONS

Reading-Strategy Instruction

INITIATING

MATERIALS   "The Three Little Pigs," adapted by Carolyn Burke

The Three Little Pigs

Once there was an old mother pig who had three little pigs. She had no money, so she sent the three little pigs away to make their fortunes.

The first little pig met a man with a bundle of straw. The little pig said to him, "Please, man give me some straw to build me a house." The man gave him some straw and the little pig built his house with it.

Along came a big bad wolf. The wolf knocked at the first little pig's door. He said, "Little pig, little pig, let me come in."

"No, no," said the little pig. "Not by the hair on my chinny chin chin."

"Then I'll huff and I'll puff and I'll blow your house in," said the wolf. So the wolf huffed, and he puffed, and he blew the house in. The wolf ate up the first little pig.

Adapted by CAROLYN BURKE

The materials prepared for this strategy lesson are expected to encourage readers' use of predicting cues derived from personal experiences and the semantic and syntactic language systems. The materials should incorporate the following qualities:

1. *Familiar story line.* The initial selections can relate directly to past language experiences: for example, stories that the reader has encountered as a listener, that have personal appeal, and that the reader is able to retell. Subsequent selections can maintain story-line types with which the reader is familiar and can include stories that pattern in ways familiar to the reader.

2. *Predictable structures.* For example, redundancy of events:

    Each of the pigs builds a house.
    The wolf visits each pig with the same demand.
    The pigs' responses to the wolf are identical.

    redundancy of syntactic patterns:

    The first little pig made a house of [noun]
    The [adjective] little pig [verb] [determiner] [noun] [preposition] [noun].
    The [noun phrase] [verb phrase] [prepositional phrase].

    redundancy of surface structure phrasing:

    Once upon a time . . .
    I'll huff and I'll puff and . . .
    Not by the hair on my chinny chin chin!

Once a piece of material has been selected, it should be searched for words and phrases that lend themselves to synonym substitution. The test for choosing an item should be the teacher's ability to produce two or three workable substitutions rapidly:

young
small
tiny

Once . . . there was an old sow with three *little* pigs.

constructed
got
built

The third little pig *made* a house of bricks.

You will need to be selective in your use of available synonym-substitution candidates, as some sentences will contain many possibilities:

The first *little* pig *met* a *man* with a *bundle* of *straw*, and said to him: "Please, *man*, give me that *straw* to *build* me a *house*."

The lesson calls for the use of the first 150-to-200-word segment of the story, the approximate amount of text that can fit on one sheet of paper when typed with a large-print typewriter. Determine the cut-off point for the segment on the basis of the story structure, making the cut at the end of a completed sequence of events.

The text segment is prepared for the strategy lesson by simply underlining the words and phrases selected for synonym substitution. Duplicate the prepared text so that each reader will have a copy, or prepare an overhead transparency that all will read from.

Tell the students that they will be reading together from a familiar story. Give them a few moments to scan the text so that they can confirm their knowledge and take note of the underlined items.

Complete the instructions by telling the readers that there is only one rule to be followed during the reading: As they come to underlined items, they must *not* say what is actually written on the page. They may say any thing they like that seems to make sense.

NOTE It is important to consider the effects of this strategy lesson on the reader's use of graphophonic information. The intention is to shift the use of the cues generated by the graphics from predicting to confirming information, so that the basic decisions the reader makes are meaning based. The intent is *not* to have the reader ignore available graphic cues.

The items selected for synonym substitution will incorporate a mixture of the immediately recognizable and the unfamiliar. In each instance the reader actually encounters and processes the graphic as an aspect of determining a useful meaning-based response. In order to produce *young*, *small*, or *tiny*, the reader has had to perceive *l-i-t-t-l-e*.

INTERACTING

Once the reading starts, it should continue at a steady pace, without interruption, until the end of the selection is reached. The focus must be maintained on forging ahead past any intervening pitfalls. The teacher maintains this focus by reading as a member of the group, maintaining silence as each underlined item is encountered, and proceeding on pace.

In any discussion that follows the experience, attention should be on interesting alternatives that are generated. There should be no attempt to reexamine methodically the choices made for each synonym slot. Nor should any attention be drawn to individual slots for which synonyms are not produced. Remember that the thrust of the experience is to demonstrate that material can be read and meaning developed even when individual items seem beyond the immediate control of the reader.

APPLYING

Following the Interacting phase of the lesson, the whole of the selected story can be made available in a learning-center experience. One variation for the center would be to have available

1. A picture-story book of the text
2. Your typed version of the story with the selected synonyms underlined (you may decide to omit the underlines for the segment used in the Interacting phase)
3. A tape recorder

The written directions for the students would be as follows:

1. This picture-story book tells a story that you know. Use the pictures in the book to tell yourself the story.
2. Now, look at the typed story.
3. Turn on the tape recorder and read the typed story out loud. *Remember, when you come to something that is underlined you may say anything that makes sense, but you must not say what is written on the paper.*
4. Listen to your taped reading as you look at the story.

Chapter 10

Integrating Semantic Cues

CONCEPTS

General Rationale

The preceding reading-strategy lessons have been concerned with raising to a conscious level readers' use of the various language systems—the graphophonic, semantic, and syntactic—always with the goal of gaining meaning. Readers who ask themselves, *Why do I want to know or understand this information?* and *Based on my reasons, what do I think the author is trying to say?* will gain from all of their reading.

In this section we focus on helping readers become consciously aware of their responsibility to be active participants in the long-distance discussion between reader and author. Readers should be encouraged to interact with and to react to authors' concepts, ideas, characters, themes, humor, propaganda, and generalizations in order *to decide for themselves* what is going on behind the surface words and sentences.

The first group of lessons in this chapter are concerned with integrating concepts. The term *concept* is difficult to define. Everything that we develop an understanding of is a concept. (If it is a misunderstanding, it may be called a misconception, but it is developed in the same way that a concept is developed.) What we know to be the color red, which animals we classify as dogs, what we consider *two* to be, all are concepts. Brotherhood, cooperation, or justice, as we understand them, are also concepts. Concepts can be concrete or abstract. They are not learned by naming a word or stating a definition. They are developed through many continuous, real, and vicarious experiences that take place over many years.

Concepts can be developed and extended through reading. But in order for this learning to take place, concepts have to be related to the reader's schema—to experience and knowledge already developed. New ideas and concepts must be related to what is already known. What the reader gains is understood in relationship to the already existing schema or storehouse of knowledge. In this way the developing concepts are integrated into the reader's schema. All reading experiences provide opportunities for students to

1. Develop new concepts and integrate them with their storehouse of knowledge
2. Expand or modify concepts that have already been integrated into their schema
3. Reject the new concepts because they cannot, for a number of reasons, be integrated into the schema or storehouse of knowledge

It is important that readers be aware that they are actively involved in their own learning. As they interact with written materials, they have the responsibility to evaluate and critique what they read. Proficient readers do this by asking questions similar to the following:

1. What is my purpose in learning this new concept?
2. Will this particular concept be important for my purposes?
3. What evidence do I have that helps me to know whether the concept is accurate and/or appropriate for my purposes?
4. Is it important to remember this concept; and if it is, how can I remember it best?

Concepts are learned from both fiction and nonfiction material. Although, from the point of view of the reader, they may be learned in similar ways regardless of the kind of material, for the purpose of strategy lessons, we shall first suggest ways of helping the student integrate concepts in nonfictional informational material and then deal with integrating concepts in fiction.

INFORMATIONAL MATERIAL: STRATEGY-LESSON PLAN

Specific Rationale

Although informational material is often read for enjoyment, and story material is often read for purposes of formal analysis, we shall treat the two types of reading material in their traditional ways. The strategy-lesson plan "Story Material" will focus on material that is read for personal enjoyment. After you have used the lessons for both fiction and nonfiction as suggested, reverse the strategy lessons by presenting informational material for the purpose of enjoyment and story material for more academic purposes. Discuss with students that informational material can legitimately be read for enjoyment whenever they wish and that story material can be analyzed and used for purposes other than enjoyment.

Informational material (as well as other material) can be difficult to read for two reasons: concept load and hard-to-predict grammatical structures.

Concept load. Many times reading matter presents too many concepts or ideas that are new or contrary to the present beliefs of the reader. The reader has difficulty integrating such ideas into his or her already developed schema. Very often texts cover a wide range of ideas over a long historical period in a few short paragraphs. Authors who write such material are often unaware that in an attempt to generalize and simplify they have overloaded the material with too many new concepts. This type of material should be avoided especially with students who are having any reading difficulty.

Consider this excerpt, which is the first paragraph of a chapter from a high-school history text, and as you read the passage, ask yourself what background knowledge a reader must have in order to understand the many concepts in it. Put a check over each word or phrase that represents a concept requiring background knowledge.

> When the Treaty of Versailles went down to defeat in the Senate in 1919, it seemed that the United States had said a loud "No!" to any role in the postwar world's affairs. But that was only part of the truth. The United States might disband its 4-million-man army and reduce its great navy in 1919. But the economic power that had already drawn the United States into the network of international relations continued to limit any American desire to withdraw from world affairs as did the conscience of those who thought American power must help a battered Europe.[1]

We used a passage from a high-school text so that you could be more consciously aware of the complexity of such concepts as the Treaty of Versailles; the postwar world's affairs in relation to the date 1919; part of the truth as opposed to the whole truth or to distorted truth; disband and reduce army and navy as it relates to concerns about being the best-armed nation in the world; economic power; network of international relations. Those who have an extensive background

---

[1]Bernard A. Weisberg, *The Impact of Our Past* (New York: American Heritage, Publishing Company, Inc., 1972), p. 661.

in history, whether developed through fiction or nonfiction, may be totally unaware of why this paragraph might be difficult to read, because a reader who has a storehouse of knowledge about any subject will find it relatively easy to read about that subject. As knowledgeable adults, teachers are often unaware of the degree to which informational materials, prepared for young readers, are loaded with new concepts.

Hard-to-predict grammatical structures. The structure of the grammar of written material may be unfamiliar to the readers and therefore hard to predict. (See the strategy lesson "Hard-to-Predict Grammatical Structures" in chapter 5.) In the paragraph from the high-school text did the use of a direct quote (" 'No'!") embedded in the first sentence cause you any problems? Why was there a shift in tense to *might disband and reduce* in the third sentence? Was this tense shift disruptive to your reading or significant to the meaning? Did the relationships developed through a variety of dependent clauses in the last sentence cause you to reread and wonder if you had understood it?

It is important to *accept* the notion that if both the structure and concept load are complex for any particular reader, the material should be discarded. Students should be encouraged to discard material that they are not understanding. They should be helped to understand that their inability to read something is due not to failure as readers; rather, they have not yet built the necessary background for the new concepts as they are presented, or the author uses too many grammatical structures that are unfamiliar to them. They need to have a variety of ways provided for them to build adequate schemata for new information they wish to learn.

When proficient adult readers decide to discard something, they seldom say to themselves, "I have a reading problem"; instead they either believe that they don't care to read the material at a particular time or that it is not well written. Often when people say a text is not well written, they mean that the material has an overload of new concepts or that the grammatical structures are hard to predict. Both of these problems are usually involved when the proficient reader decides *not* to read something.

The role of the teacher becomes very important when the student wants to read something and the material immediately at hand is too complex, for the reasons stated above. There are at least three ways to help a student in such a situation:

1. *Provide concrete experiences prior to reading.* Reading to learn is limited by background knowledge. Schemata have not yet been built to integrate all the new information students need to learn in school. It is therefore necessary to have many real-life experiences on which to build a storehouse of knowledge before written material can even begin to take on meaning. It is almost impossible to learn to knit or to put together a disassembled toy from written material unless some prior real-life experience has preceded the reading of the knitting or assembly instructions. When students become interested in aspects of science, social studies, or math, firsthand experiences will not only make the subsequent reading easier but will provide the motivations necessary for them to want to read the material in the first place. If field trips, experiments, or demonstrations are not possible, visual aids including filmstrips, movies, or still pictures should all be prerequisite to reading. If there are some things necessary for required reading, the teacher should go through the material and place a check mark over those concepts that will cause problems. Real or vicarious *nonreading* experiences should then be planned to provide the background to support developing schemata. Then if the students have difficulty in comprehending, the previous concrete experiences can be explored to help them integrate their own schemata with the knowledge they are beginning to develop from their reading.

2. *Develop a bibliography of easy-to-predict reading materials related to significant concepts.* There are many single-concept informational books that often go into a particular concept in greater depth than an overall text can afford to do. A variety of such material should be part of the classroom library. As such a collection is developed; a major criterion to consider in the selection of the material is that the grammatical structure should be easy to predict so that the students do not have to deal with complex sentence structures at the same time that they are learning new concepts. Start this collection by compiling a bibliography that can be added to over time. Students can be

involved in both developing such bibliographies and adding to them as they find new reading materials about a particular concept. Magazine and newspaper articles may also be good sources for such materials.

3. *Select or write materials for strategy lessons.* Strategy lessons such as those that follow will help students become more consciously aware of their own responsibility in developing and integrating concepts as they read. In addition, other strategy lessons from this book may also be used; apply the procedures suggested in those lessons to informational material.

EVALUATION

The strategy lesson for Informational Material will benefit

1. Students who read informational material but are unable to discuss any significant information; and who tend to recount surface facts and detail.
2. Students who state that they do not understand informational material when they read it.
3. Students whose miscue-analysis profile shows that more than 60 percent of sentences produced are acceptable but 60 percent of sentences show extensive change of meaning.

Reading-Strategy Instruction

INITIATING

MATERIALS   "Spiders," by Yetta Goodman
Read-for-Information Guide

Spiders

How many spiders have you seen in the last week? If you are observant—that is, if you watch the world around you carefully—you have probably seen more than one. Spiders live in most places in the world. They live both indoors and outdoors. They come in many sizes, shapes, and colors.

Although many people are afraid of spiders, they are not harmful animals. They do not usually bite unless they are disturbed, and very few spider bites are poisonous. Spiders are really helpful. Each year they eat many thousands of harmful insects, which they trap in webs.

The body of the spider has two parts joined by a slender neck or waist. It has eight legs. The top or front part of the body contains the spider's head. The bottom or back part of the body is called the abdomen. On the bottom of the spider near the back edge are its spinnerets which make the silk used not only for spider webs but for the spider's egg sacs as well. These spinnerets look like tiny tubes.

When a spider starts to spin a web, it presses the spinnerets against something hard and out comes some of the liquid silk. This silk hardens in the air. Different kinds of spiders make different kinds of webs.

Many people have been interested in spiders. Scientists have studied the behavior of spiders under different conditions. Some people can tell exciting or scary tales or superstitions about spiders. What do you know about spiders?

YETTA GOODMAN

References: *Comptons Dictionary of the Natural Sciences*, vol. 2, (Chicago: F. E. Compton Co., 1966), pp. 598–600, and *The World Book Encyclopedia*, vol. 17, under the word "Spiders" (Chicago: Field Enterprises Education Corporation, 1966), pp. 611–15.

Read-for-Information Guide

1. Think about why you want to know this information.
2. Make a list of some of the things that you already know about the subject. Call it *What I Know*. Keep adding to this list as you find out important information that you want to remember.
3. Make a list of questions that you have about the subject. Call it *What I Want to Know*. Keep adding to this list whenever you think of a question that is important.
4. Think about where you can find the answers to your questions.
5. Look for answers to the questions that are most interesting or important to you.
6. Organize the important information by putting ideas and concepts about the same things together.
7. Share your information with others. Present it in the form of a play or a TV show, lead a discussion about it, or think of another interesting way to share it.

Explain to the students that the group will go through the steps of *one* way to organize informational material in order to *present* it to others. They should know that *presenting* information not only gives new information to others but gives the presenter an opportunity to understand the information better.

The Read-for-Information Guide may be reproduced so each student can have a copy. You may want to read the guide aloud with the group to give them a chance to ask any questions they may have about the procedure. Tell them that the topic of spiders will be used as a sample, but when they work on their own presentation, they should choose something that is of special interest to them.

Using the Read-for-Information Guide, begin looking for information about spiders.

Step 1. Have the students discuss possible reasons to know more about spiders.[2]

Step 2. Have them list on the board, under the caption What I Know, important things they know about spiders. Encourage them to use short phrases. If anyone raises questions or challenges while the statements are being listed on the board, have the challengers write their questions under the caption What I Want to Know. Label each question and statement with the name of the student who provides it. The student will then assume responsibility for the concepts in his or her particular statement or question. Whenever the student learns new important information, it should be added to the What I Know list.

Step 3. Ask if anyone has additional questions about spiders. Add these to What I Want to Know, or if no questions were raised earlier, start such a list. Continue to add to this list all questions or challenges that students raise throughout the lesson. The two lists might look like the following:

What I Know	What I Want to Know
Eight legs (Gregory)	Is the silk spit from spider's mouths? (Georgetta)
Spiders bite (Darryl)	Won't the webs cause infections? (Georgetta)
Spin silk webs (Susan)	Insects have six legs, how can spiders be insects? (Sandy)
Webs can stop bleeding (Georgetta)	Are they poisonous? (Carl)
Spiders are insects (Darryl)	Can they grow into big monsters? (Bob)
Good for gardens (Susan)	Is it bad luck to kill a spider? (Tracy)

Step 4. List names of books that the students know or places that they can look for all kinds of print information about spiders. The students may suggest encyclopedias and dictionaries. Accept these suggestions, but try to encourage them to examine a wide variety of books, magazines, and newspapers as well. Encourage the students to find out where books about spiders are located in the school and/or local libraries. Provide the students with a few suggestions to get them started, but leave the bulk of the work to them. Let librarians (at both school and public libraries) know in advance that the students will be looking for all kinds of materials about spiders so that they too will be prepared. List nonprint resources (pet-store owners, science teachers, exterminators). Help them understand what kinds of questions a parent or older sibling or such experts as biologists or leaders of nature centers may be able to answer.

Step 5. Ask the students to select from the list of questions those that they think are most important or interest them the most. Pass out a copy of "Spiders" to each student. Have them read through the material to themselves one time keeping their questions in mind. They can put a light pencil mark at any point that they find information that answers their questions. They should also mark anything that they think significant but do not quite understand.

INTERACTING

QUESTIONS FOR DISCUSSION

1. *What information helped you answer your questions? Was the information important? Why do you think so?*

---

[2]The number of this step and those of all subsequent steps in the Initiating and Applying phases, correspond to the item numbers in the guide.

Have the students add only significant information under the What I Know list. Encourage them to use short phrases and their own words. Have them explain to others what they think the ideas or concepts mean, and encourage cross-discussion, challenges, and questions.

2. *Do you think the new information is true or not? Why do you think so?*

Help the students question what they read. If they are not sure if something is correct, have them leave it as a question under What I Want to Know. When they believe they have accurate information, they can then put it under What I Know. Help them conclude that the fact that something is in print does not make it accurate.

3. *Did you find out that any information on the What I Know list was not correct or should be changed? What evidence do you have?*

Cross out any statements the students believe to be inaccurate or change any that they think should be changed.

4. *Is there any other new information that you think is important? Why do you think so?*

Have the students discuss any new concepts that they have formed. As the students discuss spinnerets, web making, egg sacs with each other, you will know the degree to which they understand each concept. If you believe their concepts are not sufficiently developed for this particular task, ask questions that will help them reconsider any narrow or inaccurate interpretations. Avoid giving them answers. List all new questions under What I Want to Know. List all new information that is acceptable to the students under What I Know.

Your list might now look like this:

What I Know	*What I Want to Know*
Eight legs (Gregory)	Insects have six legs, how can spiders be insects? (Sandy)
Spin silk webs and egg sacs (Susan and Georgetta)	Can they grow into big monsters? (Bob)
Webs can stop bleeding (Georgetta)	What do spinnerets look like? (Georgetta)
Spiders are insects (Darryl)	Do all spiders have spinnerets? (Carl)
Good for gardens (Susan)	Is it bad luck to kill a spider? (Tracy)
Few spider bites are poisonous (Carl)	What different sizes, shapes, and colors do spiders come in? (Bob)
Spiders can help people (Tracy)	Do all spiders make webs?
Silk comes from spinnerets (Georgetta)	What kinds of webs do spiders make?
	What superstitions do people have about spiders?

5. *Which of the questions are you most interested in finding more information about?*

Have the students select a few questions they wish to read more about as they continue to follow the Read-for-Information Guide. Help them think of questions that are related in some way. Provide options for those who wish at this point to read for information about topics of greater interest to them.

APPLYING

This phase focuses on helping the student organize information for presentation purposes. See statements 6 and 7 in the Read-for-Information Guide.

Step 6. Organizing information involves at least two separate activities: categorizing the material and selecting significant information.

As the list of What I Know increases, have the students place their concepts or ideas into related categories. They can cut their list apart and paste each statement on index cards so they can rearrange the categories when they need to or add to them easily. Or they may wish to number all statements related to a particular concept, say, 1, all information related to a second concept 2, and so on, until all the significant information is similarly numbered. Suggest *ways* of organizing, but allow students to discover their own ways as well.

Students often want to present everything they have learned. Suggest that they select *only* those concepts or ideas that are most interesting or important to them. Or if they have found a lot of information about a single concept, they may want to limit their presentation to that. For example, *How Spinnerets Work, How Spiders Weave Webs, Superstitions about Spiders,* are each sufficient for an individual presentation, even though each topic deals with only one of the questions asked by the students.

End this lesson by having the students evaluate the Read-for-Information Guide. They should add to it or change anything that made finding and understanding information easy and helpful. They should cross out anything they did not find useful. Through this evaluation they will develop a new Read-for-Information Guide. This type of evaluation should be done periodically so students can consciously think through the strategies they find to be most useful in helping them read selectively and organize their thinking for reporting purposes.

Step 7. Encourage students to share what they have learned with others. Suggest a variety of sharing possibilities, avoiding the traditional written report or presentation in front of a whole class, although these can be among the options for students at some time during the year. For example, students may wish to keep a log of their observations of a spider making a web and then compare this experience with what certain authors have written on the subject. They can share the information by showing the web and providing a time line with slides or pictures of how the web changed. Using information from books, students can apply fine light-colored thread to black paper to reproduce the different kinds of webs made by different spiders.[3]

Possible presentational forms include

diaries or logs	filmstrips
plays	T.V. shows
travelogues	scrapbooks
documentaries	discussions
demonstrations	debates
paintings	time lines
photographs	panels

EXPANDING

LANGUAGE   Encourage students to use their new concepts in a variety of ways. If spelling and vocabulary study are part of the ongoing curriculum, the students could add the new words or phrases to that part of the curriculum. Encourage the students to use the new concepts in both oral and written language whenever the opportunity arises.

Encourage the students to present the information a second time to some younger children in the school. Help them with any necessary arrangements with other teachers. The classmates who saw the original presentation could help reorganize it so that it can be presented in a way that will be interesting and exciting for younger children.

WRITING   Take any reports that the students write from their information search, and produce a class encyclopedia. Have editors verify the information developed by the author or authors of any original article. Write to encyclopedia companies to find out how they insure accuracy of material and how they update their material.

SOCIAL STUDIES, SCIENCE, AND MATH   Have the students use a similar method when they read informational material in all subjects.

STORY MATERIAL: STRATEGY-LESSON PLAN

Specific Rationale

Much of the background information for this strategy lesson has been developed in the preceding sections of this chapter. When students are reading for their own enjoyment, the process should not be interrupted by instruction. Therefore, in these lessons students will read the story material all the way through and then consciously think about these concepts that they developed through reading the story and ultimately integrated into their schema. Proficient readers

---

[3]This can be shared as an exhibit when the student who made it is available to answer questions from the others.

learn a variety of concepts when they read, even though they may not be aware that they are doing so. The purpose of this lesson is to help all readers become consciously aware that when reading takes place, the reader is learning a lot more than the story itself.

EVALUATION

Similar to the Evaluation section for Informational Material (see page 201) with a focus on story material.

Reading-Strategy Instruction

INITIATING

MATERIAL Any well-written folktale

Provide each of the students with a copy of the folktale. Ask them to read to themselves silently. Tell them that whenever they come to any words or phrases they do not understand, they are to say "blank" or provide a synonym substitution and then continue reading. Tell them that the main purpose of this lesson is understanding the story, but they should try to keep in mind any significant words and phrases that are unfamiliar to them or used in an unusual way. When they finish reading, ask them to look through the story and place a light pencil mark over any significant words or phrases that are new to them or used in an unusual way.

INTERACTING

QUESTIONS FOR DISCUSSION

1. *What did you like or dislike about the story? What were the most important parts of the story?*

    Lead an open-ended discussion of the story so that the students are aware that their understanding of the story was the main purpose for reading. Permit discussion among the students and have them justify their points of view.

2. *Which words or phrases were unfamiliar to you or used in an unusual way?*

    Have students write the text sentence on the board that contains the words or phrases, underlining the specific word or phrase. Do not focus on pronunciation.

3. *Have you ever heard this word or phrase before? Have you ever seen it before? If you have, relate that experience to the way the word or phrase is used in this story?*

    Discuss with students how words and phrases take on different meaning in different stories. They should know that this is how their ideas or concepts grow. Explore with the students any different meanings they have for specific words or phrases. Point out to students that there are many words that readers know only from reading and that they may never hear spoken, just as there are many words used in oral language that may seldom or never be seen in print. (See Expanding phase below.)

4. [Now point to the sentence on the board that contains the word or phrase just explored.] *Can you say this sentence another way without changing the meaning? Who else can say it another way without changing the meaning?*

    Encourage the use of familiar language. Keep asking for additional suggestions as long as the students have something to add and are interested. Have the students react to each other's restatements in regard to what degree of change they think is involved if any.

5. *How did you find out what the words or phrases meant in this story? What language cues in the story helped you know what the words or phrases meant?*

    Help the students understand that meaning changes depending on context, and when they relate new words, concepts, or ideas to what they already know, they can often figure out meanings for themselves.

6. *Are there lessons to be learned from this story? What are they?*

APPLYING

Have the students develop a notebook called My Language Power Book. In this book they are to record, after their reading, sentences that contain words or phrases that are unfamiliar to them or used in an unusual way. They are to underline the specific word or phrase in the sentence. On the next line they are to rewrite the sentence in their own words without changing the meaning. After the students have collected a few pages of new words or phrases have them arrange these items alphabetically so they are easy to find. They should leave space following each item so that they can add complete sentences, whenever they encounter them, that use the particular phrases in other contexts. They may want to share these lists with each other periodically to see which ones have words or phrases in common and to compare the various concepts related to the same word or phrase. These lists may also be discussed in individual conferences with the teacher to monitor concept development. Many students will enjoy this activity as long as it is used to stimulate discussion about language and not made into a rigid chore that must be done at certain times in specific ways.

EXPANDING

LANGUAGE   If you use spelling or vocabulary lists, have the students select one or two words a week from their reading and add them to the lists.

Have one student write his or her favorite word or phrase on the board, and allow it to remain there for several days. Have others in the class try to find the word or phrase in some context and share it and the meaning with the person responsible for the selection. When a number of students have some ideas and examples, let the originator lead a group discussion about various meanings that words or phrases can have depending on context.

WRITING   Remind students to incorporate words or phrases from their language power book into their creative writing when they are appropriate.

Students can begin collecting different kinds of words or phrases to help expand their language concepts:

1. Words or phrases I've known and loved
2. Words or phrases the author used that made me HEAR, SEE, SMELL, FEEL

ART   Have the students make a collage related to one or two words or phrases in their Language Power Book. They can use the word or phrase as a title. They are to cut pictures from magazines, newspapers, postcards, greeting cards, and paste up a collage to represent the words or phrases. If they wish, they can add original artwork to their collage as well.

CHARACTERIZATION AND SETTING

General Rationale

It is through their characters that authors tell their stories. Authors produce a setting to establish the living space and time for the characters, and a mood and background in which the characters carry forward the action or plot of a story. The proficient reader comes to know the place, the time, and the characters significant to the story in an intimate way. When proficient readers like a story, they believe that they could recognize a significant character if she walked down the street or recognize the setting if transplanted there. It is no wonder that avid readers are sometimes disappointed when their favorite stories are brought to visual life in movies or on television, since the people and places seem so different from the ones they so vividly imagined from reading.

The purpose of the strategy lessons that follow is to develop in readers an excitement about, and desire to know intimately, a story's characters and the time and place in which they live.

RELATING CHARACTERIZATION AND SETTING TO ACTION: STRATEGY-LESSON PLAN

Specific Rationale

As they read, proficient readers become interested in the dreams, aspirations, beliefs, and inner motives of significant characters. They need to know what makes any one character different from others and how the characters interact with and relate to each other. Age categories, family memberships, occupation roles, and social status are established for each character in the story. Such understandings are developed not only through the facts of character's life—age, family membership, occupation, social status—but also through the way in which they operate within the settings in which they are placed. For example, an eighty-two year old female character who lives in a twenty-room, three-story mansion in suburban Connecticut in 1975, and has servants and a chauffeur-driven limousine, will evoke different reactions in readers than would that same character depicted as living in a one-room farmhouse in rural Appalachia in 1932 with neighbors coming in and out of her house daily to provide food and seek advice.

Even nonproficient readers are able to recall surface detail about significant characters in a story. They know familial relationships among characters, sex characteristics, age-groups, but they do not often integrate the significance of the time, place, or plot of the story with the characters.

As you discuss with your students the lessons that follow, keep in mind that each reader views people in different ways; therefore, each may react in a different way to characters in stories. Readers' own views of the world, including their personal values and attitudes, will color their responses to the people, the places, and the times about which they read. Readers' already developed schemata—with regard to, say, men and women of the 1920s or the 1970s, people who drink or are teetotalers, people who work in mines or in executive offices—will be projected onto the characters in stories or articles. People of the same age, coming to a given experience with idiosyncratic views of their own, respond differently to the same characters, times, and places. Certainly, then, it is easy to understand that young people view the world differently than do adults; students, differently than do teachers. Young readers may not recognize abstract characteristics such as greed or jealousy as easily as an adult might. However, they are often aware that they do not like a particular character because of a specific action taken in a story. Or, based on their own experience, they may not think (as would some adults) that it is unusual for a stable, likable character to be living in a one-parent family or to be smoking weed.

We found quite a variety of views toward characters in a story that was used extensively with middle-grade students. Although many students recognized the officious nature of the television executive in the story—a "very busy man"—and said he was silly, others allowed that he was a nice person because "he spent time with kids" or "he gave the family some money," while still others said he was hard working because he gave orders to others. A few students thought that one of the story's main characters was a girl. The story is told in the first person by a young male whose name is never mentioned. Except for one picture, however, there are a few subtle references to the fact that the storyteller is a boy. The story opens with the storyteller baby-sitting for a younger brother. These baby-sitting experiences continue throughout the story. The view that some readers have of what kind of person baby-sits—boys or girls—could help them conclude that the storyteller must be a girl. This particular bit of misinformation is not significant to the plot, theme, or basic understanding of the story but does reveal much about schema that readers bring with them to the reading material.

Teachers cannot expect readers to develop similar views about any character in a story, nor should teachers expect them to develop the same views teachers have. If readers have good reasons for saying why a particular character acts a certain way and can justify their answers, their viewpoint must be accepted as legitimate. Through open-ended discussions with peers, students will find other opinions to support or amend their own points of view. As students support their conclusions from their reading, and from listening to other students, they will gain insights and become aware of the range of possible interpretations. Teachers should offer their own opinions as long as they are also substantiated and the students are given the opportunity to disagree. Teachers' opinions about interpretations of characters and settings should be *one* of several possibilities to think about but never the *last word* or the *correct* interpretation.

EVALUATION

The strategy lessons for Relating Characterization and Setting to Action will benefit students who need to focus on relating characterization and setting to action.

Reading-Strategy Instruction

INITIATING

MATERIALS   "Sally and Andrea Went Shopping," adapted by Barry Sherman from a news article

Sally and Andrea Went Shopping

Yesterday, I heard a story about what happened when Sally and Andrea went shopping on Saturday. Sally bought a suit at a department store and had it wrapped in a very nice-looking box. They were on their way to a nearby restaurant to have lunch.

As they were driving down a beautiful street, their car accidentally hit a cat that was running across the street. Sally and Andrea stopped the car and got out to see if they had killed the cat. Yes, the cat was dead. They were very upset because they both loved animals. They decided to try to return the cat to its owners. They removed the suit from the box in which it was packed, and put it in the trunk of the car. Then, they picked up the dead cat carefully and put it into the pretty box.

Sally and Andrea knocked on doors all over the neighborhood, but they couldn't find the owners of the cat. At last, they decided to take the dead cat to the animal shelter. But they were very hungry, so they decided to have lunch first. They stopped for lunch at a restaurant and parked their car in the parking lot in front. They left the cat in the department-store box on the rear seat of the car.

The table in the restaurant was near a window, so they could see their car while they were eating. As they ate, they suddenly saw a well-dressed, middle-aged woman walk past their car. Then she stopped, walked back to the car, and looked in the rear window. She looked around to make sure she wasn't being watched. Then she opened the car door and reached in and took the box from the rear seat.

Sally and Andrea couldn't believe what they saw. This woman had just robbed their car. Should they call the police? They were trying to decide what to do when the thief walked right into the restaurant and sat down at the counter. She put the box on the seat next to her, looked at the menu, and gave her order to the waitress. Sally and Andrea decided to do nothing for a few minutes. They would watch the thief and see what she would do.

As the woman who stole the box was waiting for her order, she turned to the box and slowly began to lift the cover of the box a bit more. All at once she screamed as loud as she could and fell to the floor in a faint. As she fell, she let go of the cover of the box, and the box closed again. No one else saw what was in the box.

Naturally, everyone in the restaurant gathered around the woman who had screamed and fainted. After a few moments, the woman's eyes opened. But as soon as she saw the box, she began to shriek. Then she fainted again. Someone called an ambulance. When the ambulance arrived, the woman's eyes opened, but she was only partly aware of what was going on around her. She was placed on a stretcher and carried into the ambulance.

Just as the ambulance started to drive away, one of the waitresses ran out of the restaurant, carrying the box and shouting, "Stop! Wait! You forgot her package!" The ambulance stopped, and the waitress gave the box to one of the ambulance attendants. He put it carefully next to the woman in the stretcher so that she would know that the box was safe beside her. Just then the woman sat up, looked around her, and saw the box next to her. She started to scream again, and her screams were almost as loud as the siren on the ambulance as it started on its way to the hospital.

For a few minutes, Sally and Andrea couldn't say anything to each other.

When they came into the restaurant, they were feeling sorry for the cat. Now they were feeling sorry for the poor woman who had stolen the box with the dead cat inside. One thing was sure to be true, they agreed: *that* woman would think twice before she ever tried to steal anything again.

Adapted by BARRY SHERMAN

Tell the students that they are to read the story all the way through silently. After they finish reading, discuss the story together, concentrating on how the characters act and interact with each other.

INTERACTING

QUESTIONS FOR DISCUSSION

1. *Who are the important characters in the story and how do you know?*
   Permit the students to suggest the most important characters and provide evidence for their statements.
2. *How do the characters in the story feel about each other?*
   Again permit discussion and have students provide evidence for their own positions.
3. *How do you feel about the characters in the story? Do you like them? Would you like to have them for friends? Would you ask them to go* shopping *or* play hockey [or any other activities your students are interested in]?
   Encourage cross-discussion among students and try to get the students to ask each other, *How do you know that?* or, *Why do you believe that?*
4. *Is the time or place in the story important to the characters? Would it make a difference if the time and place were different? In what ways would it make a difference? How would the characters act differently if the time or place were changed?*
   Help the students put the characters in a different time or place. How would the story be different if it had taken place in a small town? How would it be different if it had taken place in the time of King Arthur, or the Civil War, or any period your students are likely to know about. Have them understand that time and place and characterization work together to help a story develop.
5. *What are the problems faced by each character, and how do they solve their problems?*
   Again help the students focus on the characters within a particular time and setting, and their ability to solve their problems.
6. *Would you solve the characters' problems in the same ways? What other solutions are there to the problems? Would they work any better? Why do you think so?*
   This helps students apply what they have read to other situations and settings as well as to their own lives. Accept any solution offered, and encourage cross-discussion to allow students to question each other and thereby expand each other's thinking.

APPLYING

Select three or four stories that have lots of information about different characters in relation to different settings.

Divide the students into groups and have each group select and read one of the stories thinking of themselves as witnesses to that story. After the reading, tell the students that they are to believe that the main characters in each story have been reported to the police as missing persons. Each group will act as witnesses to the story they have read and will become detectives for a second story using information they receive from the first group of witnesses. The procedure is as follows:

1. Divide the students into groups. Have each group read a different story. They are to read this first story as if they were witnesses to the story. Each reader in the group reads the selected story silently.
2. When they finish reading independently, the group works together to make a list of characteristics of each of the main characters and the most likely place where each could be found. Encourage the students to be concerned with significant aspects of each selected character rather than specific detail. They are not to share their story with any other group.
3. Decide which group will be the detectives for which story. Provide the detectives with the list of characteristics made up by the group of witnesses to the story they will work on. They are to have time during which they can interview the witnesses about the

characters in the story. Again minimize their concern for specifics by asking them to concentrate on significant aspects of the characters' personality, and interrelationships with time and place. Remind them of the kinds of questions you asked during the Interacting phase of this lesson.

4. Have the detectives write a report for the Bureau of Missing Persons, which describes the characters and settings. They are then to read the original story and compare it with their report.

EXPANDING

LANGUAGE   Have the students add a section to their Language Power Notebook called Words or Phrases I Like. They are to list those words and phrases they especially like that refer to people, places, or times. Have them list the whole sentence in which they found the word or phrase embedded. As they begin to develop a substantial list, they can also begin to categorize the words or phrases in various ways. For example, their organization may include physical characteristics, such categories as emotional or psychological characteristics, social characteristics, economic characteristics.

Use students' favorite comic strips to explore the interrelationship between time, place, and characterization. Think of Snoopy and his doghouse; *Doonesbury* and the college setting; or *B.C.* and prehistoric times. Have them rewrite an episode changing the time or place or certain personality traits, and discuss with each other the impact of these changes on their cartoon.

WRITING   Ask the students to think of the person in their lives who has had the most important influence on them and then write a story about that person. Have others read the story and discuss with the author the person described. They can discuss the similarities and differences between what the reader and author believe about the person in the story. In a similar assignment students may write about a person who has had a very negative or bad effect on their life.

SOCIAL STUDIES, SCIENCE, MUSIC, SPORTS, MOVIES   Have the students read about famous people in real life, and the place where that person lives. After the reading they can tell a small group or the class—their favorite sports, TV, movie, or music personality—

1. What about that person's personality helped make him or her become famous
2. In what ways, if any, the place in which the person was born or lived affected the person's becoming famous
3. In what ways the other people in the person's life affected his or her fame

ART   Have the students draw or paint a favorite character from a story that has no pictures.

Have the students select a favorite character and develop a collage that represents what that character is like. They can cut pictures out of magazines and do a paste-up on shirt cardboard.

GETTING TO KNOW THE TIME AND PLACE: STRATEGY-LESSON PLAN

Specific Rationale

There are many human characteristics that are universal and characters in stories will reflect this universality, regardless of the time and place in which they live. All people have some kind of family relationship. They have similar emotions and needs. It is not difficult, consequently, for readers to relate to how people in stories act and what causes them to act in the way they do. On the other hand, there are many respects in which a character's life experiences and those of the reader may differ. Such differences, moreover, may be far more related to the time and place in which a character lives than to the personality or physical characteristics of that character. For example, understanding how aspects of rural life affect the experiences, dreams, and hopes of a character depends on the reader's concepts of (a) rural life and (b) how the character's aspirations may or may not be fulfilled in certain kinds of environments. The problems motivating characters of times past, or those problems imagined by authors for the future, may not easily be related to the modern experiences of the reader. Setting is therefore somewhat more difficult for students to deal with than is characterization. Often in simplistic material setting is not developed in relation to the character and it makes little impact on the story. Therefore readers are often not so consciously aware that time and place can be significant to the action in a story as they are that significant characters are indispensable to the development of the story.

This strategy lesson will help students explore the significance of setting in a story.

EVALUATION

The strategy lesson on Getting to Know the Time and Place will benefit all students who need to focus more on integrating meaning as they read.

Reading-Strategy Instruction

INITIATING

MATERIALS   "A Summer Visit to Grandmother," by Irlene S. Sherman

A Summer Visit to Grandmother

Spending my summer vacation with Grandmother Rosa was the most exciting thing that happened to me every year. I could hardly control my excitement when we would all start getting ready for the long trip to Grandmother Rosa's big house in the country. Every June, together with my mother and father I would pack a few clothes in a small suitcase. Then, after a few more days of preparation, we would take a taxi to the railroad station.

The old train was always waiting for us, its noisy steam engine ready to start the long trip from the big city to the small, quiet village where Grandmother lived. That village was hundreds of miles away from the city and dozens of years back in time. It took 12 hours for the old train to make the trip to Grandmother's village.

It was a very small village that had not grown or changed for many, many years. Grandmother's house was built on the highest spot on a hill. From the house, we could see all the other houses, the few stores, and the river down below. The Iguape River was a very important part of life in the village. Men and children fished in there, women washed clothes in it, and it also served as a highway to get from town to town. The only way to get across the river was to ride the old-fashioned ferryboat. The river overflowed every year in the rainy season, its water spreading over its banks to form a large lake. When it stopped raining, the river became narrower and narrower, until, many days later, it was back to normal.

We had to cross the river to get to Grandmother Rosa's house. And every year, by the time the train arrived at the station, it was night and very dark because there was no electricity in the village. If the moon was out and full, we could see where we were going. If not, we couldn't even see the ground we were stepping on. It was like being blind, trying to guess what lay ahead of us. But we always got to the river safely. After crossing it on the old, creaking ferry, we walked up the slope of the hill that led to Grandmother's house. Finally, we arrived at the old house on top of the hill. We saw the flickering light of the oil lamp shining through the front windows, telling us that we were welcome.

No matter how late the train arrived at the village, Grandmother Rosa was awake and waiting for us, burning her small oil lamp. She sat on a chair near the oil lamp, among the shadows dancing on the wall, waiting for her visitors.

The large table in the kitchen was filled with lots of food that she had been preparing for days. There were all kinds of foods, and she had prepared each dish herself. Grandmother Rosa was a small woman, and she lived alone. She raised chickens, pigs, vegetables, and fruits. She took care of all the chores by herself. She was her own butcher and cook; she baked all her own breads and cakes, and canned her own fruits and vegetables. She chopped wood for the ovens and stoves, and even took care of her own flower garden.

In the kitchen, Grandmother Rosa had a large woodburning stove. When it was lit, it made a lot of smoke. Over the years, there had been so much smoke that the kitchen walls were black. Outside, in the yard, my grandmother had a big oven for baking. Is there anything like the smell of fresh-baked bread?

Every year, when we arrived, after the long walk and crossing the river in darkness, Grandmother Rosa opened her door and hugged us and kissed us again and again. As we walked into the warmly lit kitchen, the delicious smells of different foods reached us.

It was at that moment that we were flooded with happiness at having reached Grandmother's kingdom, with all the gifts that she so lovingly offered us. It was then that we suddenly knew why we had traveled for so many hours, and why we walked so far in the darkness of the night to get to the flickering light in the house at the top of the hill. Here was Grandmother waiting in the middle of the kitchen, with her heart bursting with love for us.

IRLENE S. SHERMAN

Tell the students that they are to read the story all the way through silently. After they read, you will discuss the story together, concentrating on where and when the story takes place.

INTERACTING

QUESTIONS FOR DISCUSSION

1. *When does the story take place? Does it take place in modern times, in the future, a long time ago, or in very ancient times? How do you know?*
   Explore with the students the cues that provide them with information about when the story takes place. Tell them to focus on what cues there are in a story that tell them whether they need to think of modern times or not. They may decide it could have taken place in more than one time because not enough information is available to be exact.
2. *What language does the author use to help you know when and where the story takes place?*
   Focus on either dialogue in the story or on any specialized language the author uses that suggests time.
3. *In what ways is this story similar to today's times? How is it different? Is it important to the story whether it takes place now or at another time? How do you know?*
   Explore with the students how the time of the story is not significant to this story.
4. *Where does the story take place? Does it take place near here? Does it take place in another country? How do you know?*
5. *In what ways is the place similar to where you live? In what ways is it different?*

APPLYING

Have the students choose two of the following three activities to develop in relation to their reading.

1. Draw a map following the action of the story. Label each place on the map, relating it to significant actions in the story.
2. Draw a time line of the story, relating it to the significant events in the story. Focus on important parts of the story rather than insignificant detail.
3. List aspects of the story related to time and setting that are most different from their equivalents in the students' own lives, and the aspects that are most similar to those in the students' lives. List only the most important. Do it in chart form as follows:

Time and Place Setting	Same or Different
12-hour train ride	fast trains now

EXPANDING

LANGUAGE   Have the students begin to collect favorite words and phrases that describe setting and record them in their Language Power Book.

Have the students begin to collect examples of language in stories that take place in a different time or setting and indicate how these differences relate to their own perceptions of time and place based on personal experiences. Provide opportunity for them to share their findings in class.

SOCIAL STUDIES   Have the students relate historical fiction to periods of history by making interrelated time lines that match the books they happen to like with a particular historical period they are studying. The westward movement in the United States, for example, can be related to Laura Ingles Wilder's books.

Have the students make maps based on stories that they believe lend themselves to map making, labeling the places where the significant action takes place.

WRITING Have the students interview members of their family who are older or who have traveled a great deal. Have them write these interviews into stories. They can then make time lines or maps about their relatives' lives. Whenever relevant, these kinds of activities should be related to social-studies experiences as well.

DETERMINING WHO IS TELLING THE STORY: STRATEGY-LESSON PLAN

Specific Rationale

Often the author becomes a character in the story by telling it in the first person. Even proficient readers sometimes have difficulty and confuse the storyteller with one of the other significant characters in the story.

EVALUATION

The strategy lesson for Who Is Telling the Story will benefit

1. Students who need to think about the storyteller.
2. Students who fail to recognize the role of the first-person character in a story.

Reading-Strategy Instruction

INITIATING

MATERIALS "Who Do You Think Told This Story?" by Dorothy Watson and Yetta Goodman

Who Do You Think Told This Story?

Characters:

Jimmy is riding his bike to school. He is small for his age. He is riding his bike fast, calling to his friends as he rides by, waving his hands at them.

Bob is the same age as Jimmy. He is tall and skinny. He is walking to school by himself. He looks at everyone and everything he passes very carefully.

Ms. Cool is Bob's and Jimmy's teacher. She rides a motorcycle to school so that she can find a place to park. She has never had an accident with her motorcycle.

Scene:

It is Monday and it has been raining.

Jimmy is riding his bike to school. He is just about to cross the driveway leading to the teachers' parking lot as Ms. Cool turns into the driveway on her motorcycle.

Bob runs into the driveway shouting. Jimmy swerves his bike. He runs off the curb, hits a tree, and falls off his bike. When Jimmy gets up, his pants are torn and the wheel on his bike is bent.

VERSION 1

My new bike is busted. It's really totaled. That kid, Bobby, I'll kill him if I get my hands on him. He yelled at me to scare me and then got in my way. If I hadn't gone off the sidewalk, I would have hit him. Bobby's going to pay for my bike. It's new and my mom just bought it for me. The light on my bike is broken and my wheel is bent. He's going to have to pay. He got in my way. Ask Ms. Cool, I bet she saw it.

VERSION 2

I just—I just—I just prevented a terrible accident. I saved that Jimmy's life. I was going to walk into the school yard and I saw Jimmy riding his new bike. He was so proud of it and was showing off and everything. Then I saw Ms. Cool turning left into the driveway. She didn't see Jimmy because he was behind the tree. But he was coming so fast I knew I had to stop him or he was going to get hit. I jumped out in front of him and said, "Jimmy, look out." I hope he didn't get hurt when he fell down. I bet he really will thank me for saving his life. Ask Ms. Cool, she'll tell you all about it.

VERSION 3

I'm really shaking. If Bobby hadn't run out and tried to save Jimmy, I would have hit him. Bob did a brave thing. I was just turning into the driveway. It looked clear to me. I saw Bob running and then saw Jimmy on his bike. He swerved away from my motorcycle. I guess we are really lucky. I can't help thinking about what might have happened if Bob hadn't done some fast thinking. It looks as if Jimmy just has a bent fender and I don't think there is a scratch on my motorcycle. I'm going to recommend to the school safety patrol that Bob get an award for bravery. I'm sure Jimmy will be grateful to him, too.

DORTHY WATSON and YETTA GOODMAN

Before providing the students with the reading material, paraphrase the following information:

Sometimes when you are reading a story or a book, the author is not just describing the story, he or she is actually a character in the story. It is important to recognize this character and to know who is telling the story. It is not as important to know the character's name as it is to be able to tell how that person acts, why he or she acts that way, how he or she acts toward others in the story, and how he or she influences events in the story.

Tell them they will be given a short story to read. First the characters and the setting of the story are described, but then each character tells the same story as it happened to that particular person. The students are to see if they can tell which character is telling each version of the story and what evidence from the story supports their answers.

Provide each student with a copy of "Who Do You Think Told This Story?" and have them read it silently.

INTERACTING

QUESTIONS FOR DISCUSSION

1. *Who do you think had the correct version of the story?*
   Encourage the students to explore the idea that each person told the story correctly. Discuss how people get different slants on a story because of their own vantage point.

2. *Do you think that Bob should have to pay for Jimmy's bike?*
   Of course, there is no right answer here. The students should explore all the possibilities. Help them anchor their opinions to the details in the story whenever possible; however, permit inferences. You may want to have a mock trial in which the three characters would be witnesses. The story can be acted out as if it has been brought to a courtroom. The trial would take place before the student body of the school.

3. *Why did* [name each character in turn] *act the way he* [or she] *did?*
   Encourage the students to use evidence from the story to provide motives for the characters.

4. *When an author puts himself in a story, does it confuse you? Is the "I" character in a story always the author?*
   Try to deal with the concerns of each student and emphasize the importance of knowing who is telling the story.

5. *Why would an author write a story in the first person?*
   Explore with the students how this device often makes a story seem more personal or makes it seem as if it were being *told* rather than written. (For another lesson, read different first-person stories to explore questions 4 and 5.) You may relate first person stories to oral storytelling.

APPLYING

MATERIALS   "The Four Doors," by Debra Goodman

The Four Doors

My name is Antonio and I live here in this big house with four doors. There are four families living in my house, but we Romeros are proud, because we have the nicest door of all. When you come see me you will know which door is mine. My door has a window so we can look out when the doorbell rings and see who is coming to visit. Every year we paint our door with beautiful latex paints. And we paint the mail slot shiny black, so the postman will say, "Ah, what fine people the Romeros are, they have the nicest mail slot I've ever seen."

My name is Felisha and I live here in this big house with four doors. Four families live in this house, but we Johnsons are proud because we have the nicest door of all. When you come see me you'll know which door is mine right away. We have a beautiful silver screen door in front of our hard brown door. In the winter me and my big sister Denise take out the screens and put in the storm windows. But now it is summer and we can open our hard brown door and let the air come in without all the mosquitos and flies. Our screen door has our initial "J" for Johnson, and there is a mail slot right in the door so the postman will say, "Ah, what fine people the Johnsons are. I don't even have to open this shiny screen door to deliver the mail."

My name is Ramona and I live here in this big house with four doors. Four families live in this house, but we Billingsleas are proud because we have the best door of all. If you come to see me you will know my door right away. We haven't painted it since we moved in. The doorbell doesn't work. My little sister broke the window with a baseball last fall. And when the mailman comes by he always says, "When are you going to fix that mail slot?" But what I like most about my door is when my mother and father come home at night, and they look at that broken window and say, "We'll have to fix this door up someday, but we're not home very often—so we'll just talk and play with our children tonight."

DEBRA GOODMAN

Have each student read "The Four Doors." Using the three episodes they have just read as models they are to write the episode of the fourth door. They are to write their episode from the perspective of the storyteller using the first person.

Then have the students read "The Foor Doors" silently, again. Then divide the students into three groups, and have each group choose to be one of the three families described in "The Foor Doors." As a group they are to select two incidents that occur in front of their door. One should involve the mailman bringing a letter. The second should involve an interaction with one of the families in the story, including families the students developed in the episodes they wrote. The students are to think through their stories and present them to the others in play form or as first-person storytellers.

EXPANDING

LANGUAGE Develop interest in oral storytelling. Begin by having the students tell a favorite joke as if it had actually happened to them. Then have them interview parents or grandparents for folktales, stories, or superstitions from their own ethnic background. Again they are to tell these stories as if they had happened to them. Later, as they become more confident in themselves as storytellers, they can begin to read stories for oral telling or make up their own adventures to pass on to their peers.

Select an exciting happening at school, such as an accident, a fight or quarrel, a problem between students and a teacher or administrator. Have the students describe the people involved and the scene. They can list on the board the characteristics of the people and the setting of the scene, using no emotional words or phrases. Then have the students write the story from the point of view of two different people, using the first person in each story.

Have the students pretend that their favorite character from a story has gotten lost. They are then to write or tell, using first-person narrative, what happened to that character.

ART Have each student make "The Four Doors" story into a book including their own story of the fourth door with illustrations focusing on the four doors.

Have the students make a wanted poster or a vote-for-me poster for their favorite character in a story that they really liked. The text for their poster should focus on the character's major personality traits.

EXPLORING PLOT AND THEME

General Rationale

Plot and Theme are traditional terms used in literature. Many people who study the field of literature have very specific notions about what the terms mean, and are often certain that they know what the plot and theme of stories are. There is, however, controversy regarding these terms and their application to literature. We do believe that reading for meaning can be expanded and enhanced if readers begin to explore aspects of plot and theme.

As students deal with plot and theme, they must be permitted and encouraged to express their own opinions about their understanding of what they read. Not only do definitions of the terms *plot* and *theme* vary among experts but there is always variation concerning the specific plot or theme for any particular piece of literature. As teachers discuss plot and theme with students, they should keep in mind that any plot or theme that readers can justify, based on their own background and what they have read, must be acceptable. When readers are confident that they have the right to make judgments of their own and that their judgments will be respected, they will read for themselves and not to please others.

PLOT: STRATEGY-LESSON PLAN

Specific Rationale

Authors set up problems or conflicts related to the characters in a story. Such is often the case with feature articles, biographies, or autobiographies, which are nonfiction. We define the plot of a story as the problem(s) and the method(s) of solving the problem(s). The plot includes the aspects of a story that relate action or events. Plots can often be stated as questions: Will Little Red Hen make her bread and eat it with the help of others? Will Little Red Riding Hood get to her grandmother's house safely?

Readers should know that authors often write stories to help the characters in those stories solve a problem or problems. When stories are long or involved, they can have a number of plots. As readers, not only can we state what we believe the problem to be and whether or not the author has solved it, but we can judge whether we like the way the problem was solved, explain why we think the problem was solved in the way it was, and perhaps even suggest some other ways the problem could have been resolved. Our research suggests that readers are often able to make a plotlike statement about a story. A reader involved with the plot of the story may be personally interacting with the ongoing story development.

The purpose of this strategy lesson is to help students interact with the author about the problems in a story or article. The purpose is not to express one critic's or one reviewer's or one teacher's idea or belief about plot but to allow readers to decide for themselves what the major problems in a story are, how they are resolved, what interrelationships cause problems or resolution, and whether the resolution seems appropriate.

EVALUATION

The strategy lesson on Plot will benefit most students.

Reading-Strategy Lesson

INITIATING

MATERIAL   Select a cartoon with a simple, clear story line or use a picture book without words. Provide each student with a copy of the cartoon. Ask them to look over the cartoon to see what is happening. Tell them that together you will decide what story the pictures tell.

INTERACTING

QUESTIONS FOR DISCUSSION

1. *What is the most important thing happening in the story? Can you tell what it is in just a few words? Why do you think that is most important?*
   Have the students focus on the main point and not simply a sequential retelling. If more than one major point is suggested by the students, ask those with differing points of view to suggest why they think their point is more important than the others. They could agree that more than one point is important.
2. *Which are the most important characters in the story and why do you think so?*
   Have the students use information from the pictures to justify their answers.
3. *Which are the least important characters? How do you know?*
   Explore with the students the notion that it is not very important to know the specific sequential events. Try to get them to understand that some sequential events in stories make less difference to a story than do others. What makes the most difference are the major characters and how they carry out the action.
4. *What problems do the major characters have in the story?*
   Again, have the students use the information from the cartoon to support their answers.
6. *How do the major characters solve their problems, or how does the author solve their problems for them?*
   Accept any answers that the students can justify, and encourage them to discuss their differences with each other.
6. *Can you think of any other way to end this cartoon?*
   For those who can suggest a different ending, have them draw the different solutions. Try to encourage more than one student to provide different endings.

7. *Which of the endings do you like best—the original or one suggested by a classmate?* It may be possible to conclude that all the stories have merit and that by changing the ending, not only has the story changed but a new story has been created, which starts the same way as another story.

APPLYING

Collect a group of folktales with similar plots but different characters (for example, "The Three Billy Goats Gruff" and "The Three Little Pigs"). The students can eventually be involved in collecting suitable tales. Have each student select one folktale from the collection, which they are to read silently. After their reading have them each choose one of the following activities:

1. They are to select the most important events in the story. They should think about the most important beginning event, some of the most important events in the middle of the story, and the most important final event. Then they are to make these into a filmstrip, television, or cartoon sequence and present their work to others who have not read the story.
2. They are to decide what the major problem in the story is and then solve that problem in a different way than the author did. They may draw the sequence of main events but end it with their solution; or write their own ending using their solution; or tape-record a version of the story that uses their solution. They are to find a classmate who has a different solution to the story and compare the endings.

EXPANDING

ORAL LANGUAGE Have the students explore the similarities and differences in the plots of their favorite detective series or family comedies on TV. Have them discuss how the characters in these shows solve their problems.

Encourage different students to pretend they are hosts of TV shows who will interview these characters. They have two minutes of TV time to tell the public each character's problem and how it was solved.

Have the students compare plots of familiar folktales or stories they remember from earlier reading. This may motivate them to look up picture-story books of such tales as "The Little Red Hen," "The Three Little Pigs," "The Three Billy Goats Gruff." They may want to do an interpretive reading of one of these tales for their own class or for younger students.

ART Have the children recall fairy tales or folktales they heard when they were younger. Ask them to draw the main events in the form of a cartoon, filmstrip, TV program, or picture book. This could be expanded into a unit on folktales and fairy tales.

Have students draw a cartoon strip of their favorite story or TV show. They will have to select only the most significant aspects of the story to develop a cartoon sequence.

STORY SCHEMA: STRATEGY-LESSON PLAN[4]

Specific Rationale

Researchers are becoming more aware that in order to understand and reproduce either a story or an article the reader must have some notions about the overall structure of stories and articles. In other words, they must build schema about storyness, about articleness, about how connected text is organized.

By listening to stories young children become familiar with certain story landmarks: beginnings ("Once upon a time . . ."); plot sequence that builds nicely to a climax and resolution; themes (good triumphs over evil); endings (". . . and they lived happily ever after"). Such landmarks are comfortable and helpful—comfortable because they allow the reader to

---

[4]Written with Dorothy Watson, who calls this a schema-story strategy lesson.

settle in quickly from author to author and helpful because they allow readers to predict the course of the story and to monitor their own reading.

In response to adults reading or telling them stories, children begin to develop a sense of story—an organizing schema that becomes more familiar and more useful the more it is called upon. The stories that young children hear provide them with general frames of reference for more conceptually difficult but similarly organized stories. As readers get older, they begin to encounter written information in a variety of formats. Essays are organized in a different way than are feature articles. Sports articles are structured differently from "Advice to the Lovelorn." A natural introduction to diversity in presentations of messages is simply to read to students from dissimilar texts (poetry, folktales, songs, math problems, science information, social studies, advertisements, menus, recipes, directions. At appropriate points, ask: *What will happen next? Does this remind you of anything else we've read? How is this similar? How is it different? Why is this organized in this way?*

For the purposes of this strategy lesson, we shall help readers focus on the cues that help them recognize different story or article schema. Since even young children have a sense of story in response to many forms of fiction, this lesson will use nonfiction formats.

EVALUATION

The strategy lesson on Story Schema will benefit most students.

Reading-Strategy Instruction

INITIATING

MATERIALS   Select an article that has an easily identifiable beginning, organizational sequence, and ending. Science, social-studies, and math texts which are out-dated and not used as regular texts are good resources for this.[5] Weekly newsmagazines such as *Scope, Sprint,* or *Weekly Reader* have a variety of selections. For readers with limited experience, stick to straightforward materials from science or social-studies texts. For readers with wide experience, use written language with which they have had limited experience. To repeat, it is helpful to read the particular form aloud to students a few times before introducing this strategy.

Cut the story into sections depending on its complexity and the ability of the students. For younger or less proficient readers, cut the story into three or four sections. As students become more sophisticated with this technique cut the story into more sections. Include the titles, diagrams, questions, and the like that are part of the text. Each section must be long enough to give students something substantial to read—even though they may be reading something from the middle of the selection. Ask each student in the group (it's usually good to have as many readers as you have sections or to pair your students on each section) to read the selection silently, thinking about what might have happened before and after that particular excerpt.

INTERACTING

QUESTIONS FOR DISCUSSION

1. *Who has the beginning of the article?*
   Have the student who responds read the section aloud.
2. *Do you all agree this is the beginning? Why do you think so? What cues are there that this is the beginning?*

---

[5]A number of times we have mentioned discarded basals and texts. These books can be adapted for many uses in strategy lessons. Good stories can be cut as is, from a basal or text and placed in a file folder; in this way a collection of short stories is easily and inexpensively added to the class library. Students can decorate or illustrate the covers. Appropriate stories can be cut up in such a way that students must stop at particular places in order to predict. For other stories, endings may be cut away so that students finish the stories themselves. And finally, appropriate articles or chapters can be cut apart for the purposes of this strategy lesson.

If two students have responded, have both read their sections and then interact with each other in response to the questions. Allow the rest of the group to enter the discussion with their views.

3. *Do you all agree that we've chosen the first section? Who has the next section?*
   Use questions similar to the above as you proceed through each section. Encourage students to make and test predictions, discuss decisions, and listen to each other.

APPLYING

Using other cut-up stories or articles, have each student reconstruct his or her own story independently. Then the group can compare their reconstructed stories or articles with each other.

Using questions similar to those raised in the Interacting phase, allow students to discuss what cues help them decide how stories or articles are structured or organized. These may then be compared with the original organization to see which cues help in reconstructing an original and which may mislead the reading.

EXPANDING

Experiment with variations of the ideas explored in the Initiating and Applying phases. When students have had ample practice reconstructing single stories or articles, you may then provide a cut-apart article and a cut-apart story on the same subject. Mix these together and explore the ease or difficulty in first separating the two and then reconstructing. Or you can use two fiction pieces that are somewhat similar and two nonfiction pieces that are somewhat similar. Stylistic differences between authors should emerge. Keep in mind that there may not always be enough cues or difference to reconstruct the original or even to separate the two stories.

THEME: STRATEGY-LESSON PLAN

Specific Rationale

Many authors write with a lesson in mind. They want their readers not only to gain the knowledge presented but also to learn some overall rules, ideas, or values about life that the authors believe to be significant. Other authors may not want to teach a lesson directly but are concerned with the readers' exploring certain rules of conduct in life's processes. When such abstractions appear in story material, we define them as themes but prefer the term *generalization* when they have to do with informational material. They have also been called *morals, lessons, overall concepts,* or *major ideas.* Some people are surprised, when they visit Canada, to discover that there is more to the country than fields and fields of corn and wheat; when in Holland, to find no one wearing wooden shoes. Generalizations about people and places that are drawn from reading can be limiting or actually erroneous, as well as expanding and productive.

The focus of the lessons that follow is NOT the "correctness" of a particular theme or generalization; rather it is helping readers become aware that authors often have a purpose in writing and this purpose may be in the form of a lesson or overall idea that a reader can express.

From our research we have discovered that some readers can respond to a question that elicits themes appropriately:

Teacher: Why do you think the author wrote this story?
Student: You can get people to do what you want for them if you tell them the opposite.

However, so much of the reading in school has focused on instruction that often readers view texts as if they were instructional aids.

Some students may respond by suggesting the author's purpose was to teach a specific skill that happened in the story but was peripheral to the plot:

Teacher: Why do you think the author wrote this story?

Student A: To teach you how to make a flashlight.
Student B: To teach you to take care of pets.
Student C: To teach me new words.

In addition to considering an author's purpose, we believe that readers must also be aware that other readers often come up with different themes or generalizations based on the knowledge and belief systems that they bring to the task.

Although it is crucial to become aware of the author's purposes, and even to find out if the author ever expresses a personal purpose or lesson in writing a particular book, the author's theme is not nearly as significant to the reader as the lessons the reader develops from the experience.

Helping readers become consciously aware of themes and generalizations should enable them to

1. Realize that in writing some authors have purposes in addition to the telling of a story about a group of people and their problems
2. Discuss and evaluate their reading so they become aware that the same reading can generate a variety of themes and generalizations for different readers

EVALUATION

The strategy lesson on Theme will benefit most students.

Reading-Strategy Instruction

INITIATING

MATERIALS   Build a collection of typical myths and folktales, some of which end with an explicitly stated moral. Use one with an explicitly stated moral for this lesson.

Ask the students simply to read the story provided. Do not prepare them with any other explanations or statement of purpose.

INTERACTING

QUESTIONS FOR DISCUSSION

1. *Why is a moral stated at the end of the story?*
    You may explore the idea that whoever originally wrote or told stories of this type wanted to make sure that the listeners understood their purpose in creating stories.
2. *Do most writers have a purpose when they write? Do you think most of them are trying to teach something to their audience?*
    Explore a variety of possibilities. Students may use their favorite TV shows as examples. Try to conclude that regardless of the type of story, the author often tries to teach, explain, or pass on significant information, beliefs, or knowledge.
3. *Most stories do not end with a stated moral, lesson, or theme. How does a reader know the author's purpose?*
    Students must understand that if an author does not state the purpose directly, then the reader literally makes a good guess based on evidence from the reading. Therefore, different readers may come up with legitimately different themes.
4. *Do you think the author could have any lessons other than the one stated at the end of the story? Why?*
    Encourage students to explore various possibilities and share their reasons with each other. Permit them to interact and argue with each other about their personal reactions.
5. *Is it possible for an author to reveal things about what he or she believes without doing so consciously?*

APPLYING

Use the collection of myths and folktales. Have the students read silently two or three of the stories. Then, working in teams of two or three they are to list as many themes or lessons as possible that each story might be teaching. Through discussion with each other, they are to decide which of the themes they think best represents the story. Have each team who read the same story work together as a larger group. They are to put their most representative themes on the board and discuss the variations. They may decide to agree on a single theme, but if there are well-documented alternative themes, they should leave all the appropriate ones on the board.

EXPANDING

CREATING WRITING   Take morals or sayings that the students know, and let them write a story to support them.

Have them find morals that contradict each other. They are then to write stories representing opposite morals or themes. Examples include

1. If at first you don't succeed try, try again, *or* Why try again, you only keep failing?
2. Better late than never, *or* Being late can cause a disaster.
3. Don't envy what others have, *or* If you show your admiration of what others have, you may get what you want.
4. Truth is greater than fiction, *or* Half the truth is often a great lie (Benjamin Franklin).
5. To be blind is bad, but it is worse to have eyes and not see (Helen Keller).
6. With all beings and all things we shall be as relatives (a Sioux Indian saying).
7. No one can make you feel inferior without your consent (Eleanor Roosevelt).
8. You can't hold a man down without staying down with him (Booker T. Washington).

GENERALIZATIONS: STRATEGY-LESSON PLAN

Specific Rationale

Nonfiction material often has a major idea that the author hopes the reader will learn. This major idea is built from the cumulation of knowledge presented in nonfiction. Readers will be helped to understand what is significant in their reading if they ask themeselves What is the most important information I can learn from this reading and Why did the author want me to learn this?

EVALUATION

The strategy lesson on Generalizations will benefit most students.

INITIATING

MATERIALS   Use social studies or science materials that the students are using at the time this lesson is presented.

The student may select sections to read that are causing problems or you may select material related to a unit of study you are exploring.

Reading-Strategy Instruction

INTERACTING

QUESTIONS FOR DISCUSSION

1. *What was the most important idea(s) presented in this passage? Why do you think so?*
   Help the students think about what idea was explained in a variety of ways, restated,

and reexplained. These cues help the reader know what the author thought was most important.

2. *Why do you think the author wanted you to know this information?*

Again we hope students will begin to understand that writers have a purpose which often helps authors decide what is important.

3. *What ideas in the article or chapter did you find most interesting, and why? What was least interesting, and why?*

With this question, we hope the reader will understand that the author and the reader are not always interested in the same things.

4. *For what reasons would you reread this article? When would you write down some of the ideas in this article?*

Explore the notion that reading at varying speeds, taking notes, or going over written information must be related to the *reader's* purpose. Have the students reread the article after this discussion. Then ask, *Did our discussion help any in your rereading of the article?* Stress the importance of knowing the purpose of one's reading in order to understand what will be most important in the reading.

APPLYING

MATERIALS   Develop a collection of science or social-studies chapters around single concepts, single-concept books, or articles from newspapers or magazines that focus on a single concern or subject, such as prejudice, conservation of energy, a particular animal or insect.

Allow the students some choice in selecting a topic to read. Before they read, they are to write down two reasons why they want to read the article. After they have read the articles, have the students who select the same articles work together as a group. They are to respond to the following questions orally in small groups. You can ask one of the group members to lead the discussion.

1. *What were the author's most important ideas? How do you know?*
2. *What ideas did you think were most important? Why?*
3. *Why did you choose this article to read?*
4. *When would you want to read more about this subject?*

EXPANDING

ART   Draw the author's main idea as a diagram, model, or political cartoon.

LANGUAGE   Explore with students the benefit of jotting down the author's main ideas on 3-by-5-inch cards for further reference, when they should do this, and why. You may discuss underlining in the same fashion. These kinds of discussions may help individual students find out what kinds of study aids help them the most.

POINT OF VIEW

General Rationale

Authors have a point of view. Their writing often reveals what they believe. Complete objectivity in writing may be nonexistent. Some people think that writers who believe they are truly objective—completely fair and unbiased—are denying "the existence of their own personalities."[6]

Even articles on the front page of a newspaper, where the most objective reporting is

---

[6]Earl Kelly, "Teaching Current Issues in the Schools," *Twenty-sixth Yearbook of the National Council for the Social Studies* (Washington, D.C.: 1955), p. 59. R. Ellsworth and O. Sands, eds., *Improving the Social Studies Curriculum.*

supposed to appear, reflect reporters' points of view as revealed by the stress placed on *selected* facts as well as by the omission or inclusion of selected information or events. It is not only in nonfiction reporting that authors express their points of view. Humor, pathos, and other writing that expresses an author's emotions, and calls forth the emotions of the reader, reflect the author's beliefs and prejudices. This is the stuff of written language. Authors who control the use of language are able to move large numbers of people emotionally and become the great writers in a society. Readers who are sensitive to these emotions but can understand their purpose and be wary of their impact become the critical readers in a society. In a democratic society where a major goal is to minimize or eliminate censorship, developing critical readers must be a major thrust at all grade levels and in every curriculum area. Controlling what an author writes is not necessary if readers learn that they can reject, disbelieve, or question what they read.

We do not want to imply that everything a students reads for the classroom should be dissected or critically evaluated. Often criticial reading has meant learning to discover the single "right" criticism or a teacher's or critic's view of the reading. Our major purpose is to impart the view that all reading must be evaluated critically by the reader and that the reader must believe that

READING IS FOR ME AND UNDER MY CONTROL

Therefore, I always react intellectually (based on what I know and believe) and emotionally (based on what I feel) to everything that I read. Not only does the author have a point of view that is reflected in his or her writing, but I also have a point of view that is reflected in my right to react to or interact with the author.

PROPAGANDA: STRATEGY-LESSON PLAN

Specific Rationale

Readers must be consciously aware that authors' points of view are sometimes subtly stated. If students are to become effective critical readers, this awareness must be developed in early reading instruction. All readers must know that

1. They have the responsibility to evaluate what the author is saying
2. They have the right to disagree with or question an author's writing but should have reasons for their reactions
3. All authors have points of view, including scientists and other authorities
4. The mere fact that something is printed in a book, magazine, or newspaper, or on a billboard, does not make it true

As in other aspects of comprehension, begin the development of critical reading by helping your students become critical listeners. Encourage discussion about the degree to which students believe advertisements on television. Ask them to share personal experiences with following the advice of advertisements on television. Explore both positive and negative results. Using local TV news, including sports reporting, discuss the problems involved in accurate eye-witness reporting. Students should be aware that different people perceive the same situation in different ways. Read through the strategy lesson and follow the suggested procedures relating to real experiences, television viewing, or radio listening prior to reading. If you help students become critical in their reaction to listening experiences, there will be an easy transfer to maintaining a questioning and critical approach in their reading.

EVALUATION

The strategy lesson on Propaganda will benefit all students.

Reading-Strategy Instruction

INITIATING

MATERIALS Two local and recent advertisements that have been copied for duplication or made into an overhead transparency. (Your choices should be legitimate ads, although they may be funny with some questionable statements.) Each should be advertising the same item and have plausible contradictory evidence.

Start with one advertisement only and ask the students to read the advertisement. Tell them to think about what aspects are true and what aspects are questionable and why. Then discuss the ad.

INTERACTING

QUESTIONS FOR DISCUSSION

1. *Why did the author of the ad want to write this?*
    Help the students realize that most of what they read is written for a purpose, often to convince others of a particular point of view. Get them to realize that if they try to explore why something was written, they can sometimes deepen their understanding of an ad, article, or story.
2. *Do you think the author is being truthful?*
    Explore the notion that it is less important that the author be truthful than that the reader be critical or skeptical. Readers should not immediately accept and believe everything they find in print. They should question everything they read.
3. *What motivation does the author have in writing? Why does the author want you to believe what is written?*
    Again, help the student realize that the author's purpose is significant to comprehension.
4. *Can you state two things that show fact? How do you know? Can you state two things that are opinion? How do you know?*

Help the students list on the board questions readers should ask themselves. Once compiled, the list can be made into a permanent chart for display in the classroom, or it may be duplicated for distribution to each student. This list may be added to as the class explores the topic at various times. Label this list Questions for Critical Readers. Since these are questions that students are supposed to ask themselves as they read, do NOT have them write the answers to these questions. Some possible questions (these are only samples—elicit questions from the students):

1. What is the author's reason for writing this?
2. What purposes does it have?
3. What ideas or facts do I believe, and why? What do I question, and why?
4. Would I buy this item or not, and why?
5. What language cues help clarify particular points?
6. What language cues confuse me?

After you have made the list with the students, let them respond to each of these questions in relation to the ad. Have one of the students lead this discussion. (Later, in the Applying phase, students, working in small groups, will be conducting a similar discussion; this will help them to learn to have a discussion with class members as discussion leaders.)

After the discussion, ask the students, *How can you find more information to get answers to your questions or to get information to support either your point of view or the author's?*

List on the board the students' suggestions. Label this list Finding Information for Critical Readers. Then place their suggestions on a permanent chart or run off enough copies so that each student will have one. Add to this list as appropriate. The list may include such ideas as (again, these are only samples—elicit ideas from the students)

1. Find other ads that have similar claims and decide if both are possible
2. Ask people if they have tried the item, and compare answers
3. Try the item yourself and make a decision based on personal experiences
4. If the ad is about medicine, talk to a doctor about it, or if it is about an electrical appliance, talk to an electrician or an engineer about it

Now introduce the second ad that you prepared for this lesson and have the students compare it with the first one. Use orally first Questions for Critical Readers and then Finding Information for Critical Readers.

APPLYING

Begin a collection of controversial issues by monitoring newspapers and magazines and getting opposed or different views about the same issues. Students can help collect such materials: for example, different views on a local desegregation suit or descriptions of a Civil War battle written by a northern historian and a southern historian.

Controversy excites and motivates reading. The readings for this section should be chosen to permit students to explore controversial points of view; some of these readings should be about the same topic, but each would present different arguments on that question.

Before the students select their readings, review the Questions for Critical Readers developed in the Initiating phase of this lesson. Ask the students which questions are still good to keep in mind while reading stories and articles. Have them add any new questions that they think will help them read critically.

In addition to the suggested questions listed earlier, additional questions may include the following:

1. Does the author believe what he or she is writing?
2. Why would an author write something he or she does not believe?
3. Will an author ALWAYS believe the ideas or facts written in his or her own stories? Why, or why not?
4. How much does the author know about what he or she is writing?

Also have the students review the list Finding Information for Critical Readers. They are to add any ways they can think of that would help them check on questions related to authors' biases, knowledge, or points of view. The new list may include the following:

1. Make a list of the most important ideas, knowledge, or beliefs that you agree and disagree with. Leave space between each one to add other people's points of view.
2. Find a variety of points of view on the same topic. In addition to reading other authors, interview various people.
3. Experiment with the ideas yourself to see if the claims are true based on your own experiences.
4. Look up information about the author to find out what he or she knows about the field that he or she is writing about.

Students should be encouraged to question authorities and not to assume that everything they write is truth. It may be interesting for them to know that some authors know a great deal about the field they are writing about, whereas others know relatively little. This fact will give the students another reason to be critical listeners and readers.

After the two lists have been added to, have the students work together in groups of two or three.

1. Each member of the group is to read one story or article silently.
2. Using Questions for Critical Readers, they are to discuss orally in their small group the relevant questions.
3. Then they are to read a second story or article that presents a different point of view on the same topic.
4. Using Questions for Critical Readers, they are to discuss the second article as they did the first one.
5. Using Finding Information for Critical Readers, they are to choose any relevant way (that is, in relation to the topic) to explore their point of view, whether or not it supports the author's point of view. (Here the students may come up with additional points to add to Finding Information for Critical Readers.)
6. They are to write a letter to the authors of the articles, explaining the ways in which they agree or disagree. (You could have the students present their reactions to the articles in ways other than letter writing. See the Expanding phase for additional suggestions.)

EXPANDING

WRITING   Write down five sentences in the story that give true facts and five sentences that show the author's opinion. Next to each one, state what cues in the story helped you distinguish the factual statements from the opinions.

Find a newspaper article in which the writer is trying to persuade you of something. If you agree with the author, write him or her a letter telling what arguments were good and why you think so. If you disagree, write a letter telling what arguments the author used that did not support his or her point of view and why you think so. Share your letter with one or two classmates and ask them to tell you what they think you meant. If your classmate misunderstands what you wrote, clarify the necessary sections. Rewrite your letter and send it to the author or the newspaper.

READING   Local controversies are relevant to many students. Exploit the opportunities the local newspapers provide. Have the students collect the different articles from local newspapers on the same controversy. The students can report the points of view for the class, and the class can discuss what they believe.

ORAL LANGUAGE   Set up classroom debates among students focusing on controversial issues about which the students are excited. If your class enjoys this, they may research the rules of debating societies and begin to follow more formal debate formats.

SOCIAL STUDIES OR SCIENCE   Younger students could focus on TV commercials for children's toys to note the claims made about the products. Students who own these products can bring them to class so that the class can examine them, test out the quality of the products, and compare their findings with the advertisers' claims. A chart can be made for each product, for comparison:

Advertiser's Claims	Actual Qualities	Tests Run
1.	1.	1.
2.	2.	2.

When students discover a serious discrepancy between the manufacturer's advertised claims and the product's actual quality, they may be encouraged to write to inform the manufacturer of their findings. A similar activity could be done with various foods or personal items.

HUMOR: STRATEGY-LESSON PLAN

Specific Rationale

As they grow and develop, people find a variety of things funny. What is funny to a six-year-old may not be funny to a twelve-year-old, and a twelve-year-old may not understand why his parents are laughing at some particular incident. In addition, an adult and a twelve-year-old may both laugh at the same incident but may find different aspects of the incident to be funny. A person in Los Angeles may see something more significantly funny in a story about smog than would a person in a small rural community in Iowa. Comments about Watergate can evoke laughter from an audience in the United States, while someone in Peking may be totally unaware why an American would laugh at such comments. What is funny and why it is funny are very much related to how a situation is being characterized and how it is understood by the reader or listener.

There are many kinds of humor and many reasons for people to laugh. We want readers to respond to humor in their reading, although we do not want to decide what is funny for them. Humor is part of reading and makes reading an enjoyable experience. This strategy lesson is written to help readers explore humor, but it is not meant to TELL readers WHAT is funny nor WHY something is considered to be humorous.

Keep in mind that what may be funny to you, may not be funny to your students or may be funny for reasons different from your own. Different things are humorous depending on age, cultural and ethnic group, as well as all the experiences people have during their lifetime.

In exploring humor with your students, you may have to deal with jokes or stories that make fun of specific groups of people for reasons of national origins, for example, Poles; racial differences, for example, Blacks; religious differences, for example, Jews; family relationships, for example, stepmothers; physical characteristics, for example, fat people.

Take this opportunity to discuss with your students how humor can be used to put people down or to keep people in their place. Jokes made at the expense of a whole group of people may hurt the whole group in the same way that jokes made against an individual hurt the individual. This is an area of controversy that can be researched and explored by your students. (Relate this discussion to the use of eye dialect. See chapter 6.) Through open-ended discussions readers can begin to see how others view humor and expand their own definition of humor.

EVALUATION

The strategy lesson on Humor will benefit all readers.

Reading-Strategy Instruction

INITIATING

MATERIALS   Three related cartoons

Reproduce the selected cartoons for use on the overhead. Ask the students to read all three cartoons. Tell them when they have finished you will discuss whether or not they find the cartoons funny and why.

INTERACTING

QUESTIONS FOR DISCUSSION

1. *Do you think the cartoons are funny?*
2. *Why?*
3. *Which cartoon do you think is funniest, and why?*
4. *Who agrees or disagrees, and why?*
   Explore all the possibilities the students suggest. Add your own ideas to stimulate and keep the discussion going. Encourage the students to interact with each other and question each other about the various answers.
5. *What makes the cartoon funny, and why?*
   Again permit as much discussion as possible and encourage student interaction.
6. *Are all the cartoons you read funny? Which are and which are not? Why do you think so?*
   Let this discussion get started and then encourage students to bring to class examples of cartoons they find funny and those they don't find funny. Continue this aspect of the discussion at another time.
7. *Why do authors like to make things funny?*
   Explore the notions of entertainment and of point of view expressed without hitting the reader on the head.
8. *What reason do you think the cartoonists had in mind when they drew and captioned these comic strips?*

APPLYING

Have the students select their favorite funnies and cartoons and read them first to a child of six or seven and then to a person over twenty—either person could be a member of their family. They are to ask their subjects why they think the cartoons are funny, or why not? They should jot down the responses to share with the group or class another day. Then discuss how different age-groups react to things the students find funny.

As each student presents his or her findings, have the other class members share their reactions to the presented selections. This way students will observe different points of view among peers as well as among different age-groups.

Have the students select and read a funny story to others and follow the same procedure.

EXPANDING

ART Have the students draw cartoons about something funny that has happened to them personally.

Annotated Bibliography for Children

PREDICTING

Primary

Aliki. *Hush Little Baby*. Englewood Cliffs, N.J.: Prentice-Hall, Inc., 1975.

> Resume: Traditional children's lullaby.

> Relationship to strategy lessons: Folk song with eye dialect in picture-storybook format.

Barthelme, Donald. *The Slightly Irregular Fire Engine or the Hithering Thithering Djinn*. New York: Farrar, Straus, & Giroux, Inc., 1971.

> Resume: A satirical nonsense story about the humorous adventures of a "person" named Matilda.

> Relationship to strategy lessons: Illustrations are nineteenth-century engravings in collage form. Captions have various types of print and are presented in varying ways and in varying placements.

Carle, Eric. *The Very Hungry Caterpillar*. New York: The World Publishing Company.
———. *The Secret Birthday Message*. New York: Thomas Y. Crowell Company, 1972.

> Resume: Both titles provide good summary statements for each of these exciting picture-story books.

> Relationship to strategy lessons: In each book Carle uses an unusual format that matches the story line and the artistic work. Pages are cut appropriately to look like rocks and doors. Peepholes in the pages are used to find surprises or to represent hungry caterpillars.

Preston, Edna Mitchell. *Popcorn and Ma Goodness*. Illustrated by Robert Andrew Parker. New York: The Viking Press, Inc., 1969.

> Resume: A nonsense rhyming poem that tells a story about the rural life of a man and a woman called Pop Corn and Ma Goodness.

> Relationship to strategy lessons: The author uses some uncommon spelling patterns in an attempt to represent a folk dialect.

Schmidt, Eric von. *The Young Man Who Wouldn't Hoe Corn*. Boston: Houghton Mifflin Company; Cambridge, Mass.: The Riverside Press, 1964.

> Resume: A young man is criticized for refusing to work as the other villagers do, but his detractors learn that other types of contributions are also valuable.

Relationship to strategy lessons: The printing style and type (ink slightly runny, lines not perfectly aligned, tails on letters) fit the time period of the story (New England, 1633). The language of that period and setting is also represented. A moral issue is also examined.

Sendak, Maurice. *In the Night Kitchen*. New York: Harper & Row, Publishers, 1970.

Resume: Max has a nightmare and experiences with the night kitchen, the Milky Way, and other adventures before he wakes up. NOTE: Max loses his pajamas through his adventures; therefore some illustrations show frontal nudity.

Relationship to strategy lessons: Although the print is always in caps, its style and shape change from page to page. It occurs horizontally, vertically, in speech balloons, in varied sizes of rectangles, on buildings.

Tanz, Christine. *An Egg Is to Sit On*. Illustrated by Rosekrans Hoffman. New York: Lathrop, Lee & Shepard Co., 1978.

Resume: A patterned book, which starts, "An egg is to sit on . . . if you are a chicken." An elephant, a kangaroo, a termite, among others, get into the story following a predictable initial sentence.

Relationship to strategy lessons: The book invites children to predict the end of the sentences and encourages a variety of responses. Children might use this to write their own patterned books.

Waber, Bernard. *Nobody Is Perfick*. Boston: Houghton Mifflin Company, 1971.

Resume: Eight short stories covering some very real aspects of kids' lives—with some ironic endings.

Relationship to strategy lessons: These little stories are written in a modified comic-book style with no dialogue carriers. Some of the endings have an O. Henry twist but are usually true to life.

Walter, Mildred Pitts. *Lillie of Watts*. Illustrated by Leonora E. Prince. Los Angeles: The Ward Ritchie Press, 1969.

Resume: A day, both special and ordinary, in the life of an 11-year-old Black girl living in Watts—her dreams, fears, problems, joys.

Relationship to strategy lessons: The author uses phrase structures and spelling patterns representative of a Black dialect. Cultural aspects are also introduced.

Primary and Middle Grades

Brunhoff, Jean du. *The Story of Babar*.

Resume: The first of the well-loved series about an elephant family.

Relationship to strategy lessons: One edition of these elephant stories is written in cursive script.

Hunt, Mabel Leigh. *Little Girl with Seven Names*. Philadelphia: J. B. Lippincott Co., 1936.

Resume: A Quaker girl finds ways to cope with an unusually long name.

Relationship to strategy lessons: The little girl's unusually long name provides the motivating device for the story. The author attempts to represent the language of the period and setting. The child's character is built through her interaction with family members.

Williamson, Mel, and George Ford. *Walk On*. New York: Okpaku Books, The Third Press, 1972.

Resume: A day in the life of a Black child as seen through his eyes.

Relationship to strategy lessons: Each page is presented as a separate vignette written in the language and thought of the boy who is walking through his neighborhood. The author uses terms and phrases representative of the language and dialect of a young Black child.

Middle Grades

Taylor, Sydney. *All of a Kind Family*. Chicago: Follett Publishing Company, 1954.
———. *More All of a Kind Family*. Chicago: Follett Publishing Company, 1954.
———. *All of a Kind Family Uptown*. Chicago: Follett Publishing Company, 1954.

Resume: A Jewish family and their everyday lives—their enjoyments, trials, and tribulations—in New York City during the early part of the 1900s.

Relationship to strategy lessons: The names used in these stories are from American Jewish culture. The characters use words and phrases related to the Yiddish language.

Wagner, Jane. *J.T.* New York: Dell Publishing Co., Inc. 1969.

Resume: A sensitive story about an urban boy's love for a cat.

Relationship to strategy lessons: The author attempts to represent the syntax used in a Black dialect. Sympathetic relationships are built among the family and community members. Moral issues are also examined.

Middle Grades and Older

Adamson, Joy. *Born Free.* New York: Bantam Books, Inc., 1960.

Resume: The life histories of a lion, Elsa, and her cubs interacting with humans and their own natural habitat.

Relationship to strategy lessons: Pronoun reference to animals provide challenge for predicting strategies.

Ball, Jeffrey. *Bristol Face.* New York: Scholastic Book Services, 1973.

Resume: An Appalachian boy's relationships with a variety of people in a rural environment, and his love for his dog. An exciting adventure story.

Relationship to strategy lessons: The author uses eye dialect in the narrative as well as in the dialogue of this story told in the first person. A positive picture of rural Appalachia is built.

Felsen, Henry Gregory. *Why Rustlers Never Win.* New York: The Crowell-Collier and Macmillan, Co., Inc. 1955.

Resume: The humorous story of a Western outlaw who decides, after everything goes wrong for him, that future outlaws should be educated.

Relationship to strategy lessons: The storyteller uses words and phrases that might represent an uneducated cowhand's speech. The outlaw, as a victim of fate, changes his character.

Kim. *The Boys of Puhawai.* New York: Scholastic Book Services, 1960.

Resume: The adventures of a Maori boy and his two white friends.

Relationship to strategy lessons: The author has attempted to represent the form of pidgin English spoken in New Zealand. Maori words and phrases are also included.

Sleator, William. *Among the Dolls.* New York: E. P. Dutton & Co., Inc., 1975.

Resume: A young girl finds out that if she treats her dolls in a mean way, it has an effect on her own life.

Relationship to strategy lessons: High level of suspense makes this a good story to read chapter by chapter, stopping at the end of each chapter to get students' predictions.

Older

Wigginton, Eliot, ed. *The Foxfire Book.* 3 vols. Garden City, N.Y.: Doubleday & Company, Inc., Anchor Press, 1971–75.

Resume: Each volume focuses on different aspects of life in the Appalachians. Volume 1 provides information on chimney building, soapmaking, preserving vegetables, and other activities. Volume 2 includes ghost stories as well as information on midwifery and burial customs among others. Volume 3 tells about banjoes and dulcimers, butter churns and animal care. But most important, the volumes provide insight into a people who are part of the cultural heritage of the United States. High-school students did much of the writing.

Relationship to strategy lessons: Much of the writing represents the speech of the people who provided the data for the books. Some of it is in eye dialect. The language includes semantic, syntactic, and phonological dialect features. For those not familiar with the dialect, it represents hard-to-predict structures.

Primary, Middle, and Older

Graham, Lorenz. *David He No Fear*. Illustrated by Ann Grifalconi. New York: Thomas Y. Crowell Company, 1971.

> Resume: The story of David and Goliath is related by a storyteller who heard it and learned it from previous generations.

> Relationship to strategy lessons: The author uses hard-to-predict phrase structures to represent English speech of an African storyteller. Two other stories by Lorenz Graham, *God Wash the World and Start Again* and *Everyman Heart Lay Down*, have structures and styles similar to those of *David He No Fear*.

CONFIRMING

The following books are well-known children's folk songs presenting predictable patterns that are confirmed by the reader-singers as they meet unfamiliar verses and different versions of their favorite songs. Although these books can be used by all ages, they are especially geared to children in primary grades. Prediction and repetition of structures are related to musical patterns. Children can add verses as well as sing along.

Boone, Rose, and Alan Mills. *I Know an Old Lady*. Illustrated by Abner Graboff. Skokie, Ill.: Rand McNally & Company, 1961.

Brand, Oscar. *When I First Came to This Land*. Illustrated by Doris Burn. New York: G. P. Putnam's Sons, 1974.

Emberly, Barbara, and Ed Emberly. *One Wide River to Cross*. Englewood Cliffs, N.J.: Prentice-Hall, 1966.

Langstaff, John. *Frog Went A-Courtin'*. Illustrated by Feodor Rojankovsky. New York: Harcourt, Brace & World, 1955.

———. *Oh, A-Hunting We Will Go*. Illustrated by Nancy Winslow Parker. New York: Atheneum Publishers, 1974.

———. *Over in the Meadow*. Illustrated by Feodor Rojankovsky. New York: Harcourt, Brace & World, Inc., 1957.

———. *Soldier, Soldier, Won't You Marry Me?* Illustrated by Anita Lobel. Garden City, N.Y.: Doubleday & Company, 1972.

Quackenbush, Robert. *She'll Be Comin' Round the Mountain*. New York: J. B. Lippincott Co., 1973.

Spier, Peter. *The Fox Went Out on a Chilly Night*. Garden City, N.Y.: Doubleday & Company, 1961.

———. *The Erie Canal*. Garden City, N.Y.: Doubleday & Company, 1970.

Primary Grades

Baylor, Byrd. *Guess Who My Favorite Person Is*. Illustrated by Robert Parker. New York: Charles Scribner's Sons, 1977.

> Resume: Two people share their favorite things with each other: colors, dreams, places to live, sounds, and others.

> Relationship to strategy lessons: Personal involvement in moods, descriptions, and images that are confirmed and disconfirmed as child and adult interact. A good book to use as a base for student writing.

Brown, Margaret Wise. *The Indoor Noisy Book*. Illustrated by Leonard Weisgard. New York: Harper & Row, Publishers, 1970.

———. *Country Noisy Book*. Illustrated by Leonard Weisgard. New York: Harper & Row, Publishers, 1970.

————. *The Noisy Book.* Illustrated by Leonard Weisgard. New York: Harper & Row Publishers, 1970.

Resume: In each book Muffin, a little dog, is incapacitated so that he is unable to see, but he can hear. The title of the book indicates the setting in which Muffin hears many sounds.

Relationship to strategy lessons: The reader is invited to be actively involved, to predict the producer of the noises, and then to confirm based on additional cues.

Primary and Middle Grades

Geraldine, as told to Charles L. Blood and Martin Link. *The Goat in the Rug.* New York: The Parents' Magazine Press, 1976.

Resume: A picture-story book describing the weaving of a Navajo rug from the shearing of a goat to removal of the rug from the loom.

Relationship to strategy lessons: A goat narrator may cause readers to rethink or reread.

Perish, Peggy. *Amelia Bedelia.* New York: Scholastic Book Services, 1963.

Resume: Amelia Bedelia always misunderstands her boss's metaphors and follows directions in her own fashion.

Relationship to strategy lessons: The misunderstandings provide the reader much opportunity to rethink, reread, and continue to read. Making sense is Amelia Bedelia's problem, too.

Middle Grades and Older

Crawford, Peter. *Australian Marsupials.* New York: McGraw-Hill Book Company, Inc., 1972.

Resume: Separate chapters providing information about marsupials.

Relationship to strategy lessons: Each section tells about a different marsupial, among them wallabies, koalas, wombats. These specific names can all be referred to as marsupials. Permits the building of new concepts.

Dolan, Ellen M. *Nefrou the Scribe.* Adapted from the original text written by Georges Orclincx. Illustrated by Marie Webbes. St. Louis: Webster Publishing Division McGraw-Hill Inc., 1967.

Resume: Historical fiction set in early Egypt that tells the story of a young Egyptian who wants to be a scribe when he grows up.

Relationship to strategy lessons: Concepts that students could build from this story include *scribe, pharaoh, hieroglyphics.* Many unusual names used during this historical period in Egypt are introduced.

Juster, Norton. *The Phantom Toll Booth.* New York: Random House, Inc., 1961.

Resume: A marvelous fantasy through the doldrums and other interesting places.

Relationship to strategy lessons: The use of concepts and terminology that relate to a wide variety of meanings causes the reader to use confirmation strategies and to develop meaning through context.

Lindgren, Astrid. *The Tomten.* New York: Coward, McCann & Geoghegan, Inc., 1968.

Resume: The simple tale of a strange but gentle creature who comes out only at night, talks to animals in Tomten language, and is never seen by human beings.

Relationship to strategy lessons: On the basis of his actions and the descriptions provided, the Tomten might go under various names, such as ghost, troll, elf.

Raskin, Ellen. *Ghost in a Four-Room Apartment.* New York: Atheneum Publishers, 1969.

Resume: The amusing story of a mischievous poltergeist who has and causes adventures among a family in an apartment house, and then moves out when their pickle supply runs out.

Relationship to strategy lessons: The terms *poltergeist* and *ghost* can be used as interchangeable synonyms because of the author's descriptions. At the same time, the reader is able to see why all ghosts are not poltergeists.

Reed, James. *Rhyming Will.* Illustrated by Edward Ardizzone. New York: McGraw-Hill Book Company, Inc., 1968.

Resume: The story of a boy who did not speak until he was seven, and then always spoke in rhyme until he was frightened into using nonrhyming words.

Relationship to strategy lessons: After a series of simple and predictable rhymes, the hero of the story begins using nonrhyming synonyms, which the reader can predict. Some words and phrases from long-ago England are also used.

Primary

Branley, Franklin M., and Eleanor K. Vaughan. *Mickey's Magnet*. Illustrated by Crockett Johnson. New York: Scholastic Book Services, 1956.

Resume: Mickey explores what things will and will not be picked up by a magnet. His father helps him make a magnet with a needle.

Relationship to strategy lessons: The concept of the bar magnet is explored by inviting the reader to be involved in the process.

Hoban, Tana. *Look Again!* New York: The Macmillan Company, 1971.

Resume: Perception is changed by a square cut in certain pages to reveal only part of an object. Then the whole object is revealed.

Relationship to strategy lessons: Helps children explore developing concepts by inviting them to talk about differences in objects caused by differences in perceptions.

Meyer, Mercer. *There's a Nightmare in My Closet*. New York: The Dial Press, Inc., 1968.

Resume: A scared little boy learns to control his own nightmare.

Relationship to strategy lessons: A story line that integrates plot and theme as the major character solves his personal problem through self-control. Humor is also explored.

Steig, William. *Sylvester and the Magic Pebble*. New York: Windmill Books, Inc.; E. P. Dutton & Co., Inc., 1969.

Resume: Sylvester turns into a rock and, through his magic pebble and loving parents, is saved.

Relationship to strategy lessons: Setting and time are important in this story in which Sylvester as a stationary rock has activities and seasons take place near his site.

Yashima, Taro. *Crow Boy*. New York: The Viking Press, Inc., 1955.

Resume: The special qualities of a culturally different child in a classroom are sensitively portrayed.

Relationship to strategy lessons: Presents a theme to which children can relate: the importance of everyone being human. Crow Boy's character and personality develop through this story.

INTEGRATING

The following folktales have plots and themes typical to the cultures they represent. Although all ages can read these picture-story books, they can be used well by children in primary grades.

McDermott, Gerald. *The Stone Cutter*. New York: The Viking Press, Inc., 1975.
————. *Arrow to the Sun*. New York: The Viking Press, Inc., 1974.
————. *Anansi the Spider*. New York: Holt, Rinehart and Winston, 1972.

Primary and Middle Grades

The *Let's Read and Find Out Science Books* series are single-concept books. These would relate to any strategy lesson that lends itself to nonfiction. The ones we have selected are published in Spanish and English.

Golden, Augusta. *Pelo Lacio, Pelo Rizo*. New York: Thomas Y. Crowell Company, 1968. In English: *Straight Hair, Curly Hair*.

Gwynne, Fred. *The King Who Rained*. New York: Windmill Books, Inc., E. P. Dutton & Co., Inc., 1970.

Resume: Humorous use of puns.

Relationship to strategy lessons: Allows for exploration of what is funny.

Showers, Paul. *Mírate los Ojos*. New York: Thomas Y. Crowell Company, 1962. In English: *Look at Your Eyes*.
————. *Tu Piel y La Mía*. New York: Thomas Y. Crowell Company, 1968. In English: *Your Skin and Mine*.

Middle Grades and Older

Binder, Otto O. "*I Robot*." In *The Coming of the Robots*. New York: Ziff-Davis Publishing Company, 1938.

Resume: The story of the creation, education, and final ironic fate of a robot.

Relationship to strategy lessons: The story is written by the robot and is therefore the robot's version of what occurred.

Bloch, Alan. "*Men Are Different*." In *Short Science Fiction Tales*, ed. Isaac Asimov and Groff Conklin. New York: The Crowell-Collier Publishing Company, 1963.

Resume: A short factual account of the differences between men and robots, written by a robot who has examined and attempted to repair a man.

Relationship to strategy lessons: The account is written by a robot who is an archaeologist studying men. The facts are from the robot's perception of what they might be in the future somewhere in space.

Burton, Virginia Lee. *Life Story*. Boston: Houghton Mifflin Company, 1962.

Resume: The life story of the earth from the beginning of time to the 1960s. The illustrations aid in depicting the emergence of the earth.

Relationship to strategy lessons: The author provides concepts of the evolution of the earth in the format of a play. There is a stage, footlights, with the reader as the audience. Each era is represented by an act. Print is varied.

Deutsch, Babette, and Avrahm Yarmolinsky. *More Tales of Faraway Folk*. New York: Harper & Row Publishers, 1963.

Resume: A collection of folktales.

Relationship to strategy lessons: Each story has an explicitly stated moral.

Fern, Eugene. *Lorenzo and Angelina*. New York: Farrar, Straus & Giroux, Inc., 1968.

Resume: A small girl and a donkey have an adventure going through the mountains on thier way to the big city.

Relationship to strategy lessons: The same episodes are told from two points of view—the girl's and the donkey's.

Gersten, Irene Fandel, and Betty Bliss. *ECIDUJERP—PREJUDICE*. New York: Anti-Defamation League of B'nai B'rith, 1974.

Resume: This book explores the concept of prejudice. It examines what it is, how it feels, and how it develops. It offers suggestions for action.

Relationship to strategy lessons: It offers the authors' point of view about prejudice and provides students with a background that could help them evaluate other points of view in regard to prejudice.

Newell, Hope. *The Little Old Woman Who Used Her Head and Other Stories*. Illustrated by Ruse, Margaret and Anne M. Peck. New York: Thomas Nelson, Inc., 1973.

Resume: Short stories about an old woman who has many problems, which she always solves in unusual ways.

Relationship to strategy lessons: The old woman's solutions to her everyday problems are always logical but unexpected.

Rodgers, Mary. *Freaky Friday*. New York: Harper & Row, Publishers, 1972.

    Resume: A daughter takes her mother's place physically for a whole day.

    Relationship to strategy lessons: Enables readers to put themselves in other people's shoes.

Simon, Solomon. *The Wise Men of Helm and More Wise Men of Helm*. New York: Behrman House, Inc., 1965.

    Resume: Folktales of foolish souls. References to old-world Jewish traditions.

    Relationship to strategy lessons: Provides obvious morals and lessons for readers to explore.